Nurturing Good Children Now

Nurturing Good Children Now

10 Basic Skills to Protect and Strengthen Your Child's Core Self

Dr. Ron Taffel with Melinda Blau

Golden Books

New York

Golden Books®
888 Seventh Avenue
New York, NY 10106

Copyright © 1999 by Ron Taffel, Ph.D., with Melinda Blau.
All rights reserved, including the right of reproduction
in whole or in part in any form.
Golden Books® and colophon are trademarks
of Golden Books Publishing Co., Inc.

This book contains references to situations involving the author's
clients. However, the names and other identifying characteristics
have been changed to protect the privacy of those involved.

Designed by Suzanne Noli

Manufactured in the United States of America

10 9 8 7 6 5 4 3 2 1

Library of Congress Cataloging-in-Publication Data

Taffel, Ron.
  Nurturing good children now : 10 basic skills to protect and
strengthen your child's core self / by Ron Taffel with Melinda
Blau.
      p.   cm.
      Includes index.
    ISBN 1-58238-009-0 (alk. paper)
    1. Child rearing. 2. Child development.   3. Self-esteem in
children.   4. Parent and child.   I. Blau, Melinda, date.
II. Title.
HQ769.T13   1999   98-35313
649'.1—dc21   CIP

To Stacey, who nurtures the light
—RT

To Jennifer and Jeremy, who have heart and soul
—MB

ACKNOWLEDGMENTS

For over two decades, I've seen people in my clinical practice go through life without ever once acknowledging themselves out loud. This is especially true for the majority of self-effacing parents I meet whose primary concern is honoring their responsibility toward others. My wife, Stacey, and I are no different. Our lives essentially are dedicated to raising our children, Leah and Sammy, the best way we can. Rarely do we pause long enough to acknowledge our efforts.

This book is about nurturing a child's core, a task that cannot be done if mothers and fathers take their own well-meaning intentions entirely for granted. If we are not proud of ourselves, our children will have greater difficulty feeling pride in their efforts to become good and strong human beings.

So, before moving on in the usual fashion, I am going to turn tradition—child-rearing and literary—upside down: I would like to first briefly acknowledge myself.

Specifically, what you see in *Nurturing Good Children Now* represents twenty-five years of sticking with patients, often feeling in way over my head, many times becoming as worried as the families themselves. Yet, in the end, trying never to let them down, even as I learned from my mistakes.

What is just as important, but far less obvious, is the continuous effort I made to not even subtly abandon my children during the writing of this book. Most of us know what a relentless struggle it is to complete a huge work assignment without making one's kids pay a terrible price. In a project about parenting, losing this battle is certainly a most hypocritical failure: telling others how to better live with their families while wreaking havoc on one's own.

Like most of us, I didn't always win; there were, indeed, a few too many weekends during which my focus was hopelessly divided. But it wasn't often and for this I am proud.

I would also like to acknowledge one of the underlying reasons I have been so successful with children. I was a difficult child myself. When I say this, I mean tenacious, easily riled up, and way, way too fearful. Many of your children are not easy, either. Because I have lived through so much firsthand, it is almost impossible for me to be judgmental of parents' and kids' experiences together. I believe this vulnerability of mine comes through. I know self-doubt and worry and still, despite it all, I keep on trying. Just as you do.

• • •

Having said this, I want to acknowledge who gave me the inspiration and much of the book's focus on strengthening the core self. My wife, Stacey, looks at our children and has an uncanny ability to see the best in them. Watching her these many years, I've grown to understand how transformative this clear-eyed love can be. And, so far, Leah and Sammy are decent kids who treat themselves and others basically well. It helps enormously to love someone whose very essence embodies what you believe to be good. Thank you, Stacey.

I've experienced the same quality in some of my old friends, especially Robert Gaines, a clinical psychologist and buddy of mine for almost thirty years. Several times during the writing process, Robbie generously helped. This was especially so when we had to decide on schools for our younger child, Sammy. For his efforts I will be eternally grateful.

Nancy Ruben and Peter Selwyn were also there when I needed them. Most writers I know go through unpredictable bouts of illiteracy. Peter and Nancy were always available when I felt most blocked and in exactly the ways I asked. Friends who respond respectfully and generously—that's what we all need.

• • •

Now to the book itself and my coauthor, Melinda Blau. Melinda, if you don't already know, is a superbly gifted writer. But after ten years of collaboration, she is much more to me than a talented journalist. The working relationship we have is remarkably fluid. It effortlessly moves from a creative partnership, to a family-friendship connection, across the dial over to Comedy Central, and then back again to the task at hand.

With Melinda, I feel like one of those blessed sports figures who is lucky enough to be able to say, "I can't believe I earn a living doing something I love so much." That's how working with Melinda feels. Most of the time we're just "in the zone."

I want to thank my assistant, Sue Marantz, now for all the times I didn't then. She's got more resilience and determination than she realizes. Plus, in order for Sue to deal with me, she had to learn an entirely new language. In this age of picture-perfect computer copy, I can still manage to turn a neatly written page into the almost indecipherable code of an ancient people.

Then, of course, there's my lioness of an editor, Laura Yorke. This is one intellectually fierce and yet genuinely tender person. Good writers out there, take note. If you're lucky enough to land Laura, you've found one of the smartest, most alive people left on the publishing scene. Like a gifted archaeologist, she immediately spots worthwhile material buried in the debris of a book's earliest days. On top of which Laura morphs the frantic negotiating process, which we euphemistically call "bringing-a-book-to-publication," into an often hilarious experience.

A word also for assistant editor Lara Asher. Her intelligent sunniness may be the real gold in Golden Books Family Entertainment. She respectfully and graciously handled the nitty-gritty details that inevitably make or break a book.

Lastly, Harriet Lerner, that most practical of visionaries, magically appeared one day from deep in the heartland. Despite being eaten alive by the success of *The Mother Dance,* she lent a hand during this manuscript's later stages. Harriet knows what's important. And she especially knows how to communicate it plain and simple.

• • •

A book of this scope takes years before a word is ever written. Along the way, there were several people who put their unique stamp on me and on the process. The no-nonsense let's-make-a-deal approach of my literary agents, Barbara Lowenstein and Eileen Cope, balanced out my finely honed ineptitude at matters of business and the marketplace. Thanks also to Peter Guzzardi and Isabel Geffner. From early on, their robust courage gave me the nerve to present this idea.

Then, there are those people who unknowingly build a deep, solid foundation, even for something so intangible as the creative process. The core attributes of each chapter in *Nurturing Good Children Now* were taught to me by my lifelong friends: Martin David, Steven Goldstein, Marc Gordon, Martin Haber, Ron Heller, Martin Rock, and Kenneth Wolpin. How many men these days bother to maintain childhood friendships, let alone develop a caretaking network that actually grows stronger with the years?

Finally, for just about every person in the helping professions, hidden somewhere in even the most impersonal audience is the presence of a living parent or the powerful ghost of one. My parents died a very long time ago. But, boy, my mother and father would have been so proud of this accomplishment! In the forthright descriptions of family life you'll find in these pages, my parents would have also seen themselves: imperfect beings ever struggling to keep their core goodness intact.

Like snowflakes swirling past each other on a winter's wind, my children and my parents never touched. But when I look at Leah and Sammy, the past and present converge. In their young, luminous faces, I see the same hope my parents must have seen in mine.

This book is an acknowledgment of that implicit promise between parent and child. It is a promise to do the best we possibly can; to try until there's just no more left to try. So that, one day, our children will have learned how to realize their hopes and how to make their own dreams come true.

—Ron Taffel
New York City

Words escape me—a sad fate for a writer—when I try to describe Ron Taffel's and my collaboration. We finish each other's sentences, laugh heartily at each other's jokes, and share the most poignant high and low points of each other's lives. We are more than collaborators and more than friends, and our books are truly labors of love. That his wife, Stacey, allows me to refer to myself playfully as his "second wife," that Leah and I share favorite TV shows and discuss at length their plots, that even Sammy is getting to know who I am, have only enriched Ron's and my bond. I feel blessed to have all of them in my life.

I feel equally grateful to once again work with Laura Yorke. It would be enough that she is such a clear thinker and good editor, but she has also become a friend. Her assistant, Lara Asher, is smart, eager, and efficient—a great asset to Laura's team. And I am always thankful to have Barbara Lowenstein and Eileen Cope in my corner, dousing me with buckets of reality, savvy advice, and many opportunities for laughter.

Finally, I want to thank my children, Jennifer and Jeremy, who do me proud. Without them, I surely would have neither insight nor compassion about parenting issues. Now twenty-nine and twenty-six, they no longer need my daily attention, but they always have my love and my appreciation—especially when they hear my distracted voice over the phone and know in an instant: Mom is on a deadline. I owe them both several batches of brownies for this book.

—Melinda Blau
Northampton, Massachusetts

CONTENTS

RECLAIMING OUR CHILDREN

Each person bears a uniqueness that asks to be lived and that is already present before it can be lived.
— James Hillman, *The Soul's Code*

Your Child and the Second Family

"How can I protect my five-year-old son's goodness in a world like this?" asked a mother who attended one of my workshops. Her simple question instantly captured everyone's attention. It was an electric moment of shared appreciation and worry. Among the three hundred or so parents in the room, some cleared their throats and nervously looked around; others nodded in agreement. I could feel the collective pounding of hearts, the deep breaths of anxiety. Then, one by one, mothers and fathers spoke up, each expressing similar concerns: *Given the conflicting messages and demands of our times, how can we make sure our children will turn out to be good solid kids who are strong enough to survive and thrive in the world?*

This theme has resonated in almost every parenting workshop I've given. Even the parents of very young children increasingly fear that their skills and authority are being challenged by cultural influences *outside* the family. It used to be that mothers and fathers would focus exclusively on the "best" parenting technique. Today, they frequently ask a question that reflects their additional concern: "How can I keep and support my child's goodness in the face of what's going on *out there?*"

Parents have a right to be concerned about strengthening their personal effectiveness as well as developing real authority. We *are* living in an uncertain world, and, given the vulnerable condition of modern family life, child-rearing today is affected by societal influences as never before. Because of the proliferation of media and easy access to computers and the Internet, kids are connected instantly to a commercially driven culture and to each other. The effects are not all bad: I see an increased sophistication and even greater adaptability in many children today. However, from the time kids are toddlers, these influences slowly shape our children's character and their connection to us. I've given these forces a name—the *second family*. It's kind of like a social smog—an almost invisible yet powerful fusion of pop culture and peer influence that wafts into our homes.

The second family is not to be confused with the extended family—relatives, friends, or well-meaning and helpful adults in the community who nurture our children and feel like kin. However, I use the term "second *family*" because of its collective power to embrace and influence our children. I see and hear evidence of it every day:

- A two-and-a-half-year-old child absently walks around humming the Burger King's "Have it your way" jingle while her four-year-old sister lobbies for designer sneakers.
- The mother of a resourceful, hard-bargaining three-and-a-half-year-old wonders where her child came up with the expression "Parents are unfair."
- A five-year-old boy angrily says "Shut up!" when his father tells him it's time to leave the playground. Dad can't help but recall his own childhood when he wouldn't have dreamed of using either those words or tone of voice with his father.
- A first grader screams in frustration, "You just don't understand" to her bewildered mother, who didn't expect that kind of complaint until adolescence.
- A seven-year-old is obsessed with being "popular" in his second-grade class and worries about being seen as "uncool."
- An eight-year-old girl acts bored around adults; she'd rather be with her own friends or in her room, plugged into TV or a stimulating computer game.

As kids get older, snapshots such as these are even more common in the family albums of parents' minds. Parents, sensing the limits of their own power, see the growing impact of the second family on their children's values. They feel overwhelmed by the pop characters and celebrities kids talk about and emulate, by the clothes they wear, the lyrics they repeat, the TV one-liners they adopt.

I must stress that this is *not* a teen phenomenon. As early as nursery school, the grip of the second family on your child's emerging character is already becoming palpable. From the time your little one starts watching TV and playing in the sandbox with other kids, the second family is vying for what I call his "core"—the seed of selfhood that contains his innate strength and potential. Your child's adolescence is too late to start worrying; teen difficulties don't develop overnight. We must *anticipate* the effect of the second family and begin strengthening our children when they are very young.

In her best-selling book *Reviving Ophelia,* Mary Pipher identified this cultural pollution, focusing primarily on teenage girls. In her subsequent book, *In the Shelter of Each Other,* Pipher suggests—as do I— that the problem affects both genders equally. Here, I further emphasize that even our youngest children are at risk and how, from the earliest years, the second family threatens to devalue and drown out your child's core self.

Some parents perceive this phenomenon but don't know exactly what to do. They may blame themselves or their kids. Perhaps family life isn't all it could be—rushed schedules, long work hours, less-than-consistent discipline. But not many parents realize the extent to which the outside is seeping in, affecting the very interactions they have with their children. Many moms and dads who do identify the problem feel too harried or helpless to combat the second family. They feel as if they stand alone, trying to hold on to their kids in a vast undertow that drags them down and away. As one mother in a workshop tearfully remarked, "It's like me against the whole pop culture."

Increasingly, therapists, accustomed to working with a troubled child's first family at home, are beginning to help parents be more aware of the impact of the second family. In fact, my article introducing this concept, which appeared in the *Family Therapy Networker* ("The Second Family," May/June 1996), elicited more attention from therapists, counselors, teachers, and clergy than any piece I'd ever written for a professional audience. The article hit a chord because many of my colleagues in the mental health field had begun to realize that the usual interventions weren't working anymore. They, too, were looking for answers.

What's a parent—indeed, a society—to do? How can we intercede effectively and early? How do we raise kids—good kids—who are attached to us and who have a strong sense of self that enables them to withstand the second family? The answers involve a radical shift in the way we think about and support children as they negotiate our uncertain, often difficult, world. Most important, we must recognize that inside every child is a fundamental essence—her "core"—which must be protected and strengthened from the moment she is born.

Discovering Your Child's Core

The key to raising a good child today is to help her recognize, nurture, and protect her core self. With the recent publication of *The Nurture Assumption* by Judith Rich Harris, some parents now fear that this isn't possible. I agree that we can't "make our children turn out any way we want," as Harris puts it. But I emphatically disagree that nurture will ever be obsolete or irrelevant. To me, as a parent and working professional, this hypothesis is a luxury. We *must* and, as I will show, we *can* help our children become "good" children—children who are moral, feel comfortable in their own skin, and are able to be their best selves despite the pull of the second family.

I know this from having worked with thousands of children in my practice and thousands more in schools throughout the country. I know this, too, from my recent study—a multicultural sampling of 150 children in public school, from pre-K to grade six. I asked these youngsters a series of questions about what kind of parenting works for them—about family time, rules, discipline, rituals, and other topics. Two important themes emerged: *They want parents to see and respect them for who they are—and they want parents to protect them.*

The notion of protection is perhaps most obvious. When I asked her to define what a "good" parent was, one child said, "Someone to watch over me." Although kids can't always articulate their fears, they are aware of the pressures that beset them. This becomes dramatically obvious when they talk about the need for rules. Children want adults to provide safe, reliable, consistent structure. They want parents to make their voices heard above the din of the pop culture and they want to be guided by *their* values.

What is less apparent, however, is that a child also needs—and will be more successful in life if he has it—parents who protect his individuality. Each child comes into this world with a unique essence. It is not something we can test for or look at under a microscope, but it does, in the truest sense, define who that child is. To describe the core, psychologist James Hillman uses terms like "innate image" and "the acorn." Inside a child's core, he says, lives the reason that child is here—his "calling." But if we're not careful, it can be smothered or ignored; it can languish. And that unique seed might never realize its full potential.

In order to better understand what a healthy "core" is, picture your child as an infant, just at the point when he or she woke up to life and to you. Remember how fascinated and curious she was about everything. That natural inquisitiveness emanated from her core. Now, picture your child a little older, perhaps between two and five years old, expressing the kind of tenderness that could melt your heart; or remember how, in one sentence, your newly verbal child expressed himself more vividly than we can in paragraphs. Those gifts, too, came from his core. Close your eyes and imagine the calm, focused face of a preteen as she masters a task for the first time. Now, picture the unexpected friendliness your young adolescent exhibits—even in the face of limits set on his comings and goings. Finally, observe her wonderful poise, when your teen feels comfortable in her body—dancing with friends or running on the soccer field. These are just some of the attributes of a healthy core self that delights in exploration, learning, growing, and taking a rightful place in the world.

Your role as a parent is to discover your child's core, nurture it, and protect it from the chaos of everyday life and cultural distractions that can affect its growth. In these pages, I offer you concrete strategies that not only will help you understand the ten key facets of your child's core but also what threatens it. I will further explore the paths that lead our children away from us; and I will explain how cultural noise obscures the parental voice at a time when children need to hear it the most. You can't get rid of the second family—it's a fact of life— but if you know what you're dealing with, you can strengthen your child's core to withstand it and even get the most from it.

How We've Been Parenting . . . Until Now

I wrote *Nurturing Good Children Now* because I believe that we're in the midst of a shift in the parenting paradigm. We're about to leave behind decades of theories that mirrored the eras in which they were popular. None is a match for today's realities. Looking back, it's easy to see why.

At the turn of the last century, Victorians believed children were to be seen and not heard, and this expectation held firm into the 1930s and early 1940s. Mothers were directed to feed their babies on rigid schedules, hold them sparingly, and not to give too much attention, lest their children become "spoiled." Given this model, a child was barely a person, no less someone with a core.

The birth of the first baby boomers in postwar America ushered in more permissive and psychologically oriented parenting. An infant was viewed as a mass of malleable humanity to be held and shaped in Mother's hands. Mom was blamed for everything that went wrong. This period continued through the sixties, marked by relatively enlightened, yet simplistic, cookie-cutter approaches to parenting.

The "therapeutic age" of child-rearing during the seventies, eighties, and nineties further embraced a one-size-fits-all model, but child-development research increasingly found its way into parenting manuals. Benchmarks of physical and emotional growth were set forth so that Mom and Dad could compare their child to the "norm." At the same time, emphasis was placed on values that nurtured a child's psychological health, such as self-esteem, confidence, and creativity.

In the last several years, largely in response to what is perceived as too many decades of "permissiveness," the pendulum has swung again. Moralists, wanting to return to the good old days when parents reigned supreme, suggest that we inculcate values. They design programs to help youngsters develop ethics and good judgment. Behaviorists recommend that we "train" children using systems that reward them for being good. Given the antics of some kids nowadays, who could disagree with either approach?

In and of themselves, the old approaches to child-rearing are extremely valuable. Among other benefits, they have helped parents better understand children's minds and behaviors. However, each only speaks to a small piece of the puzzle—mind or body, or heart or soul. None truly reflects the concept of a core self that incorporates *all* of who your child is.

Toward a New View of Parenting

For years, whenever journalists called to ask about a specific child-rearing problem, I've always said the same thing: "Tell me a little about the child—his temperament, the way he expresses himself, how he deals with his moods." The fact is, one-size-fits-all approaches often meet with failure and frustration. Why? Because each child has a unique core that seeks expression, and child-rearing strategies must be tailored for that specific child.

In my view—confirmed by the latest child-development research—*children get into trouble out of a thwarted need to connect with their core*. The parents of younger kids often come to me with worries about tantrums, disobedience, unrelatedness, learning difficulties, or poor friendships. Preteens and teenagers end up in my office with signs of eating disorders, drug problems, petty theft, or precocious sexuality. All of these are the familiar stuff of professional texts and pop psychology. But from my experience, the defining problem is that these children lack substance. They don't feel connected to a strong internal self and, absent this resilient and solid connection to their core, they (sometimes dangerously) act out, filling the void with bad relationships or losing themselves in the pop culture.

Unlike approaches that swing to either extreme, advocating control *or* indulgence, my model of parenting integrates and balances both: I'm suggesting that you make clear your expectations of how you want your child to behave and, at the same time, employ parenting techniques that fit your child's core self. Hence, the skills I suggest throughout *Nurturing Good Children Now* reflect the notion that each child must be treated as an individual—for all the inherent possibilities he or she possesses. As James Hillman reminds us: "There is more in a human life than our theories of it allow. Sooner or later something seems to call us onto a particular path. You may remember this 'something' as a signal moment in childhood when an urge out of nowhere, a fascination, a peculiar turn of events struck like an annunciation. This is what I must do, this is what I've got to have. This is who I am."

In fact, research proves that even our youngest infants undeniably evidence distinct personalities and styles. Children are not shapeless masses, just waiting for our input. Such findings both reflect and confirm the dawn of a new age of personal and specific parenting. This approach takes into account who your child is, rather than trying to make her conform to a preconceived mode. It stresses that we need to think this way from the time our children are infants, not only because every child is different, but also because we want each one to grow up knowing her own core and her right and responsibility to nurture and protect it.

Children need to be seen for who they are—unique individuals. If you require proof, look around you and notice the vast numbers of adults today who are seeking answers about themselves. Hillman believes (and I agree) that "we have been robbed of our true biography . . . and we go to therapy to recover it." It's no accident that so many adults nowadays are also seeking *spiritual* answers to their problems. They are desperate to get in touch with their core selves.

About the New Parenting Skills

The primary goal of *Nurturing Good Children Now* is to give you the skills to strengthen your child's core from his or her earliest days. A second, equally important goal is to make you aware of, and better able to combat, the negative aspects of the second family. You don't have to feel overwhelmed. You *can* discover and protect your child's core—and thereby arm yourself and your child to withstand this cultural challenge.

To that end, I have isolated ten core-builders—applicable to toddlers or teens—traits children need to connect successfully with themselves, with you, and with the world. Each one speaks directly to your child's core self—and has a corresponding "Basic Skill" to guide you:

Mood Mastery	*Basic Skill #1:* Teach your child to soothe himself in healthy ways that match his temperament.
Respect	*Basic Skill #2:* Encourage your child to listen to and be comfortable with responsible adults.
Expressiveness	*Basic Skill #3:* Promote your child's unique style of talking about what really matters.
Passion	*Basic Skill #4:* Protect your child's enthusiasm and love of life.
Peer Smarts	*Basic Skill #5:* Guide your child in her relationships with playmates and friends.
Focus	*Basic Skill #6:* Help your child to pay attention and love learning.
Body Comfort	*Basic Skill #7:* Help your child accept his physical appearance and feel comfortable in his body.
Caution	*Basic Skill #8:* Encourage your child to think ahead and weigh the impact of her actions on self and others.

Team Intelligence	*Basic Skill #9:* Inspire your child to develop her capacity to be part of a group without losing her individuality.
Gratitude	*Basic Skill #10:* Expect your child to be grateful and, thereby, nurture his faith and spirituality.

The Research Behind the Skills

Each chapter in this book is based on one of the above core-builders. As you read through these pages, you will see that I frequently draw from research and clinical work inspired by early-intervention programs that target children with serious problems. I recognize that the vast majority of children are not—and should not be—clinically diagnosed or treated. However, in our culture, all children are at risk. Let me offer some examples of what I mean:

• Relatively few children have attention deficit disorder, but given the variety of competing media and other distractions, many children have difficulty focusing.

• A very small number of kids are clinically depressed, but because children are often overscheduled, many of them have trouble developing meaningful interests that sustain them—and make them happy.

• A minority of children are actually hyperactive, but in our frenetic, supercharged culture, many children can be impulsive, sometimes dangerously so.

• Very few children have true anxiety disorders, but because the culture puts a premium on appearance, many children are unhealthily preoccupied with their bodies.

• Most children don't have learning disabilities, but because they're exposed to excessive video and TV at early ages, their imaginations are dulled, and many find it difficult to express themselves verbally or on paper.

Because childhood difficulties are often culturally reinforced—therefore, pervasive—and because parents are swimming in the same seas, it's easy to accept certain problems as normal. So what if Johnny can't sit still long enough to do a jigsaw puzzle or is overly rambunctious after playing too many video games? Many of the boys in his class are like that. So what if Janie flits from one activity to the next or is indecisive about which outfit to wear and obsessed about looking good? She's just like her friends. Often, when we see a child struggling with homework or agonizing over peer situations, we rationalize that the behavior is normal and decide to just wait it out. Or, when more serious trouble develops, we trot our kid off to a specialist. The good news is that there's effective action to be taken between either extreme.

Appropriate intervention—steps you can take *before* a difficulty ensues—is based upon research with so-called problem populations and drawn from programs designed to help such kids. I've adapted the best of what's out there, translating it into everyday skills and techniques that any parent can use. I might add that I've only taken the tried and true. Any strategy I suggest has a measurable, long-term track record of success in research settings, clinical use, or experience with ordinary families.

I've also gathered countless stories from my own work with thousands of parents and children I meet doing consultations and through various research projects of my own. I'm particularly excited by my recent study—a sampling of 150 schoolchildren, ages four to twelve, who represent all socioeconomic levels and a cross-section of ethnic groups. I've often said that parents are the real "experts," but I have to add that kids are quite articulate when it comes to reviewing what parents do and don't do. I listen, I take their opinions very seriously, and—given such attention—children often speak right from the core.

Using This Book

You could, of course, read *Nurturing Good Children Now* from cover to cover. However, knowing myself as a father and from talking with as many parents as I do, I think that is probably unlikely. We parents barely have time to read one magazine article, no less snuggle up with a three-hundred-page parenting book! Besides, there's a lot between these two covers—ideas, research, strategies—too much to be absorbed all at once. Instead, I suggest that you begin by going directly to the chapter that focuses on whatever core-builder seems to fit your child's immediate needs. They are singularly important, but, over time, you will see that they all interconnect and strengthen the others.

Each chapter encourages you to use an approach best suited to your child's personality and style. Accordingly, every chapter offers:

- A deeper understanding of the Basic Skill—its importance to the core self, and how it protects children against the pulls of the second family.
- A view of core "threats," or ways the second family works against each core builder.
- Specific parent skills that foster the development of the core-building attribute.
- Specific skills that children can master (with parents' help), which will reinforce the core-building trait.

I've also liberally seasoned the book with appropriately named acronyms—for example, in the Caution chapter, I suggest one for children called "STOP," in the Team Intelligence chapter, you'll be encouraged to do "LAPS," in the Gratitude chapter, you'll be reminded to "THANK." Parenting techniques can be hard to remember in the everyday rush of our busy lives. The acronyms are meant to help trigger strategies you need in the moment, which, of course, is when you need advice the most but are least likely to run to your bookshelf.

Finally, I want to stress that although this book is full of solid information, I hope you will find that it provides inspiration as well. The notion that we can actually protect our children—that we can honor and nurture who they are—is a heartening one. I hope that these new skills motivate you to bring out the best in yourself as a parent—and the best in your child.

CHAPTER 1

MOOD MASTERY

Basic Skill #1: Teach your child to soothe himself in healthy ways that match his temperament.

Children You May Know

For all time, parents have understood that each child enters this world with his or her own unique personality. Regardless of fashions in child-rearing practices, which alternately stress nature or nurture and levy varying degrees of "blame" on parents, deep down inside, every one of us knows the truth: A child's *fundamental identity* is not really a function of anything we do or don't do. Her inborn nature is no more the result of "good" child-rearing than her innate difficulties emanate from "bad" practices. Especially those of us with older kids are able to look back on their first weeks and see now that certain threads of behavior have been consistent from day one.

Let's look at four children who exemplify this point. One of them, I'm sure, will remind you of your own:

- Three-and-a-half-year-old Sylvie is BIG in every way—tall for her age and very intense about practically everything that she wants or does. When Sylvie eats strawberries, she eats the whole carton. She wants every toy she sees. And Sylvie plays so rambunctiously that within minutes of her coming into a room, it looks as if three kids have been there, not one. Sylvie's eager and friendly, but her in-your-face manner tends to put off her peers. So does the fact that when she doesn't get her own way, she blows up.
- Matthew, a happy five-year-old, was right on schedule when it came to various developmental benchmarks, like walking, talking, socializing. He makes friends easily, because he's so likable. At the

same time, however, Matthew is also hypersensitive to stimuli: noises, lights, the ways certain kinds of clothing feel. To avoid being bombarded by such irritants, he retreats (leaving the room, for example, if music is too loud) or rebels (tearing off his shirt, claiming it's "too itchy").

• Four-year-old David often withdraws. When he doesn't get his way, he whines a lot, sulking or becoming petulant. He finds it hard to socialize, especially with kids he doesn't know well. Predictably, during his first week of nursery school, he clung to his mother's skirt and cried bitterly when she attempted to leave.

• Jessica, now six, started sleeping through the night when she was two months old. She was a hearty eater and a delightful child; her "good disposition," as everyone described it, has stayed with her. Sure, Jessica has some fears and sensitivities, but they are moderate. While Jessica occasionally gets cranky, she is, for the most part, a balanced child. Her mother says Jessica's been "easy" since the day she was born.

After twenty-five years of clinical work—not to mention raising my own two children, Leah and Sam—I've seen firsthand that the old model of child development, while having been tremendously helpful, can be vastly improved. I say this for two reasons. One, because much of a child's personality—in the form of genetic makeup and temperamental predisposition—is already in place before he or she is born. Two, because cookie-cutter solutions don't work.

Recent child-development studies make it abundantly clear that successful child-rearing is not, as we once thought, about kids being shaped by one-size-fits-all parenting techniques, but about our adapting specific practices to the very specific and inborn personalities of our kids. Once, professionals like myself could only describe personality; now, drawing from the latest research, we also can prescribe certain parent skills and behavior that can help you deal with your child's basic personality. With such tools, you can teach your child how to manage his temperament and interact positively with his environment. I call this process "Mood Mastery," and it is the skill upon which stands everything else that strengthens your child's core.

Why Mood Mastery Is Important

Teaching a child Mood Mastery—the ability to identify and soothe his own emotions and/or anxieties—is the primary challenge for today's parents. It is a fundamental ability that enables a child to live in the world—in synch with herself and in control of herself when she's with others. And here's the bottom line: Teaching Mood Mastery involves finding an approach to self-soothing that is particularly suited to your child's temperament.

Since the late fifties, researchers in the field of personality study have called the general constellation of physiological, psychological, and emotional attributes "temperament." Child-development researcher Jerome Kagan defines temperament as those "stable behavioral and emotional reactions that appear early and are influenced, in part, by genetic constitution." Often, we parents just think of it as our child's personality. It's the fundamental stuff from which his or her core is built.

We don't really need a formal definition, of course, because even with our newborn, we intuitively sense his basic essence—the nature of our child's core. Almost immediately, we start thinking of that tiny bundle as a "tiger" or a "delicate flower" or as "quite a handful." We put together a picture of who this baby is based on her eating and sleeping habits, whether she cries a lot or seems content most of the time, is resilient or sensitive. We unconsciously make a mental note of how outgoing or introverted she is, if she reacts to things mildly or intensely, or can go with the flow. We become especially cognizant of temperament the day our second child is born. I remember thinking when Leah's younger brother, Sammy, came along, "How could my two children be so *different?*" It was as if my wife, Stacey, and I had to learn how to be parents all over again.

As our children grow, we are amazed to see the consistent nature of their personalities. Indeed, every parent knows intuitively: What you see is what you get! And in the last several years, surprising and hopeful research, conducted (among others) by Stanley Greenspan's Zero to Three Foundation in Washington, D.C., Jerome Kagan at Yale, and William Carrey at Children's Hospital of Philadelphia, is finally proving what we've always known: Temperament causes different children to react differently to their environments, to people, even to their own internal states.

Remember four-year-old David? A very sensitive boy, he deals with intense physical feelings—such as hunger and fatigue—by crying. In contrast, Sylvie, who is aggressively strong-willed, copes with her discomfort by demanding attention or having a tantrum.

What can parents of such fundamentally different kids hope to help their children achieve? Psychologists call it self-regulation—the capacity to handle your own temperamental disposition. David's and Sylvie's parents may not use that term, but they know they want to connect with their children and get them to stop the negative behavior. They want to teach more effective strategies that will help calm and soothe the disturbance as it's happening. And they want to build trust—their children's trust in them and, ultimately, each child's trust in his or her own ability to self-regulate.

Now, here's the critical point: A sensitive, likely-to-be-withdrawn child, such as David, needs a different approach than does an aggressive child such as Sylvie. In other words, David needs to be spoken to softly and given firm but gentle limits, whereas Sylvie needs to be distracted or spoken to in a crisp, sharp manner that leaves absolutely no room for power struggles. Over time, as each set of parents uses appropriately tailored approaches, David and Sylvie will begin to self-regulate, in the process developing Mood Mastery.

IT'S A FACT: MOOD MASTERY IS INSURANCE

Since 1990, the Johnson Institute in Minneapolis has been studying patterns of substance abuse through its national StudentView surveys. Among other suggestions for prevention, they cite "mood maintenance" as the foundation of self-esteem. "People most likely to fall in love with intoxication are those who live in the high-range intensity of feelings—anxiety, anger, frustration—or the low range—boredom and depression," says Bud Remboldt, president of the institute. "We must teach children to live in the middle zone—calm but excited about life."

Mood Mastery is the cornerstone of a solid core identity. Again, the research is indisputable: We parents can make our children's road a lot easier and increase their chances of success if we simply adapt, rather than fight, who they are. David, Sylvie, and any child who acquires Mood Mastery will feel more in control—and, not so incidentally, they'll feel better about themselves as well.

A child who has learned Mood Mastery can:

express his needs;
temper his emotions;
improve his connections with others.

Mood Mastery enhances your child's sense of well-being and strengthens his experience of himself—as genuine—in the world. Instead of wondering who he is, or, worse, feeling bad about himself, your child will think:

"I'm okay the way I am."

"I can get the world to understand and help me."

"I love my parents because they understand who I am."

"I feel comfortable and proud of who I am."

What greater feelings could your child have about himself? Hence, our first Basic Skill:

> Basic Skill #1: Teach your child to soothe himself in healthy ways that match his temperament.

As this description implies, Mood Mastery begins with an understanding of who your child is. Later in the chapter, I'll help you zero in on particular traits to be aware of when I describe the four types of temperaments. However, Mood Mastery—as well as the nine other Basic Skills I present in this book—is not just a matter between you and your child.

Core Threats: What Works Against Mood Mastery

For every core-builder I cite, there are certain counterproductive factors, some that exist within the family, and some that emerge from peers and pop culture—the collective power of the "second family." As I explained in the introduction, this aggregate force of the pop culture and your child's peers can have a profound effect on your child. No matter what you would like to teach, no matter what parenting strategies you employ, the second family can begin to affect your child's expectations, beliefs, and experience from the time she is preverbal.

Let me say up front that when I warn about the influence of the second family, I'm not moralizing about the evils of television or commercialization—and I'm certainly not advocating that we turn back the cultural clock. In fact, as I noted earlier, media and computers bring a world of valuable information into our homes and into our children's lives. However, looking at what it takes to strengthen and protect a child's core, it becomes clear that the second family also works in specific, subtle ways against each of the ten Basic Skills.

Though there has been much talk about the negative impact of television and media on children, few critics address what I believe is their most serious threat: the messages of the media and the pop culture fight self-regulation. In fact, the second family often encourages attributes that are the exact opposite of what children need to learn Mood Mastery.

Aggression and impulsivity. Television, computers, and video games are the main arteries by which media and pop culture—the second family—are transfused into our families. The problem is that in many American homes, TV and, increasingly, computer games act as a babysitter—we rely on them too much. In my clinical practice, for example, it's not unusual for me to hear about kids who spend up to ten hours on a weekend, four to six hours per weekday, involved with television or video games. The national figures, according to the American Academy of Pediatrics, the American Psychological Association, and the Center for Science in the Public Interest, are not much different (see box).

Granted, television in limited, carefully chosen doses can educate and even soothe kids, but those figures border on what researchers define as too much television—according to most studies, anything over three hours a day. Obviously, certain types of children are more vulnerable and will have different reactions based on their temperament—where Sylvie might get revved up from watching a scary program, the same show might frighten David. But regardless of individual response, too much TV is neither calming nor conducive to Mood Mastery. In fact, it often exacerbates precisely those areas of self-regulation in which your child has the greatest difficulty.

Furthermore, over one thousand separate studies attest that exposure to heavy doses of television increases the likelihood of aggressive behavior. Analyzing the research, the Center for Media Education in Washington, D.C., concludes that children who watch four hours or

TV FACTS

- The average American household has 2.24 television sets; 99 percent have at least one.
- Over 50 percent of American children, ages six to seventeen, have TV sets in their own bedrooms.
- The average young American spends nine hundred hours a year in school, fifteen hundred hours watching television.
- Saturday mornings account for only 10 percent of children's viewing time; the balance is weeknights and weekday afternoons, when our young kids are likely to be watching adult programming, rife with high action, sex, and violence.
- By the time an average child finishes elementary school, he has witnessed 8,000 murders on television, and by age eighteen, 200,000 acts of violence.

more daily are less likely to be physically active, will tend to favor using physical aggression to resolve conflicts, and are more likely to demonstrate impulsive behavior. Clearly, none of those outcomes promotes Mood Mastery.

Video games—a bastion of the second family—sabotage Mood Mastery in a similar way. An emerging body of research, in which psychologists are studying how these games affect different types of children, is already hinting at the reasons kids find them so compelling. The very elements that define computerized play—it is interactive, stimulating, and the frustration level can be self-controlled—help us understand why children spend so many hours at it. While those features also make for a powerful learning tool, only a small percentage of children actually use computerized games for educational purposes. That figure drops dramatically as kids get older—among fourth graders, for example, only 18 percent of girls and 3 percent of boys play educational games; by eighth grade, only 6 percent of girls and .5 percent of boys do.

Bear in mind that, despite your good intentions when you bought those expensive instructional CD-ROMS, 50 percent of both genders—consistently across grade levels—prefer what researchers Debra Buchman and Jeanne Funk characterize as "fantasy and human violence" games. These high-action programs feature scenarios in which the rewarded "skill" is impulsive aggression. The earliest findings indicate that these games rev kids up to a point that works against Mood Mastery. Emotions aren't processed; problems aren't thoughtfully solved. The winner is someone who is able to quickly strike out at others and boldly defend against the invaders. Such values, repeatedly reinforced, are not a boon to self-regulation.

The "gimmes." When that first TV commercial wafts over your baby (even though its message is beyond her comprehension) or when she's lying in her crib, staring at her Rugrats bumpers or hugging her Muppet Baby blanket, the messages of the media come at her. And when she starts going to the playground and eyes other children toting various pop culture artifacts, she enters a culture that puts a premium on material things—especially merchandise related to the latest media trends. Commercials propagate the idea that satisfaction and relief must come from the outside, and even our youngest kids sometimes begin to compete with one another over their "stuff." The problem is, we want to teach our children that soothing and self-regulation come from within, but it's an uphill battle when you consider that the average child sees more than twenty thousand commercials a year—cleverly crafted thirty-second spots that are bound to put his gimmes into high gear.

Instant gratification. In the average child's lifetime, TV advertising will have occupied more than a year and a half of her life, each commercial communicating a similar anti-Mood-Mastery message:
"Do it!"
"Have fun!"
"Do it now!"
"Don't compromise."
"Obey your thirst."
"Just do it!"
In the media-dependent second family, the ability to withstand frustration and delay gratification—integral parts of Mood Mastery—is an outmoded notion. When you factor in computers, video games, MTV videos, and so many of the movies targeted at our children, it's easy to see how kids come to expect—or demand—instant solutions and instant satisfaction. Video games are, in fact, a ritualized, two-dimensional embodiment of the "Just do it" message. No need to wait, to measure one's words, thoughts, or actions—get in there and just start moving that joystick.

To be sure, while the technology revolution offers valuable resources, education, and information, the above aspects of the second family bombard our children and undermine Mood Mastery. But there is one additional threat to Mood Mastery that originates from within the family—and it may surprise you.

Parents' denial. For decades, my colleagues and I have been trying to address parents' denial of inborn temperament. Some moms and dads ignore their children's basic makeup; others fight it or just wish it would be different. And even when parents do see children clearly, they often don't have faith in what they see. There are complex and deeply entrenched causes to explain why parents don't trust their perceptions. It may be fear ("Is she just like me? Will she make the same mistakes?") or guilt ("I made him clingy [noisy/aggressive]—his behavior is all my fault"). And it's almost always because of love. Most mothers' and fathers' hearts are in the right place—they truly want to be good parents. Yet, for reasons I'll describe later, their strategies continue to be mismatched with their child's temperament. Battles ensue, with parents feeling genuinely disappointed in themselves and their child. And that, in fact, makes the situation even worse.

Let's say six-year-old David's mom and dad secretly wish he would be a different kind of kid—more assertive, less shaken by every little thing. With the aim of toughening him up, they approach him more brusquely than their other children. Hurt and confused, feeling that his parents don't "get" him, David becomes even more sensitive and high strung. On the other hand, if his parents stop hoping that he'll be different, if they instead accept and protect his basic temperament and help him with Mood Mastery, David will feel better understood. He may continue to be a cautious and reflective child—his fundamental core will not have changed—but the way he behaves and feels about himself will be vastly different than if his parents continued fighting who he is.

In a similar vein, if Sylvie's temperament is not accepted and dealt with clearly, if her parents keep hoping that her aggressive, strong-willed nature will one day magically disappear (and who among us hasn't wished for such a miracle?), she could easily develop into a stubborn, argumentative girl. But if Sylvie's parents embrace who she is, those negative qualities can be transformed into self-confidence and assertiveness. One day, that stubborn kid who ate all the strawberries could be the head of a multinational corporation!

Clearly, though, acceptance is a hard-won parenting skill. As one parent admitted guiltily, "I still wake up every day and hope that my son will be a little more rugged and less sensitive. And, every day, I feel disappointment. I think I'm unfairly angry at him just for being the same child." It may be an understandably human response to keep wishing that your child were more like others. But, remember, wishing makes it tougher to see your child clearly. The good news about denial is that you can conquer it. They key is to be mindful of your own bias and aware of the kinds of second-family influences that undermine self-regulation. That said, there are a number of concrete steps you can take that will enable you to look at your child through more discerning, realistic eyes to help her develop Mood Mastery.

Parent Skills: Fostering Mood Mastery

As I explained earlier in this chapter, the research on temperament is quite clear: You can't change your child's fundamental temperament—it's inborn. But you can adapt your own response and you can help him recognize and regulate his temperament.

Hence, teaching the primary core-builder, Mood Mastery, involves three key principles:

1. Recognize and accept your child's temperament.
2. Modify your approach to teaching Mood Mastery so that it specifically fits your child's temperament.
3. Reward your child when he demonstrates constructive, self-regulatory behavior; create and maintain consistent consequences when he exhibits a lack of self-monitoring.

Accordingly, I've divided the parent skills below into three sections: The first will help you understand more about temperament—specifically, the four types of temperament observed in children. The second will help, if you happen to be wearing blinders, by enabling you to perceive your child more clearly and specifically adapt your approach. And the third offers numbers of concrete skills that will help you promote and sustain Mood Mastery.

Recognizing your child's temperament
As soon as their child is born, most parents instinctively begin to foster Mood Mastery through empathic responses. This process, known

as attunement, was originally described by child psychologist and researcher Daniel Stern. By videotaping mother-infant communication, Stern vividly demonstrated that attunement begins when a mother sees her infant's emotional-physiological state clearly and acts to soothe and engage her child.

Other researchers now suggest that attunement is important throughout the parenting relationship, *no matter how old your child is.* In other words, we continually mirror and affect each other's emotional states. Thus, your child's reactions to developmental challenges and your reactions to him as he tries to master them are of equal importance.

For example, Tracey, a young mother, is attuned when, sensing her infant son Kian's discomfort, she coos empathically and follows up with a diaper change—actions that immediately make her baby feel more comfortable. Louis, the father of preschooler Skylar, understands that his son's tantrum needs space, not another round of choices, so he patiently stays available in the background. Likewise, Belinda, the mother of Jerrod, who is in elementary school, knows from observing her son's body language and confused expression that she needs to ask him questions about the day's events. In each instance, Mom or Dad responds to a specific need and, in so doing, allows the child to feel both seen and heard.

However, those parents are not only able to gauge their child's needs because they are aware of what's happening in the moment. They also are aware of the larger issue—each child's particular temperament. Tracey has already observed that Kian is very sensitive to physical discomfort and can't stand a soggy diaper. Since son Skylar was born, Louis witnessed his crying jags and tantrums; he learned that it's always more effective not to talk to him when he's so upset. And Belinda has gone through years of Jerrod's separation problems; she has found that asking him questions gives him an important sense of connection.

In order to encourage Mood Mastery, then, it's critical to look at the bigger picture—not just the event of the moment—and to remind yourself of your child's temperament. Although researchers have come up with many classifications and numerous descriptions, I've learned from parents that less and more practical is better. Below are the four types I've observed most often in my clinical and school consultation work. The children you met at the beginning of this chapter reappear as examples in the following descriptions. Your child may exhibit greater or lesser variations, but, in all probability, one of these temperamental/emotional styles will predominate.

Intense/Aggressive. Children like Sylvie have a high activity level. They may be aggressive or simply outgoing, or seemingly "get into everything." They are prone to tantrums, often can't tolerate frustration or delays, and have a hard time containing themselves. They tire us out. If you have this type of child, you've probably said or thought the following many times:
"What a handful."
"It's like having three kids in one."
"She's a born leader, she just takes over."
"I'm actually a little scared of her reactions."
"I don't know if I have the energy to keep up with her."

Intense/Sensitive. Children such as Matthew have an extra dose of sensitivity. Like Intense/Aggressive children, they, too, can be a handful. These kids tend to be more reactive, and are easily thrown by transitions, or by what they *perceive* as criticism. Responding to even the slightest verbal disapproval from an adult, for example, Matt is likely to scream, "Why are you yelling at me?" The phrases we use to describe a Intense/Sensitive child are:
"He's so finicky."
"He's all male."
"He has to have everything his way."
"Dealing with him is like walking on eggshells."
"What a high-maintenance child."

Reserved/Clingy. I adapted this term from Alan Sroufe and June Fleeson, child-development researchers at the University of Minnesota, who have studied many children like David. He and others like him are fussy, fearful, fragile, and cautious. They cry easily. They have trouble making friends, are frightened of separations from a loved one, and want to avoid new situations. This is a child who hides behind Mom or Dad for the first few minutes of a visit—even to Grandma's house. He may warm up, but it takes time and coaxing. Things parents often say about such a child:
"I can't leave him very often."
"Everything is such a big deal."
"He's a bottomless pit of needs."

"Why is he so dependent?"

"He'll never learn to be by himself."

Easy/Balanced. Children like Jessica embody every parent's fondest wish. They are good eaters and sleepers; they are sociable, with moderate emotions and behavior. As the name implies, Easy/Balanced children are typically on an even keel. No child is perfect, though. So, at times, these children evidence some characteristics of the three other types, but *usually* to a lesser degree. In a word, nothing is overblown or extreme. Other parents eye the mom and dad of an Easy/Balanced child with a mixture of admiration and envy. Parents of these children typically remark:

"She's a low-maintenance child."

"We're really lucky."

"I don't know when it'll change, but up till now . . ."

"I could have ten children like her."

Chances are you recognized your child in the above descriptions. Parents are almost always right when they say, "This is who my child is." The trouble arises when they might not trust their perceptions or be in denial about them.

Taking off the blinders

You need to trust what you see as well as what the research shows: Innate temperament exists and each child is unique. Recognizing and accepting these truths are prerequisites to understanding how to adapt your parenting practices to his core.

For example, since Oliver, an Intense/Sensitive child, was two, his mother, Margaret, has been saying, "What's wrong with my son? Why is he so moody and sensitive around strangers? Why does he tire so quickly and can't seem to keep up with the other kids?"

During the past eight years, while Margaret's perceptions have stayed the same, she continued to vacillate about acting on them. Some days, she thought she was being an alarmist, a view her husband shared. "Let's face it," Peter would say. "Oliver's behavior isn't *that* different from other kids'—or *mine*, for that matter." On other days, Margaret blamed herself—she must have done *something* to "make" Oliver the way he was. Was it her genes? After all, her own mother had forever threatened: "Someday you'll see what it's like to have a child like you." Oliver's pediatrician was laid back. "Give it time," he'd say. "I saw a hundred kids like him just this week." Despite all different and plausible explanations—not to mention Oliver's occasional carefree mood—his mom's worry persisted.

Margaret's difficulty in accepting that her son wasn't the easy child she'd wished for, is, as I've noted above, a common phenomenon. The following reminders may help you think about the factors that are influencing you.

Temperaments run in families. We tend not to notice that which is familiar. However, when you do notice a particular behavior in your child—say, aggression—your family history might lead you to think there's nothing that you can do about it. For example, Sandra was resigned about her son, Paul, an Intense/Aggressive child. After all, the men in the family were "hard-asses." No one thought twice when Paul hit other kids or got angry when someone set limits for him. That's just the way the Walker men were.

You're blinded by your own temperament. Perhaps one of your parents was like my mother. Frustrated by my picky eating habits when I was a kid, she repeatedly warned, "Someday, Ronnie, it'll be your turn. Then you'll understand how tough it is to be a parent." My finicky reputation was so solid that when our daughter, Leah, was born, the first question asked by her excited aunts and uncles was: "Is she a bad eater, too?"

You think you're doomed to repeat history. You feel like Margaret: "Mom was right. I just have to live through this the way she did with me." Somewhere in the back of Margaret's mind was a belief in retribution—she was destined to suffer for the disappointments and difficulties she had inflicted on her mother.

You want your child to be a "model" child. It's only human to compare your child to others, to hope that she's as sociable, as quick to

---

PLAY IT AGAIN, MOM OR DAD

You know you probably have an old tape running in your head if:

- Interactions with your child sound very familiar.
- You believe nothing can help your situation.
- You quickly label your child. It doesn't matter what the label is—stubborn, finicky, crybaby—it sticks.
- You say your child's temperament is "exactly" like yours. The label you use for her is something you were called.

---

learn, as adept, as popular. It feels bad when we think our children are somehow not what we wished for. Those yearnings—and, of course, the guilt that goes with them—can blind us to our child's core self. We try to fit them into a mold we'd like, rather than helping them feel comfortable in the mold in which they've already been cast.

The good news is that you don't have to stay locked in denial about your child's temperament. Nor do you have to try to change what you believe are "bad" traits. Time and again, parents have come to me upset about a child's behavior. In reality, the only reason they're having so much trouble "controlling" their son or daughter is their own determination to change the youngster's basic temperament instead of going with it. Once they understand this, and accept their child for who she is, parents can take concrete action to maximize the child's strengths and minimize her difficulties. Taking off the blinders involves three important steps.

Be a family detective. Look for mood strands that help explain your child's biological and genetic endowment. Temperaments *do* run in families. Go on a fact-finding mission and talk to older relatives. Ask them not only what you were like as a child, but also your parents, your grandparents, aunts, uncles. Try to focus on *specific* questions. Instead of a blanket "What was I [or he or she] like?" ask about moods, first days of school, eating and sleeping habits, socializing patterns, popularity, obedience, diligence. For example, you may find that Grandpa was the original "absent-minded professor"—is it any wonder that his son *and* grandson never seem to pay close attention to anything going on around them? Remember, colloquial descriptions often hide real temperamental issues, so listen carefully for expressions and phrases that mask deeper meanings, such as "orderly," "quiet type," "kept to himself," "go-getter," "always into something," "ball of fire."

Draw a mood map. Among the Walkers, the Intense/Aggressive theme was obvious, and once Sandra took a closer look at the family, she saw the pattern immediately. But these aren't always so obvious; you may need help. Therefore, I suggest that you draw a family mood map—called a genogram—which will give you an effective overview. This is what highly paid family therapists often do to identify generational patterns of behavior.

Below is a sample genogram I drew to represent the Samson family. It helped Garrett and Caroline Samson understand why their son Alexander was having trouble with transitions and cried so easily when they changed plans at the last minute. Neither parent knew much about their grandparents, but by just looking at the three generations, a pattern became obvious. Alexander's paternal grandmother had a reputation for being "high strung," his maternal grandfather was always seen as "moody," and Caroline admitted that she has always been called "touchy." In part, this generational snapshot explains why Alex is an Intense/Sensitive type—and why his sister is Easy/Balanced.

Following the three simple steps below will allow you to draw a genogram for your family. Look at your child's generation, yours, and your parents' on both sides. Chances are, you'll begin to see that your child is not the only one to have a particular temperamental profile.

1. List the members of each generation on both sides of your family: parents, aunts, and uncles; you and your spouse and your respective siblings.
2. Chart your extended family on a big piece of paper, representing males with a square symbol ■ and females with a round one ●. Use the example below as a model.

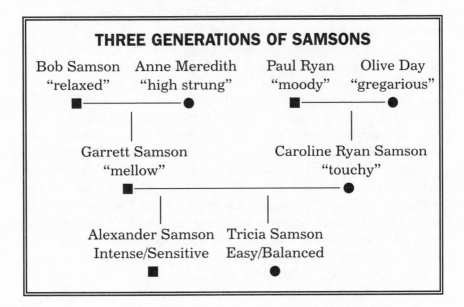

THREE GENERATIONS OF SAMSONS

Bob Samson Anne Meredith   Paul Ryan   Olive Day
"relaxed"   "high strung"   "moody"   "gregarious"

Garrett Samson   Caroline Ryan Samson
"mellow"   "touchy"

Alexander Samson Tricia Samson
Intense/Sensitive Easy/Balanced

3. Try assigning one of the four basic types to each family member: Aggressive, Sensitive, Clingy, Easy. You also may spot patterns of idiosyncracies, like bad eating habits, disorganization, learning problems, attention difficulties.

Remember that different generations have distinct standards of behavior for children. For example, at a time when children were raised to be "seen and not heard," being "obedient" was important. Take into consideration that even a mildly spirited child might have been considered "disobedient."

Also, prior generations may have called certain traits by other terms. Therefore, you will have to unlock the code phrases of specific eras. For example, today we might call aggressive kids "hyper." A generation ago, such children might have been labeled "a bad seed" or "wild."

Move from awareness to acceptance. Once you've identified certain patterns, you're less likely to deny your child's temperament or blame yourself (or him)—and more likely to respond appropriately to his behavior. I saw this in my own family. As if Leah had heard those family questions when she was born, she soon began to evidence the same eating difficulties I was so famous for. Luckily, because of my training, Stacey and I mapped out our family histories. My mother, labeled a "skinny marink," had been the worst eater in the neighborhood—until I came along. Then, the genogram revealed the exact same problem with two of my cousins on my father's side.

Doing a genogram showed me in a very concrete way that finicky eating was simply part of being a Taffel. Leah wasn't being bad or mean to us any more than I had been to my mother. Nor were we "defective." My cousins and I all lived through childhood without contracting any dread disease; we were just skinny. Maybe one day gene-mappers will find a finicky eater's gene; if so, we definitely have it. Instead of my fighting with Leah over that last drop in the bottle, or getting upset with myself, I was literally able to say, "This is who she is, and there's no point in my trying to change her into a good eater."

But I have to add one important point here: Don't expect yourself to read your child correctly every time—you can't and it's not even necessary. Jerome Kagan cites research done by psychologist Doreen Arcus suggesting that being a "perfect" parent is not what children need—getting it right more of the time is.

Fostering Mood Mastery

Once you accept your child's basic temperament, dramatic changes are possible—even with older children. Current research proves what Haim Ginott and the earlier generation of parenting experts suggested: Children can be taught to find their own solutions to everyday problems and emotional challenges. If (with parents' guidance) children are allowed to slog through ordinary moments that test their behavior, they will develop Mood Mastery and, in the process, gain the confidence to face—and solve—such problems on their own.

The following strategies and skills are not complicated. Some may even seem obvious, but, believe me, they will have a profound impact on your child's ability to self-regulate his temperamental predisposition.

Respond—don't fight. Too often an inability to accept a child's temperament causes us to push—sometimes even bully—him into changing. This just about never works. Pamela's way of fighting her son Ian's natural shyness was to overschedule Ian for activities that she expected would "bring him out of his shell." After several frustrating years, Pamela finally began to adapt to Ian's Reserved/Clingy temperament; she stopped wishing that he'd suddenly become an outgoing child. Once Pamela accepted her son's true temperament, the concrete strategy was simple and obvious: schedule fewer activities.

Miraculous as it sounds, two weeks later, Ian was a changed kid—more relaxed and more imaginative in his play. He experimented with difficult Lego and Duplo models, first at home with his parents, then with playmates in his nursery school. Pamela was deeply encouraged. Seeing Ian's shyness as caution stopped her from expressing disapproval or being annoyed. Instead, she was able to embrace him *as him*. This strengthened their relationship and brought them closer together.

When I say, don't fight, I mean, emphatically, *don't engage in chronic yelling*. For each type of child, habitual yelling takes a toll.

• For an Intense/Aggressive child like Paul, being yelled at only amplifies his need to get what he wants. For example, when Paul and his mother are shopping, he rudely demands that Sandra buy a new toy for him. She responds by saying sharply, "No! How many times do I have to tell you, you can't have everything you see?" Paul screams in defiance, "I want it!" and Mom, unwittingly upping the ante, screams back. She doesn't notice that her son has wandered away and he, feeling angrier and more frustrated, ends up shoving a child two aisles over who has the toy he wants. In this kind of scenario, yelling kindles a bonfire that heats up the whole environment. Your "handful" becomes a "roomful" and you're left feeling like an ogre or overpowered by your child. Either way, you've both lost.

• An Intense/Sensitive child hears and feels everything in bold relief. If an angry intonation is experienced as "yelling," imagine what a raised voice sounds like. My son, Sam, is in this group, and I've come to realize that he actually hears me differently than our daughter does. If I deliver a brief but sharp rebuke, not a word I say gets through to him because he's overwhelmed by my intensity. To avoid this abrasive stimulus, an Intense/Sensitive child like Sam responds by retreating, or crying. Once you start yelling, in other words, the meaning of your words is lost, and your child suffers without understanding what's going on. It's a lose-lose situation.

• A Reserved/Clingy child becomes more needy or withdrawn if you yell. Either way, there's no getting through once that wall goes up around him—and each time you yell, it grows more impenetrable. For example, Evelyn was exasperated and even a little embarrassed because every morning her three-year-old Tina was the last to let her mom leave the pre-K classroom. Evelyn's frustration peaked because her daughter's behavior regularly made her late for work. More than once, she yelled, "I can't take this. You're going to have to be a big girl," and she'd leave to the sound of Tina's wails. Her child then became even more reluctant to separate. Even worse, the battles increased, moving to bedtime, when Tina cried, "Don't leave, Mommy! If I go to sleep, it'll be soon before I have to go to school."

When Evelyn came to see me, I suggested that before anything else, she needed to cut down on yelling at her daughter—that Tina's temperament simply could not be badgered out of her. Two weeks later, Evelyn reported that once she'd eased off, Tina started talking. It's amazing, but one good conversation with Tina freed both mother and daughter from their destructive pattern.

• Because the Easy/Balanced child often can adopt any of the above coping styles, she may react by yelling back and upping the ante, by tuning out, or by withdrawing. In any case, yelling will only exacerbate the behavior.

ACT before your child gets out of emotional control. Observing young children at play, researchers have documented the self-stimulating momentum of aggression. A kid like Paul, for example, often goes into overdrive. His dad, Roger, described the pattern to me by relating a typical incident: Paul was out in the yard playing with his siblings and some of the neighborhood boys. At one point, everybody got a little too excited, the roughhousing escalated, and, Roger said, "It was as if Paul would just flip a switch." He flew out of control—hitting, yelling, grabbing toys, and pushing kids off the swing.

Each time Roger witnessed such a scene, he felt horrible, because, in fact, he had seen it coming; his son's "horsing around" inevitably turned into over-the-top aggression. And after each incident, Paul felt awful about himself. He knew what everyone was thinking: "Paul the troublemaker." He knew it; his dad knew it; the other kids and their parents knew it.

How often have you said to yourself, "I saw that coming" or "I could tell he'd be upset," and yet you did nothing to prevent what you knew would be inevitable? Countless times, I'm sure. We all have those moments; we sometimes beat ourselves up afterward wondering why we didn't *do* something. I've come up with a simple acronym—ACT—that will help you remember to intervene before your child gets carried away. ACT stands for:

Anticipate *your child's typical reaction—and step in before it's too late.*

Calm yourself and your child.

Teach your child how to handle the situation differently.

ACT can help you stop *wishing* that your child's moods or reactions would change, and start *doing* something to facilitate the process instead. Once you intervene early, you'll be surprised at how easy it is to come up with productive ideas to minimize difficulties. Let's look at each of the components.

Anticipate your child's typical reaction—and step in before it's too late. Researchers find that almost half the kids who have difficult or negative temperaments early on do not develop emotional problems later in life. Therefore, we must be doing something right by simply using our intuition, which includes anticipating. Listen to yourself—to your "gut." As you become better at acting on what you know about your child's typical responses, you will help her learn to recognize and regulate herself.

In Roger's case, for example, I asked, "If you could accept that given Paul's basic temperament, he will almost always flare up when he gets overstimulated—what would you do differently to help him stay in control?"

He thought for a minute and said, "Well, first I'd stop waiting ... waiting for it to pass or for him to change. I guess I'd watch for the earliest signal and then immediately step in." I suggested that he try just that whenever he had a gut feeling that trouble was about to start. Over time, both of Paul's parents became better at anticipating the typical cycle of events and were able to step in before their son got out of control.

Likewise, when Tom and Mary began to anticipate and accept, rather than trying to change, Intense/Aggressive Sylvie into a child with delicate manners, they could prepare themselves and her in simple ways. For one thing, Mom stopped placing large boxes of strawberries in front of her! And knowing Sylvie's tendency to grab everything for herself when friends were over, Mom and Dad always made sure to have plenty of toys for Sylvie and her playmates.

Calm yourself and your child. Stepping in means interrupting the situation at hand. But don't even try to talk until both you and your child are composed. Relationship researchers, notably John Gottman at the University of Washington, author of *Why Marriages Succeed and Fail,* have shown that when we try to communicate during an intense moment, we diminish our chances of finding solutions and teaching self-regulation. If you're too upset to talk, take a break; don't even deal with the problem. And if your child is already over the edge, calm her down first; below, I describe specific calming techniques—distracting, soothing storytelling, relaxation techniques, but some children just need the time and space to cool down on their own. Sylvie was like that; once she got going, her parents had to ride out the tantrum. Therefore, I urged Mary to wait for a quiet time to speak with Sylvie in a unruffled and positive way about how to regulate herself:

Mary:	You think you might have trouble sharing when Becky comes over this afternoon?
Sylvie:	Yeah.
Mary:	What could we do?
Sylvie:	Hide all my toys from her?
Mary:	Well, what would you play with?
Sylvie:	I want to hide my special dolls.
Mary:	How many?
Sylvie:	All of them!
Mary:	How about three? Want to hide them now?
Sylvie:	Not Samantha. I want to play with her.
Mary:	Okay, so which three shall we put away?

Teach your child how to handle the situation differently. In the above conversation, Mary began to show Sylvie a new approach to circumstances that in the past were problematic for her daughter. For shy Ian, too, once his parents, Pamela and Joe, began to ACT, they also helped their son learn that new behavior is possible. They developed signals to remind Ian that he was baby-talking (which he did when anxiety got the best of him) or appearing rude by not answering someone's question. Mom or Dad acted like a coach, touching their nose as a signal for "baby talk" or scratching their head whenever they saw Ian averting his eyes.

In addition to teaching him these signals, Pamela prepped Ian specifically for a visit to Aunt Selma—the fond relative who often expressed affection for her nephew by zealously pinching his cheek. "Sometimes, Aunt Selma gets so excited that she pinches way too hard," Pamela said to Ian. "I'd hate that, too. Maybe if you make the first move—give her a big hug—she'll hug back and won't be able to reach your cheek." His dad added, "And I'll be right beside you, just to make sure it works." Feeling prepared and protected by his parents, Ian didn't shrink from Aunt Selma at Thanksgiving, the next family gathering. He only began to cling to his mom late in the afternoon, when he got tired.

After a few successes, Ian began to say after such occasions, "I did good with baby talk today, right, Mommy?" He was developing the self-awareness and pride that goes along with Mood Mastery.

This simple sequence—anticipating, calming, and teaching—almost always works. In Paul's case, after several months had passed, he began to know what it felt like to be overexcited and came in from outside to tell Sandra, "Mommy, I don't want to get too wild, now." He, too, was beginning to attain Mood Mastery. "I can see he's much happier with himself now that he's more in charge of his life," remarked his father. Because Paul experienced the increasing benefits, he became more and more motivated to change his behavior: other kids liked him better and enthusiastically included him in their games; his relationship with his parents was easier—everyone was glad to see the old tensions fade away. This is not unusual. When old patterns start to change, Mood Mastery will create its own self-perpetuating motion.

Distract without discounting. Helping children learn how to distract themselves is an essential part of self-regulation. At the same time, though, you want your child to feel heard. Try this two-step strategy:

1. Acknowledge your child's feelings. Before your child can move on, it's important that you first acknowledge what he feels ("I know you're scared") and then offer him ways to get out of that emotional space.

2. Come up with a diversion or an alternate plan. This doesn't mean telling a child to "get over it," but rather helping her move on by giving her something else to focus on.

Paula, for example, knows that when she says "Enough" or "Stop" in a firm tone, it invariably throws her four-year-old daughter into a tailspin. As with a lot of Intense/Sensitive kids, Rebecca hears such a tone in an exaggerated way and reacts accordingly. She complains about being "yelled at" and all head-on attempts to explain or convince lead to nothing.

After I'd spent several sessions with Paula pointing out the futility of her approach, she finally tried another tack. One evening when the family was driving home from a day's visit with Grandma, Paula and Joel were playing a counting game with their daughter, who was in the backseat. Every time Rebecca counted to three, her dad switched on the inside light. Delighted at first by his four-year-old's giggles, Joel began to find it difficult to drive with the on-off, disco strobe-light effect. He kept saying, "Okay, Becca, this is the last one," but each time he threatened to end the game, Rebecca became more upset.

Paula finally stepped in. Rather than the dreaded "Enough," she said, "I know you're having fun, Becca," and followed up quickly by distracting her: "But I think the light will burn out if we keep this up. Then when we go to Grandma's birthday party next week, we won't be able to play with it at all. What do you think we can bake for her, a chocolate torte or an upside-down cake?" All of a sudden, Rebecca was able to switch gears. Her mom acknowledged Rebecca's feelings (that she wanted to play) and then, without locking horns, gave her something else of real interest to focus on.

Use (indirect) storytelling to calm your child. Distraction may not work with an Intense/Aggressive child, but storytelling usually does. This is not surprising. Just about every great healer in the world has been a brilliant storyteller, and the tradition continues. Without labeling it as such, a psychiatrist taking a patient through a guided imagery exercise or a native shaman soothing a collective wound of his people uses stories to teach Mood Mastery. Listeners learn to reach inside to soothe themselves. Unfortunately, we parents often confuse storytelling with lecturing. The message of a lecture is: "I want you to change." In contrast, indirect storytelling offers a message that will not increase your child's resistance—it gives her another way to think about it.

Soothe, don't "fix" your child. When a child is emotionally hurt, we often rush in with a solution. But "fixing" doesn't help Mood Mastery. Children use stories to find their own way. Here's how this strategy worked with a younger child: A bigger boy in nursery school class pushed ahead of three-and-a-half-year-old Madeline when the teacher was distributing stickers for good participation in gymnastics. Maddy didn't want to discuss it. But from her silence on the way home, it was clear to her dad, Saul, that his little girl's feathers had been ruffled. Because Saul knew his daughter's Intense/Sensitive nature, he was able to guess that whatever happened had wounded her ego. Instead of trying to fix her feelings or asking directly "What's wrong?" he kept quiet until they got home. Then Saul picked up Doggie, Maddy's favorite cuddle toy. He gave him a hug and said, "Doggie's upset about something. Put him on your lap so he can calm down. Maybe we can talk to Doggie and help him feel better."

Stay in the story. If you try to teach the lesson or make a direct point, it won't work. Therefore, as Saul began to talk to Doggie, he neither looked at Madeline nor did he direct the narrative toward her. He patted the stuffed animal on her lap, looked into its eyes and said, "Doggie, you look like you need a good story. Well, there once was a little girl who hated when kids pushed her. It scared her, and she wanted to cry, but she was afraid that the other kids would laugh at her. So, she kept her feelings secret. Then, one day, she saw a little boy crying in a corner of the gym. 'What's wrong with you?' she asked. And to her surprise the little boy said he was scared of being pushed, too. He told her, 'I feel better, though, because now I told someone what's wrong.' "

Allow your child to resolve the dilemma. Maddy's father paused for a heartbeat, hoping Madeline would jump in—most children will—and she did. "Oh, Daddy!" she exclaimed. "That little boy needs a friend. Maybe Doggie's sad because he does, too." Even though the story was several characters removed from her, it calmed Maddy and, after a few more minutes imagining what "Doggie" might do, she began talking about herself. The soothing story enabled her to bring her fears to the surface and deal with them.

With school-age children, stories can be a little more personal. For example, when six-year-old Lauren had trouble separating for a first sleepover, Mom told a story about her own first night away from home, emphasizing the similar circumstances and feelings between then and now.

Younger children like to identify with their parents; it makes them feel more secure. With an older child, such parallels are less effective because these kids are trying to develop their own identity. They reflexively rebel against being like their parents—and will resent the implication. Therefore, you need to be a little less directive. Tell your story through a fictitious character or person you both know. A mother who was getting a divorce used the movie *Rich Kids* to help elicit her children's feelings; one child was an Easy/Balanced type, the other Intense/Sensitive, so each had different reactions to the family reorganization. However, the movie, which follows the reactions of two preteens whose parents are divorcing, provided an appropriate springboard for discussion for both children.

Use rewards without bribing. The findings are unequivocal: Both researchers and clinicians who work with intense children—whether intensely sensitive or aggressive—find that we cannot do away with

HOW TO USE STORIES EFFECTIVELY

1. Speak in a voice that is calming, but consistent with your child's mood.

    If he's angry, have a slight edge.

    If she's sad, use a softer voice.

    If he's withdrawn, be neutral.

2. Situate the problem "outside" your child so he has some emotional distance from it: Another person is upset; a puppet is angry; other kids feel this way.

3. Use an object, like a stuffed animal, that your child relates to in a positive way.

4. Stay in the story. Don't break the mood by saying different forms of "Get it?" or "Do you know what I'm talking about?"

5. Help your child resolve the dilemma by asking how "Doggie" can make himself feel better; offer multiple-choice self-soothers: "Did Doggie sing a song? Talk to his parents?"

6. Don't interpret the story. When it's over, just let it end. Don't ask whether your child understood, or repeat the moral to make sure it got through.

rewards. Most constructive moves in the direction of self-regulation need to be recognized, at least minimally. And nothing motivates like sincere, realistic praise. For example, after Ian's triumph at Thanksgiving dinner, when it was obvious to Pamela that he had taken small steps to conquer his shyness, she told him how proud she was of him. She praised him honestly, providing a simple and very important reward that meant a great deal to Ian. Each little victory was met in the same way, and slowly Ian moved from disappointment toward feeling better and fortifying his core self.

Imagine our Intense/Sensitive child, Matthew, now struggling to contain his emotions on the playground when one of the older boys takes his baseball cap and calls him "a wimp." Because of Dad's coaching at home, Matt could be heard saying to himself under his breath, "I want to be brave." Instead of bursting into tears, he approached the teacher and told her what was going on. When he reported the incident to his father later that night, Dad said, "Good going, Matt. You're beginning to stand up for yourself more."

Dad also suggested to Matt that they go shopping for that baseball

Matt had been asking for. Even though it wasn't Matthew's birthday yet, his father knew that it would be a good idea to associate this gift with his victory on the playground. It would serve as a reminder of Matt's important step toward Mood Mastery. That big kid may be back to taunt him, but each time Matthew manages to assert himself in some small way, he's strengthening his core.

Inject humor to teach resiliency. We've always known that kids love humor. But, in the last couple of years, researchers have found that it ranks among the top qualities children value in parents. As a spokesperson for the Yankelovich Youth Monitor reported to me in 1996, "Recently, for the first time, we have found humor in adults to be one of the traits that children admire most." And in the hundreds of interviews I've conducted with children, this has been mentioned repeatedly.

You must learn to tailor humor to your child's temperament. For certain kinds of kids, especially those who are sensitive, humor at any age may be experienced as disrespectful. As with other temperamental predispositions, fighting a child's sensibilities will only make her feel worse. Don't expect to change your child's taste in humor—use whatever *works*. Keep dipping into the same well as long as you can get a positive response.

One evening, five-year-old Devon, an Intense/Sensitive child, was balking about the smell of the new shampoo his father, Keith, was using to wash his hair. None of Keith's jokes or wisecracks made a dent. However, remembering Devon's love of sight gags, Keith jumped into the tub *fully clothed*. Devon erupted into gales of laughter, still giggling without protest through a second wash and rinse.

You needn't go to such extremes, of course—just go with your child's natural disposition. When the Peterson children, Seth, four, and Lara, ten, got upset because their parents turned off Nickelodeon before it was over, a funny-sarcastic comment worked wonders with their Easy/Balanced daughter, but only made their Intense/Sensitive son sulk. The Petersons are savvy enough not to fight this basic difference in tastes. So, while Mom traded wisecracks with Lara, Dad helped Seth calm down by doing a pratfall.

Regrettably, I rarely hear modern parents talk about humor as a way to teach self-regulation. We tend to take child-rearing so seriously. But humor that fits your child's temperament can help her regulate herself and get through the rough spots. Best of all, children eventually learn to humor themselves.

Make "smart" play dates. Most parents recognize that peer pressure starts early. We have all, at times, caught ourselves whispering to a spouse, "I don't like it when John plays with Bill. That boy is such a bad influence." Parental chauvinism aside, research shows that we're right: Children do affect each other's capacity for Mood Mastery.

Even at the youngest ages, children come home from play dates having absorbed the mode of self-regulation that predominates in another family. For example, when four-year-old Lara, an Easy/Balanced child, came home from a play date, her parents could always tell which friend she'd spent time with. If it had been Rachel, with her demanding, passionate temperament, Lara came back primed to complain and express dissatisfaction. If, on the other hand, she'd spent the afternoon with her good friend Amanda, who was more even-tempered, Lara would come home quieted by a fresh reserve of patience. Her parents saw this same phenomenon with younger brother Seth, who was easily upset by loud noises and commotion. When he played with Brian, an Intense/Sensitive boy like him, there was no problem. But after a morning with Julian, who was Intense/Aggressive and a bit of a tyrant, Seth often came home in tears.

It's critical to begin monitoring peer connections early—when, in fact, you can still govern them. If you make smart dates for your preschoolers and, later, help them pick friends best suited to their nature, they will be more likely to make better choices for themselves—and more likely to develop Mood Mastery (see more about kids' friendships in chapter 5, "Peer Smarts").

When arranging play dates, consider the other child's temperament as carefully as your own child's. Often mothers tamp down their instincts and hope against hope that two Intense/Aggressive kids won't have a difficult time or will play well without supervision. As Linda, mother of three-year-old Alvin told me, "I know that whenever Alvin and Danny get together, someone usually ends up with a bloody nose. The best we can hope for is that the house won't look like a bomb hit it."

Careful monitoring is important when it's possible. Remember that your best friend's daughter may not turn out to be your daughter's best friend or, worse, the two could be like oil and water. Few combinations of temperament present an insurmountable challenge, mind you, but by taking both children into consideration, you can try to insure that they stay in control of themselves and their time together.

Put a cap on media consumption. Entire books have been written about smart TV viewing over the last several years—and with good reason. As I pointed out in the "Core Threats" section of this chapter, television and video games can counter efforts to help your child develop Mood Mastery. However, television doesn't have to be The Enemy. Just use it sparingly. As I mentioned, most of the experts agree

---

A GUIDE TO PLAY DATE MONITORING

Two Intense/Aggressive children: Plan a shorter, structured date, perhaps with more than one parent supervising. They'll both be bouncing off the walls if you don't.

Intense/Aggressive child with an Easy or Reserved/Clingy child: Step in at the first sign of tension with firm but gentle limits, so that one child doesn't feel overpowered.

Two Reserved/Clingy children: Remember, they're not antisocial, they're just uncomfortable. Create bridges—developmentally appropriate games and activities.

Two Sensitive children: Think ahead to encourage interaction; act as the "interpreter" so neither child will take things the wrong way.

Intense/Aggressive with Intense/Sensitive: Not an easy or constructive pairing; try to avoid it.

---

that anything over three hours per day of media is considered "excessive." We parents seem to have trouble limiting television, though, either abdicating entirely or becoming totalitarian rulers who try to ban TV altogether. My suggestion is to *look at what kind of child you have*— and then come up with a reasonable limit based on your child's reactions. Intense/Aggressive children are most at risk, but what is less obvious perhaps is that too much TV can make an Intense/Sensitive child feel fearful and a Reserved/Clingy child feel more isolated and, ultimately, more clingy.

With any type of child, however, it's a good idea to be watchful about content. Over a thousand separate studies and reviews attest that exposure to heavy doses of television violence increases the likelihood of aggressive behavior. This is most critical for Intense/Aggressive children, who get revved up by this kind of TV action, but violence impacts on the other three types, especially Intense/Sensitive children, as well. Indeed, a number of studies indicate that excessive television correlates with a child's belief that he or she will be the victim of a crime.

Model Mood Mastery in your own daily affairs. Research is very clear on the fact that children learn how to soothe uncomfortable emotions in part by absorbing their parents' behaviors. Years ago, Salvador Minuchin, one of the great early family therapists, demonstrated this principle in a study with diabetic children and their parents. Dr. Minuchin asked children to sit behind a one-way mirror, observing their parents with a therapist who was purposely goading them to fight. Before and after the argument, researchers measured the children's physiological indicators of stress and anger. They documented clear evidence that the emotions traveled through the one-way mirror.

Research aside, parents' fighting obviously has an impact on kids. And it makes a difference whether children see them spinning into a full-scale battle or whether parents are able to take a time-out. Going a step farther, I believe that parents' behavior toward each other and their ability to manage individual moods influence the development of Mood Mastery in their sons and daughters.

Children are always watching—so it's essential for us to model healthy behaviors. Easier said than done, right? But imagine the beneficial differences in your child's mastery when you consistently express your emotions in healthy ways. Practice arriving at the second statement in each of the following sets:

Instead of:	I'm so angry, I'm going out of my mind.
You say:	I'm really angry, so I'm going out for a run.
Instead of:	I'm so sad about George, I feel like I'm gonna die.
You Say:	I'm so sad about George, but I think a little music will make me feel better.
Instead of:	My boss is ruining my life.
You say:	I've had a hard day at work and I need to calm down, so I'm going to take a hot bath.

Statements such as those exemplify healthy Mood Mastery. They will give children ideas for self-soothing and distracting strategies—and will have the opposite effect from lecturing a child who is already upset. Our self-regulation shows kids that they have options—ways of processing feelings or putting them aside for a while.

Help your child learn to generate self-soothing phrases and activities. Mood Mastery is an ongoing challenge for children. They face new situations every day—sometimes every hour—with very few concrete skills to help them deal with their feelings. As parents, we need to make specific suggestions: "Maybe you'll feel better if you sit quietly and read for a little while" or "Why don't you help me in the garden? That might take your mind off the fight you had with Jerry." I call these suggestions "planting seeds." In time, your child will learn to harvest them—and come up with their own soothing strategies.

For example, Amanda, an Easy/Balanced eight-year-old, sometimes feels left out of the popular clique in her class. Her parents are avid readers and have been gently recommending it as a mood-soother since Amanda was six. It's not surprising that she picks up a book whenever she feels a little down, now deciding "for herself" that reading can be both comfort and company.

Likewise, Deirdre, a Reserved/Clingy child, had anxiety every spring as she anticipated leaving for camp. Despite her difficulties when at age seven she was first physically separated from her parents, Deirdre made it through the summer and had two more enjoyable camp seasons after that. However, each time, without fail, she missed her parents deeply when they left. Now at eleven, the difference is that Deirdre *anticipates* this feeling. Last summer, she asked her mother for a pack of personalized stationery as a going-away gift. "Her" idea evolved from her parents' suggestion that letter-writing could make her feel more connected to the family at home and have a soothing effect as well.

Children aren't born with these skills in place. They need our help to learn soothing words and techniques. For example, when Sylvie is told she has to wait until after dinner to have her ice cream, she's liable to go over the edge with anticipation. When Oliver's mom is not home on time, he gets very nervous. When Tommy, a neighbor's Reserved/Clingy five-year-old, scrapes his knee, his first reaction is to cry uncontrollably and look for the nearest pair of legs to grab.

Now, when Sylvie jumps out of her skin in anticipation, asking every five minutes, "Can I have my ice cream?" her mom tells her, "When the dishes are all cleaned and everything's done, you can." After a few times, Sylvie can be heard muttering under her breath, "When everything's done, I can have ice cream."

Oliver's parents remind the baby-sitter to assure him that when one of them is late, "it's usually because of traffic." Now, Oliver can tell himself, "Mommy's coming home. Mommy will be back. It's just bad traffic."

And, touchingly, I've heard Tommy whispering to himself after a minor fall, "I'll be brave. I'll be all right. I'm not going to cry."

It's poignant and inspiring to watch children in these moments. You can actually see the wheels turning as they struggle to remember words to help soothe their spirits. The more peaceful look on their faces—the self-confidence and pride they feel mastering the moment themselves—demonstrates the core-building potential of Mood Mastery.

Be patient. These strategies may fail sometimes, and your attempts to get through may be foiled. Your child might even act as if he didn't hear you—as if you'd said nothing. Younger children might complain loudly or scream hysterically when you attempt to help them achieve Mood Mastery. And get ready if your kids are older, because preteen years often respond with a sarcastic "Yeah, right!"

Don't be discouraged. Believe it or not, the seeds of self-regulation will germinate, and just when you least expect it, your child will surprise you with her growth and mastery.

Child Skills: Self-Soothing Techniques

As new cognitive behavioral and developmental research shows, most kids, regardless of specific temperament, can be *taught* from an early age to better regulate and soothe themselves. The following is a series of strategies that can begin to develop in children as young as two or three.

Recognizing body signals of anxiety— and patterns of distress

Children often experience and express their emotions in terms of their bodies. Anxious or overwhelmed, they even say things like "I feel funny in my stomach" or "My head hurts." And chances are they don't make the connection until we point it out. Notice what's happening and encourage your child to describe it so that, together, you can identify the *what, when,* and *where* of his feelings. Then he can *do* something about it.

Help him notice the patterns. When Matthew came home from kindergarten looking anxious and ashamed, saying that he "hated" school, his mom asked him questions about his body. What did it feel like? He said he had "butterflies" in his stomach.

Inquiring further, Mom realized that the "butterflies" always arrived at a particular time—when Matt sat next to Dexter. As it turned out, Matthew didn't hate school. He was terrorized by Dexter, a much bigger boy who bullied him by yelling right into his ear. Mom stepped in, asking the teacher to never seat the boys together. Equally important, she congratulated Matthew for noticing his "butterflies," and told him to pay attention whenever he felt them. That was his body "speaking to him," she explained. In this instance, the butterflies were telling him to move away from Dexter. Over time, Matthew was able to grasp that the feelings in his body had meaning, and not feel embarrassed by them. He could then do something with them—in other words, self-regulate through constructive action. He no longer felt helpless and ashamed.

The goal is to help your child read her own emotional thermostat. Six-year-old Tamara sulked and withdrew from friends over little skirmishes, which was a reactive and self-defeating response. So, her parents problem-solved, hoping to come up with a proactive response that would enable her to behave in a way that might prevent her from feeling rejected. Mom and Dad asked, "What does it feel like when you get upset?" She told them she felt "mad inside." They helped her see that it was important to do something when she was feeling just a little angry about being left out—before the feelings built up and she became really upset. Her dad explained, "If you wait and don't do anything, you'll just feel worse." Then her mom asked, "What could you do when you feel a little bit mad?" Tamara thought for a moment and said, "I could leave the game or circle before I really get mad." This simple discussion made Tamara feel as if the anger was under *her* control and wouldn't take her over. She saw that she could do something before a situation got out of hand—something that would allow her to rejoin her friends more easily.

Asking a parent for help

An important way for children to take care of themselves is by learning how to ask for help in ways that create positive responses. This is critical because sometimes children use negative behaviors to get attention. These tend to put off the adults in their lives. Kids who don't know how to ask for help are often tagged as "difficult"—they're "too" something: loud, shy, pushy, scared, you name it. And whatever label they're given follows them throughout school; eventually, the label becomes who they are—whiny Theresa, grumpy Greg, obstinate Charlie. I cover the child skill of developing relationships with other adults in the next chapter, but this skill is first honed at home, with you, the parent.

When something is hard or troublesome for your child, let her know that the way he asks will make a difference. Role-playing is a wonderful technique, allowing your child to hear herself while giving her a chance to become more self-aware. Abbie, four, is prone to whining, which is understandably annoying. But rather than snap at her with a terse, "Stop that whining!" Mom suggests playing a game in which she pretends to be Abbie, and Abbie plays her. Mom starts to speak in a grating whimper, "You're not fair. You never let me do anything fun." Abbie laughs at Mom's portrayal, but the message sinks in—Abbie *hears* herself. Mom then helps her come up with a better approach. "See if you can think of a way to ask me for something without whining. I might hear you better."

When seven-year-old Bart wanted something, he often stood too close and talked too loudly. This drove his mom, Delia, crazy—especially because she has a somewhat reserved temperament. Delia helped him understand how his decibel level affected her (and, most assuredly, others): "Watch me, Bart. Whenever I do this," she said, holding her hand up like a traffic cop, "it probably means you're asking too loudly. Say it softer and see if you can make me lower my hand."

Anticipating difficulty

As you work on these Mood Mastery skills, sensing trouble will become part of your child's internal repertoire of skills. He will eventually learn to regulate himself *before* a hard situation gets worse. This comes with time and teaching. Consider the way Sandra helped six-year-old Paul. Paul would regularly get into fights about sharing. As I explained earlier in this chapter, his behavior was particularly bad when he played in the yard; something about the full run of the outdoors really made his aggression kick in. Sandra kept coaching Paul to ask for help *before* he went too far. "If you feel you're getting too excited, Paul, like when you start yelling instead of talking, and you feel like you might break a rule, *ask me for help.*"

It didn't work right away. Sandra had to prompt Paul on several occasions, but she did so by reminding him that she was there for him. One day, Paul's self-monitoring kicked in. He and the boy next door were given water pistols with the rule of not aiming at each other's eyes. After about five minutes of play, Paul suddenly stopped and ran to Sandra: "Mommy, I want to aim at Howie's face." She recommended that he take a one-minute break—a time-out at Mom's side. At other times, Paul would have resented her suggestion, but now he understood. Sandra told Paul how proud she was that he was getting to know his own mind.

"I can't believe how pleased he looked," Sandra told me. "Afterward we went for a spur-of-the-moment treat." Mom's praise—and the ice cream cone—were rewards that helped reinforce Paul's good behavior—and helped him internalize his new skill.

Reframing, or finding positive attributes of one's own temperament

"Reframing" is a term psychologists use to describe a technique whereby we shed a different light on a particular behavior. This usually means changing a negative description into something more positive. Take Rob, for example: He is not a "bad" child, but he has been acting up at home and in school. It was his way of getting his parents, who were drifting apart, to talk and work together. A different perspective shows that he's quite a "smart" child.

Reframing helps people think—and thereby *act*—differently. In his groundbreaking research on depression, psychologist Martin Seligman, author of *The Optimistic Child,* found a direct correlation between depression and how a child thinks about failure, defeat, loss, and helplessness. The meaning is clear: If someone thinks negatively about himself or an event, then his behavior will be geared accordingly. If he expects to be a failure, to be defeated, or to be helpless, he might just be. Seligman and other cognitive behaviorists find, however, that changing the way a person thinks can not only change his outlook but often the outcome as well.

Why not teach your child to do the same thing? Instead of sitting by while he chastises or criticizes himself, you can help him think about his behavior more constructively. Remember Deirdre, who experienced anxiety about sleep-away camp? Her mom, Amy, *hoped* her daughter would adapt to camp easily that first summer. But based on Deirdre's past difficulties around separations, I explained that it was far more constructive not only to expect the inevitable but also to *reframe* it in a positive way. Hence, Amy told Deirdre, "Saying that you'll be 'homesick' makes it sound like you're going to catch a disease. Of course, you're going to miss us and cry when we're gone. I'll cry, too, because I'll be sad to have you out of the house. Missing each other is normal. It's a good sign. I'd be upset if you didn't miss us."

Amy's acknowledgment of her daughter's feelings and reframing of "homesickness" gave Deirdre permission to experience her natural insecurity and loneliness without feeling deficient. Equally important, by not arguing about her experience, her mother gave Deirdre a chance to relax and come up with a constructive suggestion. Deirdre called it her "home-missing plan": They would speak on the phone for two minutes every other day, until Deirdre felt she didn't need to anymore. In essence, Amy's acceptance of her child as "normal" allowed Deirdre to be who she was.

Margaret did something similar with Oliver, who had difficulty with new baby-sitters. She pointed out that Oliver was very "smart" to wonder about any new person and acknowledged that having someone new around would be hard for anyone. Then Margaret said, "I've checked this sitter out, but I want to hear a report from you, too." This put Oliver in a different mind-set. Feeling safer and more in charge, he got out his Legos to busy himself when the sitter arrived. Mom also suggested that he watch the clock, because she knew that would make him feel more concretely in control. By the time Margaret came home, Oliver had built a new Lego empire. He also had soothed his anxiety by making a mental list of the baby-sitter's good and bad points, which he proudly spouted the moment the sitter left.

RECIPE FOR RELAXATION
(SUITABLE FOR ADULTS, TOO!)

Have your child lie down on a bed or a pad on the floor. Tell her in a slow, calming voice:

"Close your eyes and take five really deep, slow breaths, counting to four as you inhale and as you exhale."

"Concentrate on how your breath feels as the air comes into your body and fills it up, and then, as you push it out."

"With your eyes still closed, feel how heavy your body gets as it begins to relax. Focus your attention on your toes. Curl them under for a minute and then let them relax."

"In your mind's eye, move up your legs; tense them and relax."

"Now focus on the middle of your body. Pull your stomach in and relax it."

"Then focus on your arms—tense and relax them. Do the same with your chest and shoulders."

"Finally, focus on your face. Scrunch it up, and then relax."

"Your whole body is tingling now. Enjoy the feeling."

This is a good time to add a "visualization" component. Suggest that your child imagine a favorite place, doing a favorite activity, or being with favorite people. With an older child, this state can be used to problem-solve. Suggest that your child imagine resolving the unhappy or difficult situation in the way that's best for her. This exercise can yield amazing insights—and problem-solving strategies.

"Take four more deep breaths. Just lie here for a few minutes, and when you're ready, slowly open your eyes."

Employing a self-soothing relaxation technique

Progressive relaxation techniques were originally developed in the seventies for heart patients and people with ulcers or other stress-related maladies. The exercises helped the patients calm their minds, which, in turn, calmed their body's response to stress. Since then, current research on the mind-body connection has become so convincing that managed-care companies are beginning to cover alternative relaxation techniques, such as meditation. The works with children, too.

Yet, I've met very few mothers and fathers who teach these techniques to their children—even when meditation is a part of their own daily routine. What a shame! Progressive relaxation is made for children. They love it. The basic principles are easy to adapt for kids as young as three or four. After a short time, they'll practice these techniques on their own—and they may even prescribe them for you. One day, Melanie came home tired and cranky after a bad day at the office. Four-year-old Jennifer, who learned and loved relaxation exercises that helped her go to sleep or ward off a cold, said, "Come on, Mom. Lie down. I'll do a relaxation for you."

If you already meditate, you probably need no help in adapting your regimen for your child. If not, follow the simple recipe in the box on page 48. Or find books to guide you. I have been reading *Moonbeam* and *Starburst,* by Maureen Garth, to my two children for years and have found them to be wonderfully calming. Both contain simple visualizations and stories that help children relax. Other good resources include: *The Joy of Ritual: Recipes to Celebrate Milestones, Transitions, and Everyday Events in Our Lives* by Barbara Biziou, and *The Joy Within: A Beginner's Guide to Meditation* by Joan Goldstein and Manuela Soares.

CHAPTER 2

RESPECT

___

Basic Skill #2: Encourage your child to listen to and be comfortable with responsible adults.

A Disconcerting Trend

A few months ago, I was at a suburban mall waiting for a friend who was several minutes late. I sat on one of the wood benches just watching people walk by. Though there were some parents and children holding hands, what I saw most were groups of kids—not only teenagers, mind you, but boys and girls as young as six, all clumped together while their parents walked several strides ahead. Despite the kids' different ages, their similar haircuts and uniformly unlaced sneakers made it clear that they were part of the same pop culture club. Even the cutest five-year-olds had a bit of a precocious air about them. The kids giggled among themselves; grown-ups sometimes seemed to tag along. That is, until it became time to purchase goods. Then serious, even disrespectful, bargaining broke out between just about every child and parent.

In our youth-oriented culture, older people can too often be seen as adversaries by children. This should come as no surprise. Given that age is associated with neither beauty nor wisdom, it's almost absurd to expect kids to truly honor adults. This is a cruel irony for most parents—the very generation that once warned, "Never trust anyone over thirty." Now we are the over-thirty crowd, and, at shockingly young ages, our children don't always take us as seriously as they should. I know, because, aside from looking around at the mall, I spend much of my time listening carefully to what kids say to the adults in their lives:

- Erica startled me with comments to her parents that included phrases such as "Shut up" or "You're stupid."
- Alvin and his great buddy, James, always gave themselves away when they were headed for trouble: They'd whisper in a deprecating tone: "Shhh . . . quiet! We don't want *them* to hear us."
- Jamie would often say with commanding authority "Mommy, stop what you're doing *right now!*"
- Corrine stopped referring to her parents' friends by their first or last names; she barely acknowledged their existence. Everything about her broadcast disdain for adults. A few years ago, I overheard Corrine say to my daughter, "If you want to play it smart, don't let the grown-ups know anything."

You might assume I'm talking about teenagers, but I'm not. Erica, Alvin, Jamie, and Corrine range in age from three to eight years old. Or you might surmise that their parents are uninvolved or untrustworthy. Wrong again! I've known all four families for at least a decade and the moms and dads are good, caring people, reasonable and highly invested in childrearing.

What's going on?

• • •

Erica, Alvin, and Corrine are expressing a profound, culturally reinforced trend in which children and adults gradually get used to viewing each other from opposing camps. Too much of the time—at first in ways that may even seem cute—children come to see adults as distant adversaries rather than as close loved ones worthy of admiration. Their parents often don't understand this trend. They don't realize that even their younger children are developing a lack of the basic corebuilder I call "Respect." And there are lots of kids like them.

That's why Respect is the second core-building trait in this book. Everyday experience tells us that our children are disregarding and moving away from us at earlier and earlier ages. The conventional wisdom—and what we remember from our own growing up—is that this orneriness doesn't happen until adolescence. In our day, the older children who seemed to be rebelling were "just being teenagers." But, today, younger kids need our help to see adults as valuable sources of wisdom and fun, of understanding and acceptance, of support and comfort. If we don't help, we're asking for problems.

For example, in December 1996, the *Rockford Register Star* of Rockford, Illinois, polled nearly three hundred teenagers, aged thirteen to seventeen. The researchers unearthed a rather startling fact: When asked how their values were formed, almost none of these middle-American youths mentioned their parents. Many other influences were cited, particularly peers and the mass media—what I refer to as the "second family." When it came to everyday ethics, these kids simply didn't view their parents as central to their lives. There was a chilling distance and disrespect toward adults that emanated from this group of heartland kids.

The Rockford poll is only one small documentation of what is happening in our culture now. Research in all corners of the country mirror its findings. If you don't believe it, just look around you. Chances are, even younger children are—in ways you might not immediately recognize—disrespecting and distancing from the adults in their lives, too. You might be eating family meals less frequently, watching TV rather than talking together, spending less time at family gatherings. And when you are together, your kids seem capable of greater back-talk, bargaining, and irreverence than you care to admit.

For reasons I will describe, even our youngest children are at risk to move away from and disrespect the adults in their world, often with sad, and sometimes disastrous consequences.

Why Respect Is Important

Before children can develop Respect, heed adults, and internalize their ethics, they must spend many of their early years seeing adults in benevolent, valued ways. It's up to us. We need to foster meaningful connections to the grown-ups in our children's lives, or else we'll watch them being engulfed by the self-referential world of the second family.

Hence, our next basic skill:

Basic Skill #2: Encourage your child to listen to and be comfortable with responsible adults.

Respect is a safety net for a child's inner core. First and foremost, it will lead a child to attach a *positive meaning* to the adults around her. By so doing, she will internalize a roster of mature characteristics that isn't available from peers or from the pop culture. She'll come to see grown-ups as people whose opinions matter, whose responses she can truly trust. And Respect allows children to honor their roots. They become interested in and willing to learn about the past and about their own family's histories and customs, which, in turn, results in greater self-understanding and compassion.

Finally, respectful kids won't become "Peter Pans" who are afraid of responsibility and the challenges of adult life. They won't cling to the child world of endless fun. But the tough part for us parents is getting them on the right track in the first place.

Core Threats: Why *Dis*respect Has Reached Epidemic Proportions

In my clinical experience, most kids love their mothers and fathers. They don't fear, or hate, or feel oppressed by parents. That's not the problem. Rather, our presence appears to be much more peripheral and less authoritative than it should be. How did this happen?

Some parents believe that self-expression is more important than basic Respect. Disrespect for parents in the form of back-talk and rude language is rife in today's culture. Erica, who you'll remember used to say "Shut up!" is only one of thousands of rude youngsters I hear about each year. Busy mothers and fathers sometimes take such rudeness for granted and don't even notice a child's disrespectful tone until he or she acts up in public.

Because they want kids who are unafraid of adults and who won't blindly follow authority figures, today's parents often allow back-talk that was unimaginable twenty years ago. Unfortunately, over time, disrespectful words wear away at a child's natural regard for the value, feelings, and wisdom of adults. And a child who speaks disdainfully towards his parents will have a hard time behaving respectfully towards less patient adults in his everyday life—older family members, teachers, coaches, and mentors.

Adults and children spend too much parallel time together. At this moment, your child may be snugly nestled on your lap. But on an everyday basis, many parents and children are like proverbial ships passing in the night. Virtually every study of family activities shows that the two generations are spending less and less time together because of schedules that relegate both kids and their parents to the pe-

DO YOU VALUE SELF-EXPRESSION MORE THAN BASIC RESPECT?

Child rearing philosophy sometimes offers rationales that unwittingly promote disrespect. Here are some signs.

• You believe rude language toward you is acceptable if it "helps get angry feelings off your child's chest."
• Your child talks back so routinely at home that you're unaware of it until a friend or relative points it out.
• When your youngster lashes out physically during a tantrum (smacking your arm, for example) you do little to restrain her for fear of being judged as abusive.
• You think it's cute that your child takes a somewhat precocious, bossy tone towards other adults—clerks, sales people, waiters, etc.
• You feel that a certain amount of rudeness and disrespect is inevitable since everyone around your child seems to be acting the same way.

riphery of each other's lives. The competing forces of work, school, and entertainment activities have, since 1960, winnowed away between ten and twelve hours a week of what used to be "family time." And distance does not make the heart grow fonder. After a while, in the hubbub of daily overscheduling, it intensifies the kind of logistical wrangling that breeds disrespect.

We might think that being under one roof is the same thing as being "together," but we're wrong. In many homes, family members are each doing their own thing and, in the process, gradually changing the definition of family time into "parallel time." And parallel time does not build the kind of connection that deepens mutual respect. For instance, the average child spends 28 hours watching TV every week, according to the Media Reform Information Center—compared with 38.5 minutes spent in "meaningful conversation" with their parents. One study found that 40 percent of six- to eleven-year-olds, and 25 percent of the two- to five-year-olds, have their own TV sets. The MRIC also asked a group of children ranging from four to six to choose between watching TV or spending time with their fathers. Are you appalled to learn that 54 percent chose TV? I was.

Interestingly, parents surveyed in a 1996 study done for *Advertising Age* said they were "spending more time with their children." But Brit Beamer, chairman of the American Research Group, the organization that conducted the study, found that the numbers didn't add up. "Being together means that they are in earshot of one another, versus sitting in proximity to one another in one room," Beamer concluded. "When families are pursuing common activities they are most likely to be watching television or movies." I would add that kids and grown-ups both are probably doing something else at the same time—talking on the phone, paying bills, doing homework or housework. Again, this kind of parallel togetherness makes it likely that kids and parents interact mostly around transitions—times that are fraught with tension and anger.

We're afraid our children will be bored. It's disturbing that so little effort is made to help grown-ups and kids learn how to be comfortable with each other, but parents themselves are part of the problem. While we understandably want our children to have fun, we are so desperately afraid of their being bored that we're perpetually hunting for child-focused venues. This child-centeredness subtly undermines adults as central, valued family members.

We begin, for example, with theme parties that are geared solely to the kids. This doesn't seem bad, except that it fosters a separate-worlds mentality. Performers on the kids' circuit, like Chuckles the Clown and Princess Priscilla, are paid to amuse children, leaving grown-ups as an afterthought on the sidelines. Usually, there isn't even food that comes close to being palatable for adults. I don't really care if I'm fed decently (well, it might be nice) or adequately entertained. However, by not integrating adults, the message that kids and parents need different activities—not comfortable *family* activities—becomes the dominant one, and everybody loses.

We also take our children to family programs, where the focus is not really on family, but rather on amusing the kids. Play centers, like Gymboree, which didn't even exist two decades ago, have proliferated beyond anyone's wildest expectation; these national chains are as much a part of the American landscape as your local movie theater or supermarket. Discovery Zone grew from 250 locations when it opened in the early eighties to 4,000. These centers may be great in terms of stimulating our children, but they can be another wedge in the increasingly parallel worlds of parent and child. The same is true of family restaurants, like McDonald's, Burger King, and Chuck E. Cheese. Many have recently added brilliantly designed kid-centered activities, which, on the one hand, is a boon—we eat in peace while our kids play safely nearby—while on the other hand, the value of our together-time is diluted.

Given the insane scheduling of modern family life and so many distractions to boot, when will our children learn how to sit comfortably with adults, to eat in a leisurely, well-mannered fashion, to join easily in conversation? Certainly not in family gatherings. The fear of kids not having fun is also why we don't often ask our children to spend time with older relatives—or, if we do, we may bribe them with goodies. I can't tell you the number of moms and dads who mention, as a matter of course, that to get one of their kids to accompany them on errands—not because their help is needed, but because it's an opportunity to have some time together—an incentive has to be put on the table. Why are we surprised when kids disrespectfully greet us with "What did you bring me?" after we've been away.

The pop culture encourages parents and children to wrangle with one another. Let's face it, TV has always made fun of parents. Some of us might have thought this wasn't a bad idea in the authoritarian America of the late fifties and sixties, when tensions between generations began to run so high. Now, however, parental authority is mocked, not as a way of airing cultural complaints, but as a means to advance the commercial goals of most broadcasts. Television has not become Big Brother (at least, not yet) but rather Big Promoter. "Want! Spend! Buy!" it shouts to kids. "Only your parents stand in the way." It's almost impossible to hold the line on kid-driven purchases that total billions of dollars. TV show after TV show convinces our children that they need to become better negotiators, so that they can win us over and have more "stuff."

Listen to Clarissa on Nickelodeon explain it all to kids, telling them that if they want parents to agree with an opinion or give in to a demand, just make sure Mom or Dad is distracted by something else when the conversation takes place. Watch Kevin on *The Wonder Years* describe with tremendous accuracy and poignancy what a "typical" parent reaction is to any given situation.

OUR SHRINKING HOURS: HOW MUCH TIME DO WE REALLY SPEND WITH OUR KIDS?

What's happening to our family time? The following facts and figures offer telling clues:

- According to a May 1997 report in *Newsweek*, Americans are working fewer hours. However, on average, they squander fifteen of their forty hours of free time every week on TV—more than time spent socializing, reading, and having fun outdoors combined.
- Researchers John Robinson and Geoffrey Godbey, who analyzed the minute-by-minute diaries of some ten thousand adults and reported their findings in the 1997 book *Time for Life*, note that our increasing free time tends to come in tiny portions—a half hour here, a half hour there. "It's much easier to fit a TV rerun into that fractured space than a mountain hike."
- In its 1981 "Television Ownership Survey," Statistical Research, Inc., found that 22 percent of households with children under eighteen had three or more TV sets. The 1996 version of the same study indicates that that statistic has gone up to almost 50 percent.
- In a 1997 *Family Circle* report, Ruth Westheimer reported that fathers spend eight minutes a day talking to children, and working mothers, eleven.

TV grown-ups also are portrayed as highly dysfunctional role models. Witness all of the (almost absent) parents on *Dawson's Creek*, Homer Simpson, the bumbling cartoon dad on *The Simpsons*, or his live-action counterpart, Al Bundy, on *Married with Children*. And let's not forget the day-to-day soap opera that Roseanne and Dan Conner touted for almost a decade as a "typical" family on *Roseanne*.

Life in these TV families is a string of crises, misadventures, and foolishness of inept parents. While some sitcoms may distort family life in the name of humor, what exactly do they do to our children's view of us? In a 1997 article in the *New York Times*, entitled "Dysfunction Wears Out Its Welcome," writer Caryn James notes, "In their quest to be realistic and relevant, family sitcoms have piled on the social issues, creating an abundance of popular shows about dysfunctional families. But as sitcoms approach dysfunction overload, they have come to resemble melodrama and soap opera more than real life."

Perhaps the most abused group on TV are people in their sixties and seventies. First of all, where are they? Although older folks are a majority of the population, kids' shows rarely include them. When there's a demand—typically, from advertisers—to track different roles portrayed on TV, few bother to check the numbers of older people. However, an informal review of current television programs and movies aimed at children reveals less than a handful of characters in the over-sixty-five bracket. When they are written in, often it's not in a particularly positive light—they tend to be foolish, nasty, forgetful, or all of the above. These put-downs—combined with the absence of vibrant, intelligent older people in the media—only reinforce kids' worst impressions of getting older. Parents are bad enough; senior citizens are even worse. Who would want to grow up and be like them?

Second-family loyalty separates children from adults—and vice versa. A fifth threat to Respect is kids' allegiance to the powerful second family. It starts as early as preschool and gets increasingly intense as youngsters approach the teenage years, promoted both by the pop culture and your child's peers. As Corrine said to my daughter, "Don't let the grown-ups know anything." On the recent Nickelodeon Kids' Award Show, Nick's favorite slogan, "Kids Rule!," was yelled out no fewer than a dozen times, confirming to kids everywhere the natural order of things: Adults don't, or at least shouldn't, matter.

To test this theory, I recently asked a group of mid-elementary-school kids, ranging from eight to twelve years old, "Can you think of a situation in which you would tell a parent or teacher about something bad that was happening to one of your friends or classmates?" Their answer was unanimous. "Only if my friend's life was in danger." There's a pretty wide gap between ordinary problems and life-threatening situations, and these relatively young children simply didn't see adults as a valuable resource.

In turn, there's evidence that disrespectful sentiments go both ways—adults don't appear to have much faith in children, either. A 1997 article by Dr. Ava Siegler in *Child* magazine, "What a Nice Kid," quotes a recent survey: "Only 12% of the two thousand adults polled felt that kids commonly treat others with respect; most described them as 'rude,' 'irresponsible,' and 'lacking in discipline.' " Is it possible that, as a society, we just don't like our kids? We certainly seem not to have faith in them. In fact, another poll indicates that only 37 percent of the adults believed that today's children will make America a better place when they grow up. Not only is there obvious strain and distance between the generations, but also when you piece together the four other factors I describe above, it is apparent how powerfully and early kids' image of the grown-up world can be skewed. And, at the end of the day, it's sad but not surprising that children aren't especially drawn to adults.

Parent Skills: Fostering Respect

We don't have to just sit back and let this happen, and we certainly shouldn't wait for adolescence to address a problem whose foundation begins in preschool years. Even in the face of monumental forces working against Respect, I believe parents can learn skills that will help kids value adults and bring them back if they've already begun to drift away. There are two themes here: We must seize authority and remain what I call three-dimensional.

Seizing authority

To foster the core-building trait of Respect, parents must be able to seize authority and maintain it. I say seize because, in our age, authority isn't conferred automatically just because we are parents; today, we need to wrest control away from all of the competing social forces. An equally formidable challenge is to maintain our authority in the face of a modern moral relativism that seriously confuses our kids, and can push us almost beyond our limits.

To help you with these difficult tasks, I have created a set of parent skills that I discuss in the following pages. These encourage you to articulate your own beliefs, and they offer effective methods that teach your children to embrace the values you stand for. Such skills will help you strengthen your authority as a parent by telling children—on a nonverbal, gut level—that you are a *responsible* adult whose guidance can be trusted. With practice, you can develop a strong parental voice that will balance the powerful influences of the second family.

Know what you stand for. Children start responding to predictability much earlier than we thought. In his work on attunement, Daniel Stern, whom I mentioned in chapter 1, as well as other researchers, have found that within the first weeks of life, infants develop expectations about *regular* feeding times, warmth, stimulation, and comfort.

Interestingly, *older* children talk to me about the need for consistency as well as predictable rules. In recent interviews with 150 prekindergarten through sixth-grade kids, they told me in no uncertain terms that parents had to make and enforce consistent rituals and rules or else, as one articulate seven-year-old warned, "There would be chaos." His peers heartily agreed. All of them nodded when another child added, "Don't tell my parents, but I think that they shouldn't back down so much . . ."

Despite what children say and despite mounting evidence from child research—one study, for example, found that only 19 percent of Americans believe that parents provided good role models or helped their kids know right from wrong—when I ask adult audiences around the country, "What do you stand for?" they are speechless. Among even the most articulate and those most conversant with child-rearing issues, few have thought about this question as it relates to their own families. Have you?

Take some time right now to think about the virtues you'd like to imbue in your child. Almost any quality you name can begin to be developed when your child is only two or three. For example, you can model empathy through your facial expressions and body language when your child is very young; later, when he becomes verbal, you can use spoken language. Or maybe tolerance and acceptance (lack of prejudice) matter to you. By age three, this virtue is already being formed. Perhaps you stand for drive and determination—not in terms of needing to win, but in trying one's hardest. Task mastery begins in earnest in the prekindergarten years. You name it—speaking your mind, politeness, even spirituality—all these attributes become part of your child's core soon after she begins to speak and certainly before she enters kindergarten.

In other words, *knowing what you stand for and acting in ways that convey the message should begin from the earliest days of your child's life.* If he has begun to absorb your values by preschool, he will be far less vulnerable to the negative influence of the second family. This is why it's important for you not only to know what you stand for, but also to communicate your expectations in a clear and consistent manner. This process is crucial to your child's development of a solid core—no matter how old she is, you need to pause and take stock. Ask yourself and your partner the question, "What do I [we] stand for?"

Now divide a sheet of paper in half. On the left side of the page, put everything that, in the best of all possible worlds, you'd like to pass on to your child. Then, move to the right side and list those qualities that you feel in your heart absolutely matter the most.

Here's one way such an exercise might look.

THEORETICAL	ESSENTIAL
1. Tries his best	1. Tries his best
2. Is popular	2. Is tolerant
3. Has good friends	3. Is open
4. Is generous	4. Has good friends
5. Is tolerant	
6. Is open	

Remember, the above is just a sample; I'm not saying what *you* should believe in. However, knowing what you stand for will help children respect you and feel connected to you. The list you'll work on most rigorously, of course, is the "essential" side. If you'd like to be authoritative and effective, these are the qualities that you want to demonstrate—not just preach about—to your child.

Teach what you stand for. Seizing authority is not to be confused with being "authoritarian," which implies arbitrarily laying down the law. In contrast, an *authoritative* parent has clear expectations, stays in charge, and, at the same time, takes into consideration a child's age-appropriate needs or feelings. Authoritative parents manage to inculcate their values in ways that strengthen their child's core and solidify the parent-child connection.

Never lose sight of the second family, whose messages, good and bad, are always threatening to drown you out. How does a parent seize authority when so much outside the family is vying for a child's attention—and soul? To begin with, you need to teach in ways that:

- are compassionate;
- send the message that you are reasonable yet firmly in charge;
- have clear expectations and practical consequences;
- make a strong impression.

Research recently reported in the September 1997 *Journal of the American Medical Association (JAMA)* confirms that, among the above points, having clear expectations lets children know where you stand about important issues. The authors state directly that clear expectations create strong connections between parent and child about such specific issues as academic performance, sexuality, and substance use. Moreover, such a connection is a strong predictor of whether or not your child will engage in high-risk behaviors. You and your child may not always agree, but at least she will have a clear sense of where she comes from and where she belongs.

Have a cache of effective discipline techniques that reinforce what you stand for. To seize and maintain authority, you'll need a good working knowledge of the kind of discipline techniques that help children listen and stay connected to their parents. Arbitrary discipline can drive your child straight into the clutches of the second family; too little authority will cause him to drift toward it. Remember, as I discussed in chapter 1, it's very important to adapt your techniques to your child's temperament. In any case, your best chance of staying connected to your child—and thereby fostering Respect—is to employ compassionate discipline, teaching him that the important grown-ups in his life are strong *and* reasonable. To that end, I've synthesized what works best: strategies that involve loving *and* limit-setting. These are the result of my working for twenty-five years with families, as well as my culling from current resources the most effective discipline techniques. I've summarized these tactics at the end of this chapter in a handy reference guide.

Be able to change your mind. Good intentions and great child-rearing techniques aside, there are bound to be times when we act in unreasonable ways that will distance our kids. Therefore, one of the most important skills is to know how to step back after such an incident and reverse your actions. Let's say the kids are quarreling at the dinner table. Big sister, thirteen, calls her little brother, nine, "dumb," and he responds by shoving her. A glass of milk is accidentally spilled in the rumpus. This touches a nerve in you. You snap and yell, "No TV or videos for a week!"

Later on, it's very clear to you what a mistake that was—especially since the punishment you levied will be harder on you than on the kids. But taking it back seems contradictory and weak, given that your kids are complaining about how "unfair" and "mean" you're being. Despite knowing that you've overreacted, you're afraid of changing your mind.

The problem is that such impulsive reactions (which almost all parents have) seem arbitrary to children. The answer to this and a thousand other such discipline dilemmas is simpler than you might believe: *Recover and reflect*. In the end, you will retain your firm, yet compassionate authority by changing your mind. Here's how:

1. Take responsibility. Say to your child, "I was upset and reacted too strongly."
2. Explain. "You were acting up, but that's no reason to take TV away for a week."
3. Adjust. Come up with a more appropriate consequence instead of the reactive one.

Don't worry, as many parents do, that your child will think less of you. I've never heard a child say, "My father's a wimp" or "My mother's inconsistent," when his parents have given a matter some serious thought and realized that a particular punishment truly didn't fit the crime. Most important, an appropriate consequence will teach your child what you expect—and leave much more of an imprint.

Learn to apologize. As one soft-spoken child confided to me, "I feel better after a fight when my mommy and daddy say they're sorry." It may seem at first as if this is a paradox, but remember that maintaining authority also means apologizing for your mistakes. This is hard for many parents to do. But admitting you were wrong is fundamental to earning and keeping a child's respect. I have met hundreds of grown-ups—maybe you're among them—who carry terrible resentment toward their parents, simply because Mom and Dad were never able to say, "I'm sorry—I was wrong."

Act more and talk less. Another irony about seizing and maintaining authority is that some of our most "in charge" moments occur during those quiet times when we don't use a lot of words. Indeed, what we *do* matters as much—often, more—than the things we say. Kindness to our children models empathy. Showing concern for a good friend demonstrates loyalty. And in addition to apologizing for a mistake, we do something to make amends. In short, we practice what we preach.

WATCH YOUR TEMPER!

The relationship research of University of Washington psychologist John Gottman, which focused on adults, indicates that it takes five to ten acts of kindness to make up for one loss of temper. Although no one has studied the effect of temper on a sampling of children, I suspect that this holds true for them as well—especially with sensitive, more vulnerable types. Inspired by that research are my guidelines for apologizing to your child in ways that build respect and closeness.

• Start early, as soon as your child is beginning to speak. This way she'll understand that thoughtfulness and apologies are part of who you are, not a result of bargaining or whining during an incident. Given how frustrating toddlers are, you'll have plenty of practice apologizing for losing it.

• Don't apologize during or just after an incident. It will be lost on a child who is probably still upset. Worse, it may seem to a hard-driving child as if he has coaxed an apology out of you.

• Make it short and sweet. Don't be overemotional. Offer a brief explanation—and end there.

• Apologize without lecturing ("Next time, I expect you to . . .") or making disclaimers ("I was wrong, but . . .").

• Offer a physical expression of warmth. Do what's comfortable for you and your child—a hug, kiss, pat on the head.

Acting on our convictions is an essential component to maintaining compassionate authority.

A wonderful example of this came from a parent in one of my workshops. Pam, the mother of four-year-old Gabby, remembered her daughter's losing a treasured Beanie Baby—"Horsy"—someplace in the mall. Instead of delivering the familiar lecture about taking care of one's prized possessions, Pam sympathetically held Gabby's hand while they retraced their steps. Sure enough, on their third stop, they found Horsy lying on a low shelf in a shoe store. The fact that Pam went to that much trouble—without a moment's anger—brought mother and child closer. And, in the process, Gabby learned about persistence and problem-solving.

Another striking example of actions speaking louder than words appeared in an essay in the *New York Times*'s "His" column: The writer recalled an incident from his early teens that occurred during a family vacation in a small resort colony. On a wild teenage spree, he and two of his friends trashed the community rec room. When their misconduct was discovered, each boy's father reacted differently: One smacked his son in full view of the others; the second dragged his boy away, shouting threats and obscenities into the night. The writer's father simply looked at him, surveyed the damage done, and, without saying a word, got into his car. He returned with lumber supplies strapped to the roof. All night long, the teenager could hear his dad rebuilding the property the boys had damaged. Looking back, the writer said that he never felt closer to or more respectful of his father. His dad didn't discipline him in the traditional sense, but in the *best* sense. Not a word about the event was ever spoken; yet, the boy learned an invaluable lesson: When you do something wrong, amends have to be made in a concrete way. And what better way for a parent to teach than by doing?

Staying three-dimensional

I use the term "three-dimensional" here to describe a parent's basic humanity—a complete portrait that shows who he or she is, not just a sketchy outline. The idea of staying three-dimensional in your child's eyes is a child-rearing concept we haven't thought about very much but one I believe will become central to discussions about raising our children. You are, after all, not a caricature but a multifaceted human being worthy of acknowledgment and consideration. When you let your many sides shine through, children sense your complexity—that you have a history, that you grapple with their dilemmas (and your own), and that, throughout it all, you try to be a decent person. Exhibiting this struggle will make you appear as you are—neither a stick-figure parent nor a distant being with whom your child feels nothing in common.

Being a three-dimensional parent is essential if you want your child to Respect you and internalize your values. There are several ways to make sure you appear as a full human being in your child's eyes. Some of the following may seem simple or obvious, but, during the past decades, each has proven increasingly difficult to maintain.

Refuse to be seen as a TV parent. Several mothers in a recent workshop complained that their *preschool* kids were using language they hadn't expected to surface for at least ten years: "Aw, Mom, leave me alone." "You're not the boss of me." "Get out of my face." It was clear that their sons and daughters had picked up these phrases from sitcom kids talking to sitcom adults.

As children get older, their media-shaped view of parents will definitely be expressed in real-life conflict. One day, my then eight-year-old daughter, Leah, was trying to tell me something that happened between her and a friend at school. I was listening patiently, but I must have misunderstood what she said. Suddenly, she blurted out, *"You parents just don't understand,"* and started wailing with a melodramatic body language I knew I'd seen before.

Suddenly, in the midst of my confusion, it became clear: "Leah, I refuse to be turned into a TV parent," I yelled without trying to hide my annoyance. "No, I don't understand everything—that's true. But I'm trying. I'm not hopelessly dense like the Brady Bunch's dad." Leah immediately got what I was saying and settled down a bit. She began talking to me more patiently—and I was the parent who had, in fact, been trying to understand and respect her feelings. It was a defining moment for both of us, especially me. I "got" that I had to fight to be seen as myself.

Are you subtly, slowly being flattened out or turned into *them*—a TV parent? Are you seen by your child as an adversary? To find out, listen for the sound of TV one-liners. Does your child "dis"—disrespect or dismiss—you? Does she make more distinctions between the grown-up and child worlds than are real in your home? If so, you must begin to say in a variety of ways, "No. I simply will not be turned into one of those unthinking, uninvolved, self-absorbed parents you watch on TV." Show a little outrage. In the face of your response, your child will have to take a closer look.

Sometimes, put *yourself* in the spotlight. In our child-centered world, it's becoming rare for parents to put themselves at the center of family life. Today, a busy mom might feel self-conscious asking kids to pitch in when she's not feeling well or to "make a big deal" of her birthday. Though parents are quick to commiserate with children's problems in school and to celebrate their successes, they are apt not to share with them when things go wrong at work or tell them when really good things happen. In other words, we rarely ask kids to focus on *us*. But this is an important way of humanizing ourselves in our children's eyes and giving them a chance to Respect us as real, multidimensional people.

Kids are fascinated by seeing their parents from a different vantage point. I discovered this quite by accident a few years ago when my wife and I hosted the twenty-fifth anniversary celebration for very old friends. The group of adults, ten or twelve in all, were assembled in our living room, talking and trading stories about the good old days. Our children, Leah and Sammy, then four and nine, were (uncharacteristically) quiet. At first, I was nervous. "Oh, no," I thought. "They're really bored. Should we do something with them?" Then I looked again. In actuality, they were completely absorbed, listening intently to the raucous stories about their parents as told by some of our closest friends.

Later, Leah asked incredulously, "Daddy, you *really* played football in the snow when you were young?" And Sammy said, "Take me fishing, too, like when you went on that boat with Marc's father." They've since referred to the evening many times. That my kids loved those three-dimensional stories came as a surprise to my child-centered mind. However, that whole evening underscored the importance of parents allowing themselves to be the special focus and of making children a part of a *grown-up* gathering.

This may seem unfair or even uncomfortable to you at first. Putting yourself in the spotlight doesn't mean ignoring your children; it means giving them a supporting role in the family drama every now and then. But we parents are so accustomed to focusing solely on our kids, it might feel as if you're slighting your children if you ask them to step out of the spotlight. In reality, moments in which *you* are the focus—

anything from asking a child to play quietly because you have a headache to asking for help with something that you really can't do (like hooking up the VCR) to having adult parties such as the above—train children to be at ease when the focus is not on them. The wonderful outcome is that most children love this role reversal. It gives them a chance to *give back* which is also essential to developing a core (more on this in chapter 10, "Gratitude").

Schedule intergenerational activities. Specifically planning get-togethers that include guests of all ages and feature a variety of conversational topics also builds children's tolerance for non-child-focused activities. When I was younger, I had to go to my Aunt Bertha's house every week for family dinner. There was no television, and I was expected to sit with the adults, sometimes for hours on end. Today, the idea of offering kids little that's stimulating and asking them to interact among older people seems "unfair" to children, if not cruel by current standards. We assume, as I did with my friends' anniversary party, that they'll be bored to tears. But they won't, especially if we give them the opportunity to broaden their social skills by interacting with adults outside the immediate family.

Friends of ours whose family is scattered within a couple of hours of each other have a weekly get-together on Sundays. This is a time when the kids and adults hang out with each other. I've been struck by how comfortable these children are when conversing with grown-ups; it's absolutely clear that they aren't just being polite. They are developing the ability to talk with and not be afraid of people of any age.

If you have a small extended family or one that lives far away, consider your "family" of friends. Also, look at what's happening in your community. There are quiet and heartening signs that intergenerational events are coming back, especially religion-sponsored commu-

---

ARE YOU EVER IN THE SPOTLIGHT?
- Do you expect/demand birthday cards for yourself?
- Do your kids observe Mother's Day and/or Father's Day?
- Do you ever discuss your day over dinner?
- Do you plan parties for yourself that include your children in celebrating an achievement or an anniversary?
- Do you ever get to play your music in the car?

---

nal activities, like potluck dinners and game nights. Pollster George Gallup, Jr. reports that the decline in church membership bottomed out and that, since 1991, it has been on the rise. Sadly, if we don't belong to these groups, we don't hear much about what they offer. It's a good idea to *talk* with other parents to find out what they know.

Teach family history. Children are steeped in the second-family notion that "all that really matters is what's happening now!" In 1995, the National Assessment of Educational Progress in American History concluded that more than half of our high school seniors do not know basic facts about American history. Judging from the children I meet, I would add that most kids don't know a lot about their own family's past, either. This breeds a sense of disconnection. If a parent's historical self is invisible, children are left with no idea of their own place on the past-future continuum. They lack any notion of the fascinating stories or family characteristics that led to their own existence. Therefore, it is vital to offer our children a sense of collective identity by teaching them about their heritage. Then, as if donning those old 3-D glasses, they start viewing their parents as multifaceted beings, not just as service providers or the source of "stuff." Equally important, I've seen firsthand that being aware of family history leads a child to a greater sense of self-respect.

Ideally, family history is brought into a child's awareness early on so that it becomes a natural part of his life. Age three or four is the best time to begin, but it's never too late to turn off the TV and get the kids interested in their own heritage. You may meet some resistance at first—kids ten and older who haven't been introduced to family lore sometimes complain that it's "boring." But it's important to begin and to persist, as my friend Marty did. For bedtime reading, his daughters, then six and nine, requested *The American Girl: Samantha* series, which recounts a fictional family's history. After several installments, Marty realized that his children knew more about Samantha's past than their own background—one that contained many dramatic stories of immigration, heroism, and triumph over adversities.

One night, he decided to tell his girls about their family. At first, they were disappointed and whined, "No, read to us from *Samantha.*" Marty insisted that they at least try one story just to see how it compared to fiction. As it turned out, the girls were fascinated; their curiosity was clearly piqued, and they begged for more. Now, their bedtime routine regularly includes an installment of the family saga—

his grandparents coming to the United States, their first years of struggle, births and deaths—Marty's own memories from his childhood, including the huge gatherings in which several generations came together to celebrate their traditions. Hearing these tales, the children feel closer to their parents and proud of their history.

Try Marty's bedtime approach. Or take your cue from the Hermans, who have stacks of picture albums that date back a century; fairly often, they sit with their children and tell them stories about the people and events in the photos. The O'Donnells got their kids directly involved in creating a family chronicle by restoring a stack of old family albums in which pictures were loose and pages were falling out. The parents bought a thick album and gave their four children the job of both reconstructing the old and incorporating the new. By pasting pictures of themselves into the new album, they symbolically included themselves in the larger family scheme.

Use older family members as a resource. Perhaps you have an aunt or grandparent who has that magical ability to remember every detail of family lore. Even if Cousin Ellen's anecdotes are a bit embellished, it will give your children a sense of connection they would otherwise never know. Remember, if you don't initiate—actively teaching your family history—your kids might never ask!

Create predictable routines and rituals. When I asked children from nursery school though sixth grade, "What is your favorite thing to do?" 80 percent responded by telling me about a variety of everyday rituals with their parents. Clearly, rituals anchor children in the safety of family life. The kids I talked to mentioned daily routines like bedtime stories, driving or walking to school together, as well as weekly events, like the board game marathon that starts after Saturday chores, or making mini-pizzas on Sunday afternoon. As long as it was ordinary, predictable, and one-on-one with a parent, it qualified as being a "favorite thing."

These findings are mirrored in the research of psychologists Steven and Sybil Wolin, who have conducted a number of studies on the role of ritual. They conclude that when a family is high in ritual—ceremonies, traditions, and everyday observances—a buffer is created shielding the family from outside temptations and even against serious threats from within, like alcoholism. Further, the Wolins speculate that children in families who don't observe many rituals "will find order and meaning elsewhere, often in destructive behaviors outside the family."

It behooves you to emphasize that family events are a nonnegotiable, respected part of life. Whether it's a monthly dinner out or a Sabbath meal at home, regular, dependable events give your children a sense of connection and lessen the great divide. When there are great distances between relatives, frequent gatherings would be impractical. But try to meet once or twice a year at least, for a holiday, a joint birthday party, or just for the sake of connection. These times also provide a perfect opportunity for kids to experience the intrinsic value of spending time with and even honoring people who are not their age.

Rituals should continue as long as people live—and in the best families, I've found that they do. For example, over the years, I've interviewed the Heller children, who grew up with many religious rituals. They are now young adults who continue the family practice of getting together with the same friends every Friday night for services and Saturday noon for lunch. The gathering continues to include the parents, their grown children, and—within the past years—a few newborns.

I watched the Hellers grow up. From the time they sat safely perched on their dad's shoulders, these kids have been respectful and completely comfortable with older people. I asked them recently, "Which childhood experiences seem truly important to you now?" They all agreed that rituals—family and religious, combined and separate—mattered most. As the oldest daughter told me, "I got to see my parents act according to their beliefs. That made a tremendous impact on me as a child—and it still does." No matter how many times I ask other kids from observant homes a similar question, they always respond by pointing to the rich experience of rituals.

Monitor your own ageism. Kids pick up what they hear. And because we parents are also victims of the culture at large, we sometimes unwittingly communicate negative attitudes toward older people every bit as damaging as what our children see on TV. Recently, I was within earshot of a family on school orientation night. A mother and father were talking about their second grader's teacher, one casually remarking to the other, "Why would they allow someone who's that old to teach such young children?" Their son, knowing the teacher from recess and the lunchroom, rushed to her defense. "Mrs. Franco is really nice. *I like her.*"

In another situation, James, three and a half, began a new preschool. His parents were disappointed by the quality of the classroom—too many kids, not enough art supplies. But what they focused on, and said to me right in front of their son, was what an "old bag" his new teacher looked like. Not coincidentally, within a couple of weeks, James, who initially liked Mrs. Foley a lot, began to call her "old and baggy."

Pay particular attention to off-the-cuff remarks you make about your own advancing years. For a young child with a developing core, hearing a parent complain about getting older sends negative signals about growing up. In one family, for example, Hal jokingly "refused" to turn forty. When his son, Jason, was four, Hal was thirty-nine; two years later, Hal was still thirty-nine. When Jason was a teenager, he told me that he'd always felt more than a little afraid of getting older, because his father so adamantly denied it.

Child Skills: Respecting and Becoming Comfortable with Adults

Creating situations in which your child can be with adults hones the following skills—each of which will help children feel more comfortable with the adult world:

Making conversation with adults

Narrowing the often invisible chasm between grown-ups and children is not always easy. For example, when families get together, adults—not realizing that they're taking some liberty with a child's privacy—may come at him with direct questions like "How's school? What do you do there? So, what's it like having a little brother? Did you love that present we gave you?" This familiar gambit can be difficult for a child—especially to a three-year-old who can't remember a single thing from the day before other than Ben's having pulled Harry's pants down! Many parents, sensing their child's discomfort with adult questions, tend to "cover" their child. We answer *for* him, or make excuses for his lack of response: "Oh, he's too young to understand."

The truth is, except for painfully shy children, kids at early ages must learn how to make simple conversation. It is, after all, the medium of connection between people. And not having this skill will only distance your child from the world of grown-ups.

Children need our help and we can give it in some easy ways: *Anticipate questions ahead of time, and role-play possible responses.* For example, say you're going to Grandma's house; from past experience, you probably know exactly how she'll greet your child. You can give your child the words and phrases he'll need to respond. Even if this feels contrived at first, before you know it, your child will expand her repertoire and begin to take such meetings in stride. When you haven't anticipated a problem and you suddenly see your child under siege by a distant relative, you can help by focusing the question or starting an answer for her: "Janie had a wonderful time on our vacation. Tell Aunt Jean what animals we saw at the big zoo."

Confiding in responsible authorities

When a child is in trouble, it's important for him to be able—and willing—to cross that "us versus them" line that separates the second family from the adult network. Remember, it's not that today's kids hate or feel oppressed by adults; at too-early ages, some children simply don't think of grown-ups as a trustworthy part of everyday life. Therefore, your child needs to be encouraged to open the lines of communication to the adults around him.

Help your child employ strategies for approaching an authority figure. As I detail in chapter 4, this includes knowing who is a responsible and welcoming adult. If your child has been rebuffed or mistreated by an authority, you may have to work especially hard to regenerate her trust and to help her choose a more benevolent adult. Remember, one of your important goals is to challenge the disdainful portrayal in the kiddie pop culture that most adults outside the family are uninvolved and unsympathetic. Finding some adults who will be kind, supportive, and available will get this important message across: "Don't write off all adults because 'the kids say so' or because one grown-up wasn't that nice." Once your child has identified a good candidate—say, one of his teachers—you can help him figure out when it's best to approach her—in the morning, after class, when the group is involved in independent work or study hall.

As children get older and more burdened by the weight of second-family values, the fear of being ostracized may grow. However, certain strategies can help them avoid peer censure—for instance, talking to authorities when other kids aren't around. Matthew, a nonathletic and ungainly fourth grader, had trouble participating in class games. At his parents' suggestion and armed with a note from them, Matthew approached his kindly teacher in private to avoid feeling embarrassed in front of his classmates.

Being polite

Politeness breeds better responses and lessens the distance between adults and kids. Children of all ages tell me that they feel bad about themselves when they're allowed to be disrespectful toward grownups. Kids I've interviewed have admitted—in front of each other—that adults *should* expect good manners from children. Certainly, grown-ups withdraw from kids who act "fresh." Children learn politeness from watching their parents. But they also need concrete reminders. Start when your child is preverbal, saying "Thank you, Daddy" for her when you hand her a toy or give her something to eat. Words like "please" and "thank you," the expectation that she'll say "hello" and "good-bye," should be among the first things she learns (see also chapter 10). Don't tolerate disrespect—at home or outside.

Taking responsibility

Adults tend to be suspicious of kids who blame their problems on everyone and everything else—and, therefore, may not be willing to help them, which will only confirm the youngster's belief that adults can't be counted on. Consider parents' reaction to six-year-old

Christopher, an Intense/Aggressive child. He was running around at a birthday party using a plastic fork to "stab" his playmates in the tush. Confronted by the birthday boy's upset mother, Chris's response was "I didn't know that they didn't like it." The mother and several other parents were incensed, not only about the boy's behavior, but also by his response. Had Chris said, "I'm sorry I did a bad thing" or "I won't do it again," he might have defused some of their anger. As it was, he put himself on everyone's black list, mostly because he accepted no responsibility for his action.

Granted, there are instances in which a child complains of being the brunt of teasing or mean-spirited pranks, and the only thing she did "wrong" was to seem nerdy to the other kids. Still, it's important for her to understand her predicament in a way that doesn't point a finger at other kids. For example, I was consulted by the parents of eleven-year-old Patricia, whom I had seen in therapy because she had trouble "fitting in." She was once again being scapegoated by her peers, this time at camp.

When her parents told me what was happening, I gave Patricia a call. To help her get past the typically selective preteen memory, I reminded her that she had dealt successfully with similar experiences in school by making her teacher an ally. And I also cautioned Patricia about her approach: "Most adults respect honesty. Explain your situation in a way that you don't put down yourself or the other kids. You might say, 'I need help. I think I'm making the other kids act mean to me.' "

As it turned out, Alice, the counselor, had a lot of good, concrete suggestions: A little change in her style of dress might help Patricia fit in better. Not standing too close to other kids would probably be a good idea, too. The gentle way Alice presented those little tips made all the difference. Although part of Patricia's success with her counselor was because she waited for a quiet, private moment before asking for her help, this was not just a case of knowing how to approach an adult. The important point was that Patricia was able to *own* her problem. Her taking responsibility, instead of whining about the other kids, made her counselor instantly willing to help—and, not so incidentally, transformed a potentially horrendous summer into a positive time of growth. Patricia didn't instantly become a popular kid. She did, however, begin to think of her counselor as an ally and Alice, in turn, developed a soft spot for her.

Trusting their instincts about adults

Children must learn how to trust their "gut feelings" about grown-ups. They need to heed their own internal warning signals—those moments when "something" tells them to steer clear of a grown-up. I don't just mean the extreme—an unsavory-looking stranger; nowadays, most kids learn early to stay clear of such threats. But, in order not to stereotype grownups, they have to learn to discriminate between trustworthy and untrustworthy adults *within* their immediate sphere. For example, Deirdre, our homesick camper whom you met in chapter 1, had seen the head counselor, Barbara, be insensitive in her dealings with other girls. Unfortunately, Deirdre ignored that protective voice in her gut and shared her feelings with Barbara anyway.

Predictably, Barbara responded like a wicked adult in a Nickelodeon sitcom: "If you don't cope with your homesickness now, you'll never be able to do anything right!" she told Deirdre harshly. I was outraged when I heard about this. Clearly, Barbara was the wrong adult to approach—her response did nothing to help Deirdre see grown-ups more respectfully. Even worse, the incident turned her off to talking to other adults at the camp. If she had just trusted herself, Deirdre could have avoided the assault to her feelings and looked for a more sympathetic adult.

Acknowledging helpful authorities other than their parents

Teachers, principals, coaches, tutors, clergy are real people and have feelings, too. Showing appreciation to these figures—say, by giving a valued teacher or coach a birthday card—flies in the face of second-family belief that adults' feelings aren't as important as kids' and that grown-ups don't matter.

Since our children entered preschool, my wife and I have learned from other parents who encourage their children to bring handmade cards to teachers who have birthdays or a new baby or other happy events. Because we began this tradition early, our children don't perceive it as "nerdy." More important, they get real pleasure from seeing the recipient's delight. For example, when one of our daughter's teachers got married and later that year when our son's classroom aide graduated from college, we helped the kids make cookies for both occasions. Such thoughtful tokens acknowledge caring authorities in a child's life.

Compassionate Discipline:
Techniques that Create Respect Toward Adults

Seizing authority in a compassionate way fosters a child's trust in adults and, thereby, fortifies her core. The following guidelines have been chosen and adapted specifically because they enhance Respect toward adults. They are organized according to developmental level.

Ages two to five

Distract. Rule of thumb: The earlier you intervene before bad behavior occurs, the more attention-getting the distraction, the greater your chance of success. Never try to distract a child in the throes of a tantrum; try to intervene earlier because, as family communication research shows, out-of-control behavior quickly escalates beyond distraction. Your child will immediately feel comforted when an adult is in charge of such a situation.

See tantrums clearly. Learn to differentiate manipulative tantrums, which you should ignore, and temperamental tantrums, which occur when a child is ill, tired, hungry, or overstimulated, and which should be tended to immediately. Your ability to tell the difference shows a child that you understand and know what to do.

Remove your child from a difficult situation. A change of context often releases parent and child from feeling locked in battle. If a child is perpetually backed into corner by his parents, there's a good chance he'll feel chronically contentious with adults.

Restrain your child from hurting himself or others. A bear hug is very effective, as you say, "I won't let you hit again." If he screams and squirms, hold tighter. When he feels your conviction, he'll stop. This shows children that we often create limits for their own good—a belief that will diminish preteen and adolescent distrust of adults.

Use brief time-outs. Remember to use short, enforceable periods and send your child to a quiet place—without entertainment. Don't add to the struggle by suggesting, "Think about what you did wrong." Explain in a *brief* sentence why you've done it ("I can't think straight when you yell like that"). Calm yourself in the meantime. This cuts down on explosive interactions—in which both parents and children do things that can be hurtful in the long run—and it can lead to more trusting relationships.

Build sequential rewards into everyday routine. Natural ways to get things moving, such as "If you get dressed more quickly, you can watch fifteen minutes more of Barney," make the notion of rewards less arbitrary. In this way, a child is less likely to feel as if she has to jump through hoops in order to please the adults in her life.

Ages six to eight

Offer sequential rewards—and negotiate. Suggest a trade-off, such as "If you put on your socks now, then you'll have five minutes later for *Ninja Turtles*." Don't expect immediate compliance to the first "deal" you offer—these children already like to bargain, and they'll try to expand five minutes to ten. However, holding a flexible line teaches kids to present arguments in concise ways—a skill that the adult world appreciates much more than endless haggling.

Offer limited choices. "You can wash your face first or brush your teeth—which will it be?" This positive approach makes a child feel he has some autonomy, rather than being completely controlled by grown-ups.

Leave a situation once it gets too hot. Refuse to engage when your child utters that time-worn favorite, "It's not fair." When you stop the escalation ("We'll talk about this later when we all calm down"), your child learns three important lessons: that there are good times and bad times to talk, that there are consequences to behavior, and that there are limits to how much he can challenge your—or any adult's—reserve of patience.

Ask your child for solutions. Elementary school kids are hungry to take on more responsibility. It lets them know that you don't have all the answers, and that you can work together. Their suggestions also give you a glimpse into their world—what they've picked up from the media and from friends. This tactic cuts down the distance that can build up between adults and children. It also prepares children for the cooperative learning and teamwork that is so central to adult life.

Use an old-fashioned star system of rewards. This age child appreciates structure and systems. But this strategy has a short shelf life, especially if it's overused. Best to do it with a specific goal—chores leading up to a particular reward. The predictability helps reinforce the idea adults keep promises when children do their part.

Post schedules and lists of chores. Like the star system, this is highly visible, systematic, and concrete. Let your child have input into which chores he does and the order in which he does them. This method seems less arbitrary to a child than expectations that come out of nowhere.

Use hypothetical situations to problem-solve. For example, "Matt has trouble sharing toys. How do you think his parents can help him?" Or use TV characters or book plots as a springboard for a talk. Don't bring the lesson back to your child ("How do you think Matt's situation applies to you?"). A hypothetical situation can move the spotlight away from him, allowing your child some breathing room, to work out solutions nondefensively with a compassionate adult.

Appeal to your child's sense of empathy. Occasionally, be direct about your own feelings. "It doesn't seem fair when you talk to me like that. You wouldn't like it." This is a far cry from a rigid "Do-it-because-I-said-so" approach.

Ages nine to eleven

Put a time limit on all negotiations. Tell your child, "We'll give you five minutes to prepare your best case; then we'll make a decision. Preteens love the art of the deal—they can easily wear parents down. When they do, they feel as if they've "gotten over"—a strategy they're likely to try with other adults.

Make specific contracts. Say, "If you come home at four [as opposed to "on time"] from your friend's house Monday through Thursday [versus "most of the week"], then you'll be able to stay out until five [versus "a little longer"] on Friday afternoon." Specificity leaves little room for interpretation or renegotiation. Specificity and predictability help kids listen to trusted adults.

Ask for solutions, but be prepared for the outlandish: "If I clean my room, can I go to Hawaii?" It helps to remember that kids love negotiating more than the privilege or object they're asking for. This insight lets you calm down and gain a new perspective on the issue ("Tomorrow, she won't feel so bereft about not going to that party"). And it takes some of the over-the-top tension out of parent/child negotiations.

Respect your child's moodiness after a confrontation or when you've laid down a law she doesn't like. Also, keep in mind your child's temperament. Such timing and sensitivity repeatedly tells your child that you understand who she is—which is more important to a good relationship than the content of the confrontation.

Try to forget "the room." Close the door so you don't see the mess. If the bedroom threatens the rest of the house—an odor, insect infestation—then draw the line by giving your child a limited choice: "You can either clean it up on your own by tomorrow, or we'll do it together, or I'll pay your brother to help me." This lets a child know you won't automatically encroach on his territory. But since he lives with others, he has to respect his encroachment on their territory. A respect for boundaries helps him coexist with both peers and adults.

Expanded privileges need to be earned; they are not inalienable rights. This is the gateway to adolescence. Since preteens are more than capable of empathy during a calm moment, link your experience with her increasing freedom. "You can take the bus by yourself if you're home by five. That way, I'll see that you can handle yourself, and I won't worry so much." Again, this three-dimensional approach brings home the point that parents are people, too.

Ages twelve to fifteen

Write longer-term contracts. You might suggest, "If you maintain a B average, you can take riding lessons next semester." Since most young adolescents think of any parental demand as a form of oppression, contracts help make the rules seem less emotionally charged. Allow a teen's input, but be sure he knows that you have the last word. Anything that diminishes his developmentally normal sense of being persecuted helps him be as reasonable as possible toward his parents.

Pick your battles wisely. With a teen, there are endless opportunities for conflict and, at the same time, increasingly powerful pulls from the second family. The more you clash, the more she perceives the adult world as alien and stifling. So, it might be wise to concede on a hairstyle while holding the line on curfew.

To gain cooperation, tap into the teen's growing empathy, taking care to share your own and other adults' perspective. Explain, "I need you to be punctual; otherwise I worry" or "How do you think Mr. Brown felt about what you did?" Questions that require thought broaden an adolescent's narrow view that the adult world is arbitrarily against him.

Be sure all consequences reflect these three points, which set limits and yet recognize your child's growing independence:

1. State exactly what you want ("I don't want you smoking at the concert").
2. State what will happen if you find out he didn't comply ("I won't trust you and will end up worrying, so no more concerts for three months").

3. Acknowledge that you won't be there to monitor him ("In the end, you'll have to make your own decision, knowing exactly what I think and what will happen if you don't listen").

Although teens are on the cusp of adulthood, the distance between two points will never be greater than at this age. However, these three steps send a rational message: While there are limits, we can't realistically enforce them all. Such a reasonable view strengthens relationships with teens who bristle at restrictions but despise and disrespect paper-tiger parents even more.

The above developmentally appropriate strategies at least position you, the adult, as reasonably compassionate—and nobody's fool. They will not only help you seize and maintain authority, they'll help foster Respect in your child.

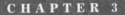

CHAPTER 3

EXPRESSIVENESS

Basic Skill #3: Promote your child's unique style of talking about what really matters.

The Articulate Generation

Eight-year-old Eric, a boy I know, is comfortable exchanging pleasantries with anyone willing to listen. At this tender age, he not only can talk about politically correct issues like the environment and different recycling methods, but he also can voice his views on a number of grown-up concerns. His six-year-old sister, Alicia, already discusses a slew of sophisticated topics, her favorite being the nuances of relationships; on various interpersonal issues such as popularity, sensitivity, and self-confidence, she sounds like an enthusiastic expert. Even their younger sibling, four-and-a-half-year-old Patty, can offer lucid opinions—sometimes to her parents' consternation—about the best fast foods and the "right" educational toys. Granted, these children come from an educated, middle-class family, but, still, they are grasping concepts you and I didn't begin to learn until junior high school.

In my professional and personal life, I'm constantly amazed by what many of today's children can talk about—if I listen with my eyes closed, I often feel that I'm in the presence of a teenager. However, I'm equally struck by many parents' complaints that despite even young children being light-years ahead in awareness and their ability to sound articulate, they still don't talk enough about things that really matter on a deeply personal level. The feelings and worries—the causes of stress in their young lives—are too often not shared. In other words, today's kids may be amazingly verbal, but they don't necessarily possess the core trait I call "Expressiveness."

Why Expressiveness Is Important

It's simply not enough for young children to be glib—no matter how cute, amusing, or endearing; there must be some substance beneath their precocious patter and pseudo-adult understanding of the world. Expressiveness—the ability to reveal and articulate what you think about and feel—is a vital key to a child's core. Its absence can cause serious consequences throughout the life cycle. The "shy" preschooler who keeps to herself is actually scared of the wilder boys in class. She is missing important social interaction with her peers simply because she doesn't know how to tell the teacher. The elementary school child who seems so personable is found later to have been unhappy because she had no "best-best" friend and didn't know how to talk about it. That junior high school girl who was always pontificating about some issue of social justice was suffering from a hidden eating disorder that grew out of her inability to express deep feelings of insecurity.

Later in this chapter, I will detail what you can do to prevent such damage to your child's core, but first let's look at why Expressiveness is such an essential core-builder.

Expressive children are more proficient children. When a child can talk up, he is less likely to act up and more likely to get what he or she wants out of life. As speech and language specialist Thomas Sowell observes in *Late-Talking Children,* frustration is commonplace among inexpressive kids; not surprisingly, it impacts social and academic functioning. You can see the pattern beginning in preschool, when a youngster gets frustrated and ends up in trouble because his feelings come out in counterproductive ways. Late talkers often tend toward a language of action. Indeed, in many of the classrooms I've visited, the less verbally expressive kids typically join in rambunctious play that can frighten the less aggressive, more expressive kids. In one nursery group, a band of three-and-a-half- and four-year-old boys, pretending to be pirates, delighted in hijacking and terrorizing their classmates. In an elementary school setting, the wilder boys were mimicking the movements and attitude of rap performers. Even at such a young age, aggression and frustration are very close to the surface, and tend to come out in physical ways when children are unable to appropriately express their feelings.

Expressive children tend to be safer children. It seems like common sense that children who hide feelings or unconsciously act them out will be more vulnerable to developmental and social dangers. Expressiveness is a major antidote. Staying in touch with feelings, identifying them, and being encouraged to share them with people who can offer guidance—most notably, parents—will lead a child toward safety. That's why it's so important to teach Expressiveness when children are young.

Michael Nerney, a school communication consultant, observes that the foundation for Expressiveness is laid in preschool years. Older kids who haven't developed this critical ability have trouble accurately identifying their own feelings and needs; they are left to take their cues from outside—from their peers—rather than tuning in to and responding to their own emotional states. Some of those pirates in nursery school who continue to act instead of talk may become troubled teenagers without the skills necessary to unburden themselves.

Expressive children are closer to their parents. The *JAMA* study I referred to in chapter 2 is probably one of the most important longitudinal studies on child development yet done; it followed almost thirteen thousand children through adolescence. Researchers suggested that a child's emotional connection to parents and his verbal openness with them were the best predictors of school performance—as well as of the likelihood that he would engage in dangerous behaviors as an adolescent. Of course, these dramatic findings only validate what parents have sensed for many years.

Expressive children can protect themselves. The power of Expressiveness seems to begin as early as age two or three. For example, three-year-old Susie was getting picked on in preschool because she wore thick glasses to correct a congenital eye problem. Even at that tender age, she was able to identify her discomfort at being called "four eyes," and she was able to talk about it with her parents. This knowledge gave Mom and Dad a chance to help her by bringing the situation to her teacher's attention. Expressiveness led to understanding and action, and this made all the difference between Susie's feeling ashamed or her being effective in the face of such taunts.

Expressive children make expressive friends. One of the most critical yet least discussed aspects of this core trait is that children who possess Expressiveness are drawn to each other. As you will read in chapter 5, "Peer Smarts," good friends protect and support a child's core. The peer relationships forged by expressive children are often centered on common interests and always based on mutual respect for skills and problem-solving. These kids are successful kids. You've seen them—they're the achievers, the specialists, the ones who have what it takes to make good choices. They're in the same cliques with other, as Mike Nerney calls them, "emotionally literate" boys and girls who are on the smart track. Unlike children who are immersed in the pop culture, these kids actually *talk* about things. Their conversations may be narrow—a "jock" talking incessantly about sports, a "techie" about computers—but their Expressiveness usually has very positive outcomes.

In short, Expressiveness is the ability to verbalize what's going on inside. For a child, this implies an emotional literacy that combines the identification of feelings with a willingness to communicate them to important adults as well as to peers. Hence, our third Basic Skill:

Basic Skill #3: Promote your child's unique style of talking about what really matters.

Obviously, Expressiveness can mean the difference between academic success or failure, social competence or isolation, connection and disconnection from the family. Because the stakes are so high, we parents have to beware of the forces that work against our helping children develop this key skill.

Core Threats: What Works Against Expressiveness

Given the openness of our culture, you would think that kids today would be more expressive than we were; however, my observations of both younger and older children offer a startlingly different perspective. Why is this?

The second family competes with Expressiveness. As I pointed out in chapter 2, kids and parents spend about 39 minutes per week in meaningful conversation—a pittance compared with the 1,680 minutes kids spend watching television. The same study shows that the average daily running time for TV sets in American homes is *seven* *hours!* Adding to that the time kids spend in front of computers and at video games, one might argue that at least children are getting a lot of information; but the sheer volume is misleading.

The pop culture promotes the antithesis of Expressiveness. Media and mass-market merchandising represent a "canned" approach to communication. Every year, advertisers and entertainment companies alike struggle to find clever catchphrases that will appeal to each new crop of teeny-boppers. The result is a language I call "PopSpeak" (see box on following page). It's the vocabulary that so many of our children latch on to nowadays—canned expressions and superficial words that diminish and depersonalize human relations.

PopSpeak separates a child from her feelings and is employed by kids as a kind of verbal shorthand, quickly and incompletely summing up a mood, expressing an opinion, describing an activity. And it is used to barter popularity. In many classrooms around the country, those most fluent in PopSpeak are not only accepted, they are preferred, part of the "in" crowd. These children tend not to be truly expressive, it has been done *for* them. Kids who are allowed excessive access to the media think the thoughts, tell the stories, and develop a universal language that's driven by the pop culture.

PopSpeak can start young. A five-and-a-half-year-old media-saturated kid told me the following story in his native tongue: "Like . . . I was like . . . it was cool . . . the boy was like 'Hey am I really getting Donkey Kong Three for my birthday? That's so fun!' "

The second family doesn't demand Expressiveness. This is an important aspect of friendship choice. When I ask a pop-culture-saturated preteen who talks the talk, walks the walk (often, an imitation of gangsta rap posturing), and dresses in baggy pants and other elements of the pop culture uniform, "What's so comforting about being with your group of friends?" he invariably says, "I don't have to *do* anything. I don't have to be good at anything. There's no pressure." As kids get older they gravitate toward others like them and, as a result, also don't have to *say* much. They often lack meaningful interests and seem unable to stick with problems and challenges. They don't know how to ask for help; they don't easily share triumphs. Instead, unexpressive kids quickly get into a pattern of wanting, as a wise elementary school teacher once characterized, "to take in and consume,

DOES YOUR CHILD TALK "POPSPEAK"?

A child's natural strength and determination, along with a strong family unit, helps inoculate against an overload of Pop-Speak—the media-inspired language of noncommunication. Many successful and accomplished kids talk the talk but are not necessarily at risk. However, some children are more vulnerable than others, and if there's a weak link in family functioning, there's a good chance the pop culture is going to become a serious influence. Those children are more likely to internalize pop culture mediocrity and become too immersed in PopSpeak. Below are signs to watch for:

• He uses certain words-of-the-moment and popular phrases to describe almost everything: *whatever, awesome, excellent, not!*— to the exclusion of a richer, more expressive vocabulary.
• She ends almost every sentence with an upward inflection, as if asking a question. This is not simply a bad habit she's picked up from her peers—it's because she doesn't want to commit herself.
• He has a lot of knowledge of pop culture—computer games, MTV hits, knows everything there is to know about popular television characters—but not very much at all about typical academic subjects.
• She talks fast, is fluent, and can even be funny, but reveals little that is personal.

rather than create and put out." This composite, continuing beyond middle school, can be a blazing red flag for behavior problems. If, in addition, any learning difficulties arise, the cycle may escalate even further, particularly as a child gets older. And then the stakes are even higher.

Tara, for example, was never particularly expressive as a younger child. By the time she reached thirteen, she was pretty much mute around her parents. Like many teens, when Tara was at home, she holed up in her room. Not surprisingly, she felt most comfortable with kids who were like her—very laid back and noncommunicative. The hidden reason for this preference was not primarily because her adolescent hormones had kicked in. Rather, it was the communication gulf between her and her parents that began way *before* her preteen years.

Sadly, Tara's parents hadn't known how to foster her unique style of communicating and, therefore, being verbal about emotional matters never became part of her core. She naturally drifted toward the less verbally demanding second family. As Tara confided to me in a private meeting, her friends, unlike her parents, "don't make me talk about stuff. We don't have to say that much to each other. We're happy just hanging out, watching TV, or playing video games." Tara's nonexpressiveness was responsible, in part, for her spiraling bad grades. She was on the verge of being expelled from school, which is why she wound up in my office.

Regrettably, I meet a lot of Taras in my work. A common denominator among these kids is their long-term inexpressiveness. As teenagers, their schoolwork slips, and they often move toward experimenting with cigarettes, alcohol, drugs, and sex. However, this problem isn't just a second-family issue.

Parents are often steeped in psychobabble. Enormous numbers of us have been in psychotherapy, twelve-step programs, and counseling of one sort or another. Pollster George Gallup, Jr., has estimated that almost 50 percent of the population has been involved with "sharing and caring" groups of the human potential movement (see page 261 for more about this). Tens of millions of readers of pop psychology books, as well as members of the various support groups, have become familiar with "psychobabble," a verbal shorthand for canned therapy maxims. Among some parents, this is almost the adult version of PopSpeak! Because parents are understandably so desperate to get children to communicate, we try to pry kids' emotions out of them by using the language of therapy. The problem is, we're not always successful. Seven-year-old Amanda said to me, "I don't like talking to my mother. She's always trying to get me to open up." A friend's son, at thirteen, put it more bluntly: "Stop trying to analyze everything I say," he said after his mom tried yet another sharing/caring tactic. And in workshops across the country, children have told me about essentially similar experiences: They are up in arms about parents acting "like shrinks," demanding that they conform to some sort of therapeutic "openness."

A related issue is that we look for an "expert" with a one-size-fits-all communication solution. In theory, there's nothing wrong with the advice in child-rearing manuals, which often contain many worthwhile tips. However, most of these—even my own first book, *Parenting by Heart*—work from the developmental assumption that kids are kids, and at different ages, their capacities change. The implication is that parents can stick to general communication techniques that are age-appropriate and assume they'll work. When they don't, either our child is "difficult," or has a learning problem, or we've somehow applied the strategy in the wrong way. But after listening to thousands of parents report to me about trying to implement various techniques, I've come away with another conclusion: *Different children have very different language and communication styles.* The idea that one set of principles will work for Johnny, with his unique expressive style, and with Janey, whose style is totally different, seems at best old-fashioned. As you will see, the latest research in language development tells us that in order to keep the lines open, we first need to recognize a child's unique communication style and then build on it.

Understanding Expressiveness

In other chapters of this book, I devote one section to what parents can do to help nurture the core trait, and another to the kinds of core-building skills children need to develop it. However, Expressiveness is unique. Communication—by definition—involves a speaker *and* a listener. The two are of a piece, and the quality of communication is determined by both parties. Even if your child already is expressive, you must take action to protect this core trait, which is always vulnerable to being dulled by the second family.

Expressiveness can be encouraged in almost every young child and adolescent. Below, I lay out this process, which begins with understanding your child's particular style of expression. I first explain the elements of communication and then the four communication "styles."

As always, I urge you: Accept what comes naturally to your child and adapt your own style to strengthen his. The specific strategies I offer later in this chapter for each of the four styles of expression should help you do just that.

The components of communication

The words "good" or "bad" don't adequately describe communication; therefore, they have no place in your own vocabulary as you help your child develop Expressiveness. Think for a moment about the ways we often describe our kids' verbal abilities, saying things like:

"He's a good talker."

"She trusts me."

"She speaks her mind."

"My child tells me everything."

"He's like a clam."

"He's a loner, he keeps to himself."

No matter how you describe your child, the important point is to understand that what you "hear" is what you have. Many of the various components of communication I describe below are inborn, a matter of "hard wiring." As you become more aware of these elements, however, you will be better able to accept *your* child's individual style. Just as important, you will see how best to modify your approach to fit that style. It's not that hard to gain a greater understanding of how your child communicates. Look at what current speech and language specialists watch for.

Pacing. Some children simply find their words and speak at a slower pace. When a child who seems to deliberate over each word has to converse with a rapid-fire talker, the two can barely communicate because the more hesitant child feels that she can't compete. For example, I recently consulted with parents who have three children. Eight-year-old Allen was—as we therapists put it—the identified patient. His parents, Elizabeth and Donald, were worried because Allen didn't talk much. When I met with the boy, however, he explained why: He didn't like talking to his mother because she constantly interrupted him. Elizabeth is really a very compassionate and well-meaning mom. Yet, when Elizabeth heard Allen's complaint, she was hurt and couldn't understand what he meant. However, after fifteen minutes of listening as the two discussed some difficulties at home, it became vividly clear that her son had a point. *In just that short time, Elizabeth had interrupted Allen twelve times without being aware of it.* The problem quite simply was that Mom's pace of thinking was so much faster than Allen's delivery. He would start saying something like "In school today—" and she'd jump in with "What period?"

Focus. As I detail in chapter 6, children have different types of focusing styles that affect not only their ability to take in information, but also their ability to stay on track. Jamie, for example, could be distracted by the least little noise or movement, confounding anyone who tried to get a story out of her. I'm sure you've met kids who seem to get lost midconversation. On the other hand, once my son Sammy's focus "locks on," he could tell a story in the middle of Madison Square Garden during a Knicks game!

Linear versus nonlinear thinking. The linear child goes from A to B to C. If Lynette is describing a play date, she'll talk about getting there, what happened first, next, and so on. If you interrupt, though, she gets confused and angry and wants to drop the subject.

Nonlinear children change the subject often—your hair could turn gray while you wait for them to make a point. Whenever five-year-old Nathan tries to tell a story, each new idea reminds him of something else, and he goes off on one tangent after another. Here's how he answered his mother when she asked him if he had fun at his friend's party: "We were playing soccer, and Jimmy was there, and he didn't let me have a turn, so I went to Mary and she had this new toy that was on TV last night. I love that new show, but I don't think it's as good as *Rugrats*." Nathan's mother is frequently lost, as are his schoolmates and teachers, because he can't keep just one story line going. Of course, Nathan doesn't realize the effect he's having on his listeners. As he grows up, he'll probably sense he's a bit "long-winded." Nonlinear adults may learn to use the phrase, "to make a long story short," but, of course, they rarely do.

Auditory Processing. This refers to both incoming and outgoing messages. Some children are simply more fluent—able to get out what's on their minds. They can also hear what they sound like and are able to correct their course when they go off. Likewise, some children are better than others at attending to and decoding what they hear—when someone talks, they get the meaning immediately. Other kids may need to hear the words more slowly in order to process what's been said.

The four expressive styles

A child's expressive style has enormous impact on relationships within the family, as well as on the kinds of friends she chooses—and both obviously affect the development of her core. Be assured, however, that no matter what your child's style is, it is possible to help him become even more expressive. Here are the four predominant styles I see in children.

Reserved. These children, usually Intense/Sensitive or Reserved/Clingy types, don't like to talk much—it's neither comfortable nor easy for them. They can't seem to describe events or things or feelings without making a real effort. A reserved child's pace may be slow or halting. She may have processing difficulties or a problem with retrieving words; but it's hard to determine, because getting her to talk is like pulling teeth. These kids also tend to be secretive. When you ask a question, they often say they don't remember; and sometimes they actually don't, but sometimes they would simply rather not share what's on their minds. Unfortunately, it's easy to feel rejected by such children—and many parents do.

The problem, very often perceived as a conflict between parent and child, is really simply a pattern of different expressive styles that needs to be recognized as such and not taken personally. Anita, who has already labeled her four-year-old daughter, Sharon, as "quiet as a dormouse," confided to me that she felt guilty about thinking that her child was "a dud." But Anita's feelings are repeatedly bruised because whenever she asks Sharon any question ("How did you like school today?"), her little girl has such a hard time opening up to her. Anita misinterprets Sharon's reserve. At the same time, Anita's hurt, frustrated reaction *is* rejecting, because to Sharon it looks like anger.

Noisy. These children—typically Intense/Aggressive types—*always* want to talk, but they take so long to get to the point, you may not want to listen! They may be slow- or fast-paced talkers; either way, they're usually nonlinear thinkers who jump from topic to topic. They say huge amounts, but may reveal very little. These children also tend to be glib, sometimes even pushy, monopolizing conversations and/or interrupting others until they get the attention they demand. Adults often find them exasperating. There's no question that such a child can absolutely drain your energy.

For example, six-year-old Pauline is a likable little girl, but her mother complains, "She's such a chatterbox. It's exhausting to be around her." Quincy's dad says of his eight-year-old son, "He can drive me crazy. When we do chores together, he talks all the time. I don't want to stifle him or discourage him from helping out, but, honestly, there are times I just want to shout, 'Quincy, enough!' "

On-off. These children are either Intense/Sensitive or Reserved/Clingy types. They're rigid: Either conditions are right for them to talk, or they won't open up; you simply can't engage them no matter how hard you try. They tend to stop speaking completely if interrupted, if they don't get what they want, or if you disagree with them. In other words, whenever conversation doesn't go their way, that tends to trigger their "off" mode. However, once your on-off child is started, you may not be able to get a word in edgewise.

Almost every parent has witnessed on-off children tune out other input when watching television. You might have to repeat a request or an instruction five times because your child is turned off to anything else. It's no wonder we say our kids are "glued" to the set. One friend of mine is certain he could do brain surgery on his son—without anesthesia—while his son is watching TV!

With on-off kids, like Belinda, off times occur for a number of reasons. For example, when she is doing any activity—a puzzle, brushing her teeth, tying her shoes—it's almost impossible for her parents to break through to her. But if she wants *their* attention, she's relentless—kind of like a talking locomotive.

Naturally expressive. These children, usually Easy/Balanced types, are flexible. Their speech and cognitive ability to communicate proceed at a developmentally appropriate pace, and even at an early age, conversation is give and take. Adults love them. Only the other day I heard one mother telling another, "My son is such a good companion! He loves to talk to me about everything." The other mother looked at the woman with a mixture of envy and total disbelief. But there *are* children like that. They have access to what they feel and can describe it. Like most children, these kids tend to be nonlinear thinkers when younger, but by early elementary school, they're eloquent and can tell stories that have a beginning, a middle, and an end. Naturally expressive children gauge their delivery by the listener's response, and therefore speak neither too slowly nor too fast. These kids exhibit a strong focus—and resilience; they're able to recover if interrupted or if they don't get the reaction they expected.

Lorena, a child who lives in my apartment building, is a naturally expressive kid. Whenever I run into her, I hardly have to do anything to get her to open up. This, according to her parents, is the way she's always been. Her mind doesn't wander. If I stop her midsentence, she doesn't forget what she was saying; she easily holds the thread of her ideas. Lorena just seems to have been blessed with an ability to tell a smooth, coherent story.

Bringing Out the Best in *Your* Child

Now that you have a sense of the various elements that make up expressive styles, it's important to listen to *your* child. Ask yourself which style seems to fit best. Following are strategies that will help you both respond to your child's particular mode, and make the most of it. Even though you'll want to concentrate most on the strategies that suit your child, it's also a good idea to read through all of the expressive styles; as your child comes in contact with other kids, these strategies will help you communicate with them as well.

The reserved child

By definition, reserved children aren't prone to Expressiveness. Remember, they are not trying to be disrespectful or withholding. If you feel this way, you might respond with anger, setting off a negative communication cycle. More often, these kids just need to be "jump-started." Here are some approaches that help:

Engage in parallel conversation. Reserved children hate to be put in the spotlight. They tend to feel self-conscious and, when spoken with face-to-face, often look down or away. You've probably met kids who simply shy away from conversation or won't look you in the eye, no matter how nice you are or how hard you try to engage them. Don't take it personally. All those tips for "intimate" conversation in parenting how-to manuals tend to fly out the window with a reserved kid. Don't look into his eyes, or try to relate "deeply," or make a big deal out of conversation. And, remember, with these children at any age, it's critical to never pounce; that kind of behavior absolutely overwhelms them.

Instead, use parallel opportunities, times when you're engaged in activities with each other. Talk while you're riding in the car, sorting socks, walking to school, cooking, or clearing the dinner dishes. Just doing an activity diffuses interpersonal intensity. This approach, which I've been teaching for almost two decades, also works well with nonreserved kids going through tight-lipped phases, such as pre- and early adolescence.

Model Expressiveness in your everyday life. We often forget how powerful our example as parents can be. Instead of simply waiting for your reserved child to open up, *demonstrate* this all-important core-builder. Tell brief stories (don't meander!) about how you felt when you were picked on in school, or how hard it was to make a decision to do something different from your group of friends. Just relate the story and keep it short; don't try to draw your child into it or expect that she'll go next. That will only increase self-consciousness.

By *showing* your children how to tell a story, how to identify feelings and talk about them, you're modeling Expressiveness. In addition, you might also jog their memory. Kids are naturally self-referential; this means that they tend to hear every story with an egotistical ear. I've seen this happen time and again with my own children. I'll come home saying that I had a hard day at work—let's say I've had a disagreement with a colleague. All of a sudden, my daughter, Leah, opens up about a fight that happened at school or she'll say, "Math was hard today." If I ask, "How come you didn't tell me when I asked about school?" she invariably answers, "I didn't remember. I forget that stuff by the time I get home."

Prompt gently. Reserved children often have trouble with what language therapists call "word retrieval." Remember that finding the right word, as well as pace and fluency, are mostly products of inborn traits. Try not to exhibit impatience or to abruptly supply the missing parts of his stories.

A far less intrusive approach is multiple choice. This allows her to think about what she's saying, pick the word that fits, and still feel a sense of autonomy. For example, I suggested to Aileen that when her daughter, Ashley, describes a play date problem without any details ("I didn't have fun"), she should prompt her little girl by asking, "Oh, really? Were you angry or sad?"

Remember that nonverbal communication matters, too. Reserved children are a lot like Geiger counters. They are incredibly sensitive to nonverbal cues. Sometimes, I give my own kids a spoken message such as "Talk to me about it—I'll understand," while my tone of voice, facial expression, or body language really says, "Hurry up, I'm busy" or "Uh oh. I know I'm not going to like this." Listen with your full body—be aware of how you might look to your child. If your child is over four, ask her to imitate how you look. My wife and I have had hysterical moments watching Sammy or Leah do impressions of us supposedly "listening."

Listen to your own pacing. This is a vital aspect of communication for the parent of any youngster, but it's particularly crucial with a combination of a reserved kid and a fast-talking parent. For example, George's machine-gun delivery often shut down his son Peter, nine, who took a while to get his thoughts together and his words out. To Peter, Dad's rat-a-tat pacing rushed him, and also made him feel scared because he didn't always "get" what was being said. George, a trial lawyer, was beside himself at not being able to get through to Peter. He was often angry at his son and, at the same time, he felt like a failure as a parent. However, their relationship improved dramatically after I encouraged George to simply talk more slowly. By matching his son's pace—and by asking only one question at a time rather than firing off several at once—he allowed Peter to keep up.

Offer your child reserved praise. I'm not suggesting that you do away with compliments all together, just that you tone them down. When a reserved child expresses himself clearly, if you overpraise him, as in "Wow!" or "That's *incredible*," he's likely to turn off. Don't make too BIG a response, and don't throw in too much information. In other words, don't offer an epic Technicolor response to a black-and-white art film kid. Roberta did that with her four-year-old. "Gee, Cathy, that's unbelievable," she would exclaim whenever her daughter described her day at school in terrific detail. "Now I really have a great picture of what it's like to play Duck, Duck Goose. You are so good at describing things!" Mom didn't realize it, but as she continued to pour on the praise, her daughter's sunny expression became more guarded. Why? Roberta's intentions were good, but the intensity of her response was too much for Cathy. Unwittingly, she was "training" her daughter not to talk as much as they both would like. (Read more about praise in chapter 4.)

Respond empathically. In the 1960s, psychologist Haim Ginott, in his much-read parenting communication guide *Between Parent and Child*, popularized the idea of "validating" your child's emotions with statements like "I can see that that made you angry." Decades later, parenting experts Adele Faber and Elaine Mazlich, coauthors of *How to Talk*

So Kids Will Listen, and Listen So Kids Will Talk, confirmed the wisdom of Ginott's work. Here, I am suggesting one additional and equally important practice: Tailor your empathic responses to fit your child. Empathy is experienced differently by different children. Reserved kids are very sensitive and often require specific, very quiet acknowledgment of their emotions.

For example, Mary, a four-year-old girl I know, needs to hear the words "I agree" from her parents; this opens her up more. Frank, six, can't even bear this small intrusion. He needs his parents to just sit back and not comment on what he's saying until he's finished saying it. And ten-year-old Maria still needs her feelings actually *named* ("I can see you're angry"), just as Faber and Mazlich suggest for younger children.

Think about the empathic words that work with your reserved child—phrases that you've learned from experience tend to work best. Most kids stick with several familiar phrases throughout their development. Keep a brief list in your mind and be prepared to use them as needed.

The noisy child

With reserved children, we rarely want to interrupt, correct, or in any way stop the flow of conversation. With noisy children, on the other hand, we feel the need to do these very things. In fact, you have to shape conversations. If you don't, discussions with noisy children have the potential to expand into an energy-draining, time-consuming, and eventually unpleasant interaction. Help them before that happens. Shaping or structuring can be accomplished in a number of ways.

Create "punctuation." Noisy kids talk like a tornado, barely pausing to take a breath. If you visualize their speech, it looks like one long, run-on sentence without any punctuation. By asking organizing questions that get him to stop and *think*, you'll help him add his own commas and periods. Teach him to incorporate time sequencing by asking, "What happened next?" and emotional description by wondering, "What did you feel like when that happened?" Questions or comments that encourage reflection tap skills that don't come naturally to fast-thinking, noisy kids:

"Take a deep breath and slow down for a second."
"Tell me: Did you know what was going to happen?"
"What were the other kids [or teacher] doing?"

Some parents have trouble with this, thinking that it squelches a child's imagination or spirit, but remember that few other people—kids or grown-ups—will indulge a rambling child. When should you interrupt? As soon as you are unable to follow the story line. With younger children, you can say, "Tell me the best part." With older children: "What's the theme, here?" "Tell me the point again." Speech therapists recommend saying, "Let me see if I understand this right." Then, state what *you* think is the main point, asking your child if that's correct. I assure you, he will not hesitate to disagree if you've missed the heart of his story.

Teach sequencing and order. Typically, noisy children stay nonlinear longer than other kids who, as young as three to four, might begin to learn sequencing. Many of the children I treat jump from topic to topic. To keep them on target and to help them recognize that the world isn't paid (as I am) to have patience, I take an active stance. I've learned from language specialists to rein in ramblers by guiding them with questions that teach order: "What happened first?," "What happened next?," and so on. This encourages kids to tell a story with a beginning, middle, and end. If a child's thoughts jump around, I stop her: "Wait, don't tell me what happened in the end. You haven't finished telling me what happened when you first got there." Try not to do this in every conversation, of course, just enough for your child to get the idea that sequencing makes a story more enjoyable to a listener.

Praise brevity and order. Because a noisy child may have trouble focusing, it's okay to heap on the compliments. Praise gets his attention and slows him down for a minute. It also helps him self-reflect—and acknowledge success—when you say, "You really told that story well." Before you know it, your noisy child might begin to notice that *he* can slow down and reflect. He'll eventually be able to tell *himself,* "I told that story well."

It's astonishing to see how the use of selective praise can influence even very young kids. For example, three-and-a-half-year-old Isabel was having trouble, as a lot of young children do, sticking to the point when she told a story. And there was no stopping her once she got going. Then, she'd get mad when her mom couldn't pay attention. I told her mother, Roz, that whenever Isabel told a *short* story and stayed on track, she should give her a hug (or make some other show of affection) and say, "That's a great story, Isabel. I could really follow what you were saying."

Honestly, I wasn't even sure this would work because Isabel was so young. But in a matter of months, Isabel not only expressed herself more effectively and to the point, she got loads of smiles and hugs from more satisfied listeners—her parents, her teachers, *and* her friends. At one point, she actually told Roz, "See, Mommy? I'm learning to talk smaller."

Break in—interrupt—if necessary. Don't be endlessly patient with your noisy child; the world certainly won't be. And don't be afraid of stifling her or hurting her feelings. This is a child for whom interruption is a good thing. The time to stop him is when *you* start losing interest. Tell him, "It's my turn to talk" or "Now listen to me." Some children react best to hand signals. Alexander, a boy I work with, loved it when I began moving my forefinger from side to side as a reminder to get back on track. He was so enamored of this method, he taught it to his mom and dad.

Look him in the eye. Be firm; use a tone of voice that's louder or softer than his—whichever one will get his attention. Some noisy children have hidden perceptual difficulties—for example, they have trouble picking up verbal and visual cues from other people—but their loud presentation masks them. If your child has a hard time comprehending spoken input, looking at him will give him visual cues regarding how you feel about his verbal presentation. If he won't look at you or he can't see you, plant yourself directly at his eye level and/or gently hold his face in your hands. Except for kids who have trouble making eye contact, this gentle "in your face" approach, used by speech and language therapists, really helps kids tell their stories more effectively.

The on-off child

These kids have certain traits in common with reserved children and noisy children. However, their style presents a special challenge: They are either in an "off" mode or an "on" mode, and getting them to switch from one to the other sometimes seems impossible. As Marie describes her on/off child, "When he is open to communicating, his face looks bright, lively, and engaged. When he's shut down, his face is altogether different—darker, as if there's a veil over it." Here are the skills that stimulate Expressiveness in on-off children.

Notice the time of day or circumstances under which your child is most often in the "on" mode. For some children, particular moments, such as bedtime, spark conversation. The questions asked at dinner go unanswered, but when five-year-old Ellen is snuggling up under the covers in her pajamas, she's good for conversation. Harry loves to talk when he's setting the table or a few minutes into dinner when he's got some food in his system. Go with these routine preferences, don't fight them. They are part of your child's makeup.

Start to notice *where* your child is when she opens up—the bathtub, sitting in the backyard, walking to school. These are your golden opportunities. Then, during these times and under those circumstances, relate to her carefully, as you would a reserved child: Engage in parallel conversation; don't "pounce" or overrespond; validate feelings and praise genuinely. Remember, for whatever reason, that invisible switch can flip into the "off" mode very easily.

Recognize and pay attention to temperamental signs. Nothing throws that switch "off" like a bad mood. I've heard hundreds of kids say that no matter what else is going on, they *never* want to talk if they aren't in the mood. A child's energy will be low and his feelings fragile when he is tired, hungry, angry, sad, or making a transition—from friends to family or from playtime to homework. At such moments, it's generally *not* realistic to expect him to open up.

Unfortunately, we parents occasionally ignore these signals. After all, we lead busy lives, and we tend to see our children most during transition times. We're afraid if we don't communicate *now*, we're not going to have another chance. But when you don't notice or respect your child's timing, you're likely to end up in a fight. As ten-year-old Lenore puts it, "When I don't want to talk, I don't want to talk. That's it. I wish people would leave me alone."

Figure out what "trigger" phrases will open up your child. Parents find that their children respond best to a variety of expressions—often phrases unique to that child and family. One mother found that her on-off daughter, who happened to have a great sense of humor, always clicked into the "on" mode when she said, "Okay, Gloria, spill your guts." Al, a father I know, found that his daughter Winona needed more gentle coaxing: "I'd love to hear what happened." Another mother in a parenting workshop told me that she appeals to her son's competitive spirit: "I bet you can't tell me that story without getting distracted." Another father praises his son's mastery: "How did you figure *that* out?"

Borrow trigger phrases and activities that work in school. One mother, Estelle, who frequently visited her son Keith's kindergarten class, noticed that Keith always settled down when his teacher would say, "Okeydokey . . . artichokey," meaning "It's time to talk." So, she started using that phrase at home—with great success. A father I met at one of my workshops realized that his preschooler, Maxine, who had been attending a Gymboree class, associated "circle time" with talking. To promote conversation, he and his wife began sitting in a circle with their daughter and her siblings in their living room.

Respond quickly. These children can get increasingly entrenched in one mode or the other, so it's best to catch them before they build momentum in either direction. For example, when your on-off child initiates conversation, immediately pay attention. Before she has a chance to switch "off," indicate that you're listening with your body language (look right at her), use active listening phrases like "Uh-huh" and "I see—go on." However, if she's just talking without saying much, quickly interrupt her, and try to get her back on track using some of the techniques suggested for noisy children that we discussed above.

Don't pressure your on-off child. When a child is in the "off" mode, he's similar to a reserved child. Don't pounce and don't pressure. If you ask a question—say, you'd like him to tell you about his music lesson—and you discover that he's in the off mode, don't pursue it further. Let the subject drop. Don't even say, "We'll talk about this later." Instead, wait until another time that's more conducive to conversation. Better opportunities will come around if you're patient, rather than trying to force them to occur.

The naturally expressive child

Although your child may rarely experience problems communicating his feelings or asking for what he needs, even these children need help at times. In certain life stages, his innate Expressiveness has to be protected, such as when he makes a significant transition. Given the increased developmental demands at those times, even a normally fluent child might tend to clam up a bit.

For example, Scott, a highly expressive and articulate boy, temporarily lost his gift for gab when he transferred from his familiar, small nursery school to a large and extremely competitive elementary school for gifted children. Because his parents recognized the tough transition, I suggested that they treat Scott with the same care they would offer a reserved child. Taking my advice, they engaged in parallel conversation, talking with him during chores rather than making direct eye contact. Mom and Dad paid attention to his nonverbal cues, prompted him gently for more details and yet were careful not to overwhelm him with a barrage of quick questions or excessive praise. And whenever he opened up to them, they responded empathically, validating that his new experience at school must be overwhelming: "Gee, Scott. This year everything seems to be so different for you. You have to sit at your own desk and do much harder work. That would be a little scary to me, too."

After a couple of months, Scott settled down and regained his natural expressive style. For most children, an illness or a family separation such as a divorce can also weaken their usual verbal strength. However, in every instance I've seen, if parents respond with the care they'd give to a reserved child, their naturally expressive child safely returns to normal.

The key to encouraging Expressiveness is to recognize your child's communication style and go with it. By adapting to, rather that struggling against, your child, you're more likely to keep the lines of communication open—from preschool through high school.

PASSION

Basic Skill #4: Protect your child's enthusiasm and love of life.

Exceptional Children

"My child doesn't seem to be *interested* in much" is a concern I've begun to hear from parents of younger and younger children over the last few years. In fact, such a remark is often indicative of a relatively new "symptom" in children—boredom. For a host of reasons, which I explain in this chapter, many kids today suffer from a lack of what I call "Passion"—the ability to maintain a deep interest in activities that require mastery. In its benign manifestation are children whose interests center mostly on TV, videos, computer games, or other pop culture amusements. In its most dangerous form are older children who turn to alcohol and find other types of self-destructive ways specifically to relieve inner boredom. We ought to listen to the teenager in Woodstock, New York, who explained, "We don't do drugs to see God and get closer to people. We do drugs to get wasted, because our everyday life is so *boring*, and we figure there has to be something better."

Over the twenty years I've been in practice, young children seem to be having a harder time developing special interests beyond what the pop culture spoon-feeds them. This is a worrisome and potentially dangerous trend, as I will explain. Therefore, when I meet the rare exception—a child who *has* Passion—I'm pleased and a little stunned. I find such children's stories worth sharing, because their deep, abiding interests protect their core selves and inoculate them against second-family pulls. These are the kinds of kids I mean:

- Heather has had a love of reading since she was five. Her parents are avid readers as well, so they nourished Heather's interest both by example and by providing books they thought she would enjoy. At eleven, Heather reads one or two books a week. No matter how busy life gets, she is never without an absorbing story in her head.
- Jeffrey, six, has a different fixation: baseball. He's a pretty good athlete but not a great one. Even though Jeffrey's never the star of a game, he gets incredible joy out of playing. Of course, like other sports buffs his age, Jeffrey also collects memorabilia; he follows every game and knows every player's stats. Whenever you talk to him, Jeffrey's either anticipating an exciting game or coming down from one.
- Jake has been fascinated by dinosaurs since he was a toddler. It was amazing to watch him, at three, reeling off those four-syllable names—pronouncing them correctly as well. Over the years, his family made regular pilgrimages to museums. Today, his room looks something like a museum, filled to the brim with books, models, and posters of dinosaurs. Along the way, Jake acquired many other interests as well, but those prehistoric creatures still captivate him.
- Kyra, a very agile child, launched a surprising love affair with soccer at age five. She wasn't the best player in her day camp where she first kicked a ball, but something about the movement and the freedom of running appealed to her. She kept at it, and eight years later is one of the best players on her junior high school team. It isn't always easy—winning, losing, sometimes juggling several games a weekend. But soccer is about more than competition to Kyra. It's about friendship, showing up, sticking with something. Soccer has also helped Kyra stay close to her parents. Let's face it—who ferried her to and from endless practices? And who have been her most ardent cheerleaders?
- Maybe because business was always discussed at the dinner table in his house, Craig has loved the stock market since he was eight or nine. His mom taught him to read about investing and to research companies whose products interested him. Not surprisingly, high-tech firms captured Craig's attention. In sixth grade, with his father staking him a hundred dollars, Craig slowly began to invest. Now, at twenty, though still an undergraduate student, he is the chief administrator of a large investment partnership.

These kids, with varying intelligence and family backgrounds, share one thing in common: They have Passion—an overriding interest and commitment to an activity or a subject. Passion can be about anything that requires mastery—a sport, a musical instrument, a collection of valuables or of seeming junk, an activity like reading or painting. Impassioned children are not one-note characters. They have friendships and get into all the regular kid stuff. But unlike so many youngsters in our culture of instant gratification, they sustain long-term interests. They're willing to devote time, and are able to develop skills, around their interests. Their passions are *not* just passing fancies or something they dabble in; they are part of who these kids are—part of their identity.

Why Passion Is Important

Having Passion is vital to a child's core. It teaches her the rules of life and leads to the development of patience and persistence, among other important skills. The three preceding core-builders—Mood Mastery, Respect, and Expressiveness—are the building blocks of Passion. In order to sustain an interest or activity, children need to be able to understand and to express their feelings, to know what calms and soothes them—particularly in the face of new situations and challenges—and to trust and be able to call on adults for help. Once a child possesses Passion, it becomes a form of spiritual fitness training and muscle conditioning all in one—discipline that, in concert with the other skills in this book, will firm up a child's core. Here's why:

Passion enables a child to forge a separate identity. A lamentable reality is that having Passion doesn't always win peer popularity points. Impassioned children can be subtly ostracized for standing out from the crowd. At worst, they are labeled. A child who collects butterflies may be called a "weirdo." One who stays after school to get in extra music practice may be seen as a "nerd." And others are often called some kind of "nut"—computer nut, baseball nut, you name it.

These children have to be secure enough in themselves to go against the group, and *be* who they are. In fact, having Passion—a strong conviction that emanates from inside—actually gives them the strength to hang in there. Because things *do* matter to them, they are able to stand up for their feelings—and for their uniqueness.

Passion encourages a love of learning. More precisely, infant researchers refer to the process of "cross modal learning"—taking in information through many different channels. Rather than being limited to a narrow realm, a child who has a deep, enduring interest in a subject or an activity is continually inspired to pursue it through a variety of channels. Thus, having Passion inspires mastery in a variety of disciplines. For example, Jeffrey, who loved baseball, learned to read from the newspaper's sports pages. He learned to draw by stenciling the walls of his room with baseball objects. He learned math via baseball statistics.

Passion helps children learn people skills. Through their enduring interests, kids meet new people, grasp the rules of social interaction, and forge friendships. Kyra, for instance, had soccer buddies with whom she made play dates; those play mates, in time, became her best pals, her buddies for sleepovers, the group she went with to the mall. She learned the rules of sportsmanship as well: how to cooperate and how to celebrate victory gracefully and handle defeat with stoic acceptance.

Passion helps a child make proactive choices. Every primary passion has a structure—an established sequence that a child must master. That structure helps him make choices that will later keep him from getting lost in the vagaries of the peer culture. For example, Seth showed an early interest in music; by preschool, he could already keep a beat and carry a tune. Because Seth's mother got him involved in a play group that played and listened to a lot of music, many of the friends Seth made there shared his interest. Later, in early elementary school, in addition to wanting the latest fast-food giveaway or fad toy, Seth also hoped for gifts that would help him become a better musician.

Passion helps kids make healthy sacrifices. If you think about it, every choice for Passion means a child has to learn to give up something else—often, another group activity. Take Yoko, eleven, who has forged her own unique path. She is very popular among her peers, even though since age five she has been taking time-consuming ballet lessons. Over the years, when her friends chose to play video games or go to the mall, Yoko often had class or had to practice for an upcoming recital. She learned how to decline their invitations gracefully. Another child might be horrified to give up even one afternoon with friends, fearing that she won't be liked, or that kids will call her a "geek." But Yoko never boasted of her choices or achievements to her friends; she didn't act as if she were better than they were because of her talent. And she didn't feel deprived either, because as much as she liked to have fun with her buddies, she also enjoyed the process of learning how to dance and gained pleasure from her accomplishments. Today, Yoko's friends stick by her, even admire her; they know ballet is "her thing." She doesn't see it as a sacrifice because, in effect, she has had her cake and eaten it, too.

Passion inspires a solid parent-child connection. There's no way for a child to have Passion without parents being intimately involved. Think about it: Behind every enduring child's interest is a frazzled mother or father who helps by researching options, making plans, figuring out logistics. You'll hear from a thousand soccer moms that the reason they put up with the endless arrangements and constant chauffeuring is that the time spent in the car before and after a game creates closeness with their children. If your child has a primary passion, you become interwoven in her life in very healthy ways.

For example, Heather often asked her parents to read along with her, so that afterward they could discuss and share ideas. Only recently, she had tears (of joy) in her eyes as she reported, "The way my dad and I read together feels so special to me." And when I brought this up with dad, he, too, was visibly moved. He wished he'd had that kind of connection with his own father.

Passion builds meaningful relationships with supportive adults outside the family. Instead of a child being totally swallowed by the peer group and pop culture, having Passion affords many opportunities to connect with adult role models who stand for mastery and dedication. When Kyra was only six, she started to get close to her female soccer coaches who modeled resilience and determination. Heather had one teacher in particular who appreciated her excitement for reading and would say, "What books am I going to feed you this week?" And, Jake's frequent visits to the dinosaur displays fascinated the museum curator, who ultimately became his mentor. Over the years, the curator also became good friends with Jake's family, all of them affected by the boy's enthusiasm for learning.

Childhood Passion becomes adult achievement. Children may not stick with the same interest, but having Passion sets them on a course of curiosity and accomplishment. As I've watched Jake and the other children grow up into their preteen years and beyond, I have seen their Passions sustain them and feed their core selves. So far, none has fallen prey to drugs; all have made wonderful friends; all are doing well academically and seem to be growing up into decent people.

Moreover, once Passion is an integral part of a child's core, the content may change—but being passionate defines his approach to life, whether it comes to making decisions or conquering challenges. In Seth's case, as with most children who have Passion, he populated his world with children and adults who also had deep interests. At eighteen, Seth still plays guitar, but he's a premed major in a fine liberal arts college, now passionate about becoming a doctor. Given his history, there's no doubt in my mind he'll make it.

The sum of these points is that Passion is vital to the creation of your child's core self. Hence, our next Basic Skill:

> Basic Skill #4: Protect your child's enthusiasm
> and love of life.

Passionate children develop a powerful inner compass. While many around them lose their heads (and, seemingly, their will) to the second family, these kids stay in touch with their cores; their lives are organized by a central interest—rather than sailing aimlessly on faddish currents. With core selves intact, children who have Passion have a stronger sense of identity and an air of self-assurance that I simply don't see in kids who drift with the pack. But the journey isn't easy.

Core Threats: How Passion Is Squelched

It has become increasingly difficult to develop Passion in our culture. This has as much to do with how we parents view our kids than with the pulls of the second family. There are several reasons.

Parents and educators tend to go overboard in their desire to help children develop self-esteem. Previous generations were afraid of children getting "swelled heads." Parents and teachers spared their compliments. While the current feel-good mentality we see today was necessary to correct often harsh post-Victorian practices, the pendulum has swung so far in the other direction that if you walk into any preschool in America, you're likely to see some display of a teacher's attempt to raise her students' self-esteem.

For example, in an article that recently appeared on the *New York Times* op-ed page, professor of early childhood education Lillian Katz cites a bulletin board in one school hallway entitled "We Applaud Ourselves." As Katz points out, "The poster urged self-congratulation; it made no reference to possible ways of earning applause." She also comments on a kindergarten classroom in which children completed the sentence "I am special because . . ." with phrases such as "I can color," "I can ride a bike," and "I like to play with my friends." Making a child feel "special" for such common, average accomplishments, says Katz, is destined to rebound. "If everybody is special, nobody is special."

Clearly, we often don't make children work very hard for their rewards. What does this have to do with Passion? When the focus is primarily on making kids feel good, children develop little tolerance for the struggle involved in attaining mastery. Instead of *earning* praise by having to investigate, with setbacks, solve problems, decisions, and perform other tasks that are involved in becoming proficient at a skill or hobby, we applaud children for just *being*. Perhaps that's one reason the average college student does twenty-nine hours a week of schoolwork today, compared with sixty hours in 1960!

In any case, we also have to look outside school and family to understand the other threats to this important core-builder.

Primary passions are crowded out by derived passions. I refer to *primary passions*—those that emanate from a child's core interests—to differentiate from *derived passions*, which are encouraged by the pop culture. Many young children today, when asked to draw a picture or write a story, re-create what they've already seen in the media or in merchandising campaigns. They gravitate to media-inspired interests because that's what most of their friends are doing as well. In 1985, according to the Media Reform Information Center, 100 percent of the top-ten best-selling toys were tied to TV shows. It's unlikely that subsequent years fell much below that figure. No wonder children's rooms everywhere (including those in my home) spill over with years' worth of handouts and toys that have absolutely no value except for their connection to media or product merchandising. Some of these rooms are virtual shrines to our pop culture, in which every detail—sheets, blankets, pillowcases, as well as toys and clothing—mirrors the interests of its inhabitant.

Now, in and of themselves, I don't object to the idea that a child might want to collect giveaways—after all, most of us had secret stashes of Crackerjack prizes, Bazooka comics, and other collectibles in our own childhood rooms. But here's where the problem is: The scope has changed dramatically. Huge cross-merchandising deals are struck between movies, toys, and child-centered restaurants, and the resulting merchandising campaigns are like nothing we've ever seen. For example, when McDonald's announced a promotion that promised children a Teenie Beanie Baby with their Happy Meals, they "turned the parenting world upside down," according to an article in *Brandweek,* an advertising trade journal. In ten days, nearly 100 million Happy Meals were sold, breaking every record for consumer response. Because of its various Happy Meals promotions, in fact, the chain is able to draw 87 percent of all U. S. children aged three through nine! Not to be outdone, Burger King gives away more than 200 million toys a year through its promotional programs.

This combined power of commercialism, media, and peer pressure—in other words, the second family—is a powerhouse phenomenon that shapes the tastes and captures the attention of almost every child in America. In many homes, "old-fashioned" hobbies, like stamp collecting and model-making, have been displaced almost entirely by media consumption. Half the children in this country between six and seventeen have TVs in their bedrooms and, based on the homes I've been in, many of them prefer the tube to activities like building, playing house, doing puzzles, and, certainly, reading.

While admittedly a lot of fun, an unwanted side effect of this pop culture invasion is that it may crowd out a child's Passion. Derived passions create the *appearance* involvement, but, in reality, media-driven preoccupations are mostly empty. They are not real passions. And they are temporary. Taste is more or less defined by what's available at your local fast-food restaurant, what toys are advertised on Saturday-morning TV, or what character is talked about in the playground. Last month, it was Barney; last week, Anastasia; this week it's Godzilla; next week, who knows? Derived passions have a short shelf life—enthusiasm wanes quickly as each blockbuster fad makes its way into kids' collective psyche. Because these ephemeral crazes almost always have to do with merchandising, they run a mile wide and an inch deep. Kids don't develop skills from derived passions. There's no knowledge to be gained, no talent developed. In the end, buying products and receiving free prizes tend to crowd out primary passions.

Passion is not cool. Another reason that it's so rare to find children with abiding interests is that as kids get older—according to the second family—it's just "not cool" to have them. By early elementary school, Passion is precisely what the second family asks kids *not* to have. I've sat in many nursery school classes where a beautiful piece of artwork drawn from a child's imagination got far less attention from other students than subjects inspired by the *Star Wars* trilogy or the latest Spice Girls CD. In short, a foundation is laid supporting the idea that nothing is more important than being "with it." Anything else is "nerdy." Regrettably, we're seeing this at younger and younger ages: a whopping 70 percent of day care centers use television during a typical day.

Thus, long before preadolescence, the second family may have a subtle impact on a child's capacity for Passion. She may have a host of derived passions, but doesn't seem profoundly interested in activities that reflect her core. Having less desire that distinguishes her from the herd makes a child even more vulnerable to the predictable merchandise-driven mind-set of the pop culture. We parents sometimes feel overshadowed by this reality, but we must take a proactive stand, to help our children develop interests that emanate from inside them. This is no easy assignment, but it can be done.

Parent Skills: Seeing and Sustaining Passion

As with each of the core-builders in this book, you must see your child clearly in order to help him develop Passion. The first section below will help you do just that. Once you see where your child's Passion lies, you can take steps to help him foster those interests—without pushing too hard and thereby turning him off. The second section will help you on that path.

Identifying your child's Passion

Really seeing your child involves noticing interests that mix natural endowment with the learning channels he is most proficient at using. For example, five-year-old Lewis loves art. Watching Lewis from the time he first held a thick crayon, his parents recognized this as his chief interest. His artwork has already helped Lewis strengthen areas he finds difficult. A child who didn't talk until he was almost four, he was nevertheless able to express himself through creativity. In one instance, after the family returned home from summer vacation, Lewis had trouble verbally talking about his experiences. But his drawings of pretty shells and other wondrous features of the shoreline spoke volumes about his delight and amazement. To this day, every new experience Lewis enjoys—bowling, fishing, Boy Scouts—is expressed through his art. By now, Lewis's classmates look to him as a chronicler of school events. The pride he takes in this identity is enormous.

Sometimes, it is equally important for a parent to *discourage* interests that don't seem to fit a child's skills and temperament. For example, Angie encouraged her ten-year-old Lila's interest in gymnastics, because from the time her daughter began to walk, she was active, graceful, and lithe. Not surprisingly, she did well and, despite a few setbacks, has progressed joyously with gymnastics. But the following year, when Lila wanted to take chess lessons, Angie confided in me, "We didn't exactly discourage her, but we also didn't do much to promote it—at our school, the chess team was cutthroat competitive. That aggressiveness didn't fit Lila's nature. We had a hunch she only brought it up because a couple of teachers at school had been recruiting really hard for the team."

Angie was right. The bottom line was that playing chess didn't make Lila happy—which is a direct indication that this wasn't a primary passion. If your child doesn't seem to experience joy in the pursuit of an interest, something is wrong. After all, these are *children* we're talking about—they should be having *fun* while developing a skill.

RECOGNIZING A PRIMARY PASSION

- It makes your child happy.
- Your child pushes *you,* not the other way around.
- The interest is a natural "fit" with your child's basic temperament and repertoire of skills.
- Your child can tolerate some frustration or disappointment without disengaging from the activity.
- Praise seems less of a motivator than simply doing the activity.
- Your child begins to identify the skill as a part of who she *is.*

Encouraging Passion

There are a number of important ways to nurture your child's Passions. The following tactics work together to provide the right balance of support and restraint.

Hold back a bit. When a child first appears interested in something worthwhile, we enrichment-minded parents immediately want to help get it started. I have even seen many financially pressured parents put the family's needs on the back burner to prematurely push a budding talent before their child has truly exhibited a deep, sustaining interest. In any case, it's critical to hold back a little. There will be a wealth of first-time experiences that will enable you to see both what your child gravitates toward and what he's good in. Don't push. It is far more important to preserve natural curiosity—which you can do by recognizing your child's emotional comfort level.

Even when a child loves something, if he's pushed too hard, his enthusiasm can turn sour. Many kids in my nursery and elementary interviews have confided in me that they feel pressured, even co-opted, by their parents. Often, albeit with the best of intentions, we do seem to take over. Children who have passionate parents tell me that whenever they get the least bit interested in something, Mom and Dad immediately jump in. It may be because of a childhood dream they never realized. Whatever the reason, the interest somehow becomes theirs, not the child's own pursuit. Hence, when a youngster shows an inclination or talent, pay attention, but try not to overwhelm her with enthusiasm. Always remember that this is your child's "thing," not yours.

Also, bear in mind that your child's temperament mediates his reaction to parental zeal and coaxing. In fact, my interpretation of research done by Dr. Stanley Greenspan's Zero to Three Foundation suggests that with Intense/Aggressive, Intense/Sensitive, and Clingy/Reserved children, it's best to begin reining in overenthusiasm when your child is very young. For example, one of their studies found that sensitive and strong-willed babies, in particular, tend to get overwhelmed when their care-givers exhibit expansive, excited reactions even if they only speak loudly or gesticulate too broadly.

Specifically, moderate your response to your child's interest so that it matches her basic temperament (see chapter 1). This is critical for the development of Passion. An Intense/Sensitive child might be scared off by her parents' overexcitement. An Intense/Aggressive child might be drawn into a power struggle if his parents become too pushy. And a Reserved/Clingy child might feel you're trying to abandon her when you push her into an activity.

Start small. Your child shows an interest in music at four, and suddenly you're surfing the Internet or thumbing through the Yellow Pages under "Pianos." Hold on! Wouldn't it be better to rent a really inexpensive instrument first, and then *if* your child shows a continued interest and asks for more, eventually move on to a better piano?

Overspending, especially with young children, can have unintended results. For example, Gretchen showed some artistic talent in preschool. By the time we met, when Gretchen was seven, she told me that her parents were so "into" her becoming an artist that she had been turned off. This made sense. After all, at the first sign of her interest, they had bought her extensive supplies and enrolled her in a junior class. With so much pressure, Gretchen lost her natural enthusiasm for art. "I still like to draw," she told me, "but not that much." Gretchen didn't lose her talent, but because of her parents' pushiness, she lost her Passion.

Having learned from their experience with Gretchen, Mom and Dad took a much more laid-back approach with younger brother George. When he began to express an interest in soccer, they bought a few pieces of secondhand equipment. They explained that if he demonstrated continued involvement, *then* they'd buy him more serious soccer gear.

Try not to overschedule. Overscheduling is the bane of practically every modern family I know. It's difficult to get precise statistics on after-school activities, but from the tens of thousands of parents I've talked to over the years, I'm convinced that the norm is between one and two activities during the week and at least two on the weekend. One reason is the cultural message that more interests are better: more options, more choices, more potential for success. By today's standards, a child's involvement in just one area is considered too narrow. We want our kids to have unlimited opportunities. Also, we keep our kids busy because *we* are so busy.

No matter what the reason, overscheduling almost always backfires. Children regularly tell me this shocking fact: "Too many things are *boring.*" While that statement might sound like a contradiction, it reflects kids' wisdom. Let's say your child goes to Gymboree on Monday,

```
┌─────────────────────────────────────────────────────────┐
│              THE SIGNS OF OVERSCHEDULING                  │
│  • Your child's negative temperamental characteristics   │
│  intensify—more whining, greater separation anxiety or   │
│  oppositional behavior.                                  │
│  • Your child yearns for increased downtime, like        │
│  watching TV.                                            │
│  • There's more fighting around the house, especially    │
│  during transitions.                                     │
│  • Your child balks at going to scheduled activities.    │
│  • Your child often complains that the groups, classes,  │
│  or lessons she's enrolled in are "boring."              │
└─────────────────────────────────────────────────────────┘
```

has MusicTime on Wednesday, and Baby Guppies on Saturday—not an unusual schedule for a pre-K child. Such busyness creates a model for learning that is wide but not deep, which, unfortunately, mirrors the ways of the second family. Kids are rarely immersed in a subject or activity long enough for them to reach a truly competent level.

When something goes wrong, don't give up—adapt. When children develop a strong interest, it is almost impossible for them *not* to run into some difficulty. For example, at four, Lila developed an instant passion for modern dance; she couldn't stop doing spins and cartwheels. Her mom, Angie, told me that most times she found herself talking to Lila's feet! Unfortunately, Lila was the youngest child in her group, and within a few months, the other kids—most of whom were six months older—started progressing much faster than she could. Lila began to get discouraged. Then, in part because she was extending herself in ways that were too rigorous for her body, she fell and sprained her wrist.

At that point, Lila became very discouraged. Her complaints and her reluctance to attend classes were strident enough that Angie considered stopping the program altogether. Both mother and daughter then could have concluded that dance was simply not for her or, worse, that she was a bit of a wimp. I suggested a compromise: a less demanding class with children at a similar level of competence. This simple adjustment worked; Lila flourished. Four years later, she voluntarily rejoined the advanced class, where she has since developed extremely high self-confidence and several solid friendships.

Determining a good "fit" involves observing your child on the field, in class, or in whatever setting his Passion is carried out. Do research and find a program suited to his temperament, and the way he learns best. Be aware of the most common problem: a teacher or coach who is too rigid or obsessed with perfection. Such pressure can instantly drive the Passion out of any child. Or, as in Lila's case, make sure your child isn't either below or above the level of the rest of the class, which is an inherently frustrating experience for anyone.

When the going gets rough, help your child come up with the "FACTS"—"counterthoughts" and active solutions. When children are discouraged, as they often are when trying something new, they sometimes fall prey to what psychologists call "cognitive distortions"— irrational thinking. Types of cognitive distortions that children favor include: catastrophizing ("I'll *never* get better at this"), mind-reading ("My coach thinks I'm a lousy player"), future-telling ("I'm going to flub at my recital"), globalizing ("If I make one mistake, it's ruined").

For example, after drawing a birthday card for his father, five-year-old Perry exclaimed, "This stinks! Daddy's going to hate it. I can't draw. I never do it good!" As if his disappointment weren't enough to make him feel rotten, that string of cognitive distortions made him feel even worse about himself.

As I explained in chapter 1, research indicates that thinking affects behavior and, conversely, changing the way a person thinks can alter his behavior. To mediate such flawed logic, it's helpful to look at the FACTS. I've coined this acronym because cognitive researchers find that children have a hard time believing anything not grounded in fact. You can use this technique when your child gets stuck or discouraged by distorted thinking:

Find out and empathize with your child's **Feelings.** Perry's mother said, "Oh, Perry, I can see that makes you angry and disappointed."

Ask specific questions. For example, "What on the card is hard for you to get right?"

Cognitive distortion—identify it. "You think you're *never* going to make a card for Daddy that he'll like."

Take a step back and come up with a realistic counterthought—an idea that points out (runs counter to) the self-defeating cognitive distortion. "Oh, Perry, just last week you did a beautiful card for Grandma. Remember how much you liked it? You started over that time, didn't you?"

Solution—find one that applies to the specific problem. "What color would you like better?" "Why don't I find another piece of paper and you can try again."

Let's look at another situation. Derris, who is five and a half, was trying to learn how to rollerblade, but he kept falling, bruising his ego more than his body. However, the thought that accompanied his spills was even more harmful. "I can't do anything right," he shouted after his fourth tumble. His mother, Nadine, remembered to use FACTS.

To find out *specifically* what was disturbing her son, Nadine expressed empathy and, at the same time, suggested what the problem might be: "Oh, Derris, I know it must feel bad to fall in front of everybody. You must be frustrated and angry." After Derris agreed that that's how he felt, Nadine identified the cognitive distortion: "But it's not like you can't do anything right." Derris looked at her skeptically until she reminded him what it was like when he first tried to ride a two-wheeler. She took a step back and suggested a counterthought: "Remember? At first, you had trouble with your balance, too, but when you stuck with it, you got better. Now you're a whiz."

It's important for a parent not to stop there, however. Don't forget step five—coming up with an active solution. Ideally, let your child suggest it. Nadine said to Derris, "What would you like me to do to help you not fall?"

"Hold me while I try again," he answered. As Derris slowly made his way around the in-line park with Mom at his side, she could hear him saying to himself under his breath, "I learned how to ride a *bike*." The positive counterthought helped Derris let go of the self-defeating notion that he'd never been good at anything. He began to relax and in a short time was racing around the park on his rollerblades.

Learn how to praise appropriately. Kids can become praise junkies if we're not careful about how and when we dole out compliments. They end up performing for applause rather than for the inherent pleasure of having Passion for a particular activity. In a series of studies, motivation researcher Edward Deci found that children and adults are more likely to retain interest in a task if they *don't* always get a reward during the process. In other words, the ability to be involved is intrinsically satisfying—to habitually replace it with an external reward is to do your child a disservice.

Whatever words of praise you use, avoid hyperbole—statements like "Unbelievable!," "Amazing!," or "That's the best cartwheel in the world." Admittedly, I sometimes forget my own advice and dole out such rhapsodic praise to my kids! However, grand pronouncements don't sound genuine. Worse, they create performance anxiety in children, as well as an unhealthy sense of entitlement. When you don't react with similar enthusiasm to every little achievement or minor victory, a child is likely to think, "Hey, you're supposed to make a big deal out of whatever I do!"

Remember to praise the child's Passion, not the product: When three-year-old Tess proudly showed her mom the finger painting she had done, her mother said, "I like how you kept at that for so long—no wonder you're happy with the way it turned out." In a similar vein, rather than telling her ten-year-old son what a "fabulous" basketball player he was—which was not true because he was just starting to learn the game—Helen praised Jeremy for practicing his set shot over and over. "You must really love it," she added.

Educator Lillian Katz also suggests "reinforcement related explicitly and directly to the *content* of the child's interest and effort." So, instead of making a huge deal over a model car that your son has built, you could offer to take him to a museum of old cars or promise to buy a new, more difficult model for him next time. Or if your child comes to you with a school project on astronomy, you could come home the next day with a book from the library that broadens her knowledge. What better praise than the acknowledgment that you're aware of and are willing to follow up on your child's interests? Remember, follow *her* cues, and try not to get too far ahead of where she's at.

PRAISE THAT FOSTERS PASSION

• Be realistic and appropriate. Rather than "That was phenomenal," say, "That was a good job."

• Be specific; don't generalize. Say, "You made a nice catch," rather than "You're the best baseball player."

• Praise effort, not result. "I saw how hard you tried," rather than "Wow! Look how many points you made."

• Be genuine. If you can't praise the whole product, find a part that you like: "Those colors are really nice."

Be flexibly available. Behind every passionate child, there is a flexible parent who understands that although we tend to think of kids' after-school interests as "extracurricular," supporting these activities is just as important as fixing meals or helping a child do homework. A passion ought to be a part of every child's life. That means making time and devoting energy toward fostering/nurturing them.

However, it's not good to go to extremes. For example, Cary and Jeanette, who are five and eight, play up to six games of soccer between them on the weekends; and their parents feel completely obligated to attend all six. The couple's relationship is strained at the expense of being available for their children. At the other end of the continuum are Iris's parents, who have little or nothing to do with her growing Passion for piano. They hired a piano teacher, but they don't urge her to practice or listen when she's successfully learned a new piece. And they go to her recitals only if it fits into *their* busy schedules. Piano doesn't have the same meaning to Iris as it would to a child whose parents are supportive and involved.

In the healthy, and more typical, middle ground are moms and dads who recognize that a necessary aspect of parenting is being flexible and making themselves available to attend events, chauffeur their kids, and see them through the triumphs and the disappointments. There may be times when these parents have to sacrifice an appointment or stay up a little later to finish a report they didn't get to because they went to a school play. And there may be times when they can't break away from their own obligations, so they ask a grandparent to go to a game or another parent to do the driving. In the end, these parents achieve a sound balance in which their child feels supported and applauded—without wrecking the quality of their family life.

Make TV a conscious choice. As I stated earlier in this chapter, the proliferation of media in our homes sometimes crowds our children's time and ability to develop Passion. This is not news to parents—in fact, one survey indicates that 73 percent of us would like to limit our television viewing. But here's another approach I've seen in families where kids develop real interests: Change the way your family *thinks* about television; make it more of a conscious choice. For example, most children ask permission when they want to go outside to play. In the same vein, shouldn't they ask to watch television or a video?

You, in turn, must try not to answer just "Yes" or "No." In *The Smart*

Parent's Guide to Kids' TV, Milton Chen, Ph.D., suggests instilling in children the notion that "we don't watch TV, we watch TV *programs.*" So, ask your child specific questions: "What's on? What do you want to watch?" Most important, ask if there's something else they've been thinking about doing—like playing outside or reading or working on a project of any sort. Try to steer them to one of those other choices. And ask yourself, "Can I motivate the kids not to automatically click on the set by involving them in something else?" You might need to take time. Set aside what you're doing for a moment in order to get them started on another activity. Even if you divert them by having them help you plan and cook dinner, it's a plus. Any activity that takes children away from passive media and encourages them to think, be creative, investigate, and engage with others is a far better use of their time and energy.

Model the benefits of having a healthy Passion. Obviously, children need us to be role models. But if you think that your having Passion is enough to stimulate children to develop their own, think again. Passion can actually be quite scary to kids. When we're intensely involved in an activity or pursuit, we often lose connection to the rest of our world. Therefore, in order to be a positive role model, you must show children that when you're deeply involved with something, it can include other people as well.

Case in point: Jonah's father, Maury, a golf fanatic, regularly disappeared for hours on end to pursue his interest. Seeing this, Jonah equated having a Passion with loss. I pointed out to Maury that if Jonah's notion wasn't debunked, he would grow up feeling ambivalent about the interpersonal consequences of Passion.

With that in mind, Maury began taking Jonah to the golf course with him. There, Jonah could see that his dad played—and had great chummy relationships—with three other men who shared his ardor for the game. Maury also began talking to Jonah about golf; the two watched golf videos together. Not surprisingly, Jonah, who loves the attention and sharing his dad's excitement, has begun to relish his visits to the driving range. So far, his curiosity about golf seems genuine, but even if Jonah pursues another sport or activity, he is at least beginning to see Passion itself in a positive light. Equally important, Dad's love of golf is bringing father and son closer, instead of creating a wall between them.

SCHOOL FOR PASSION

The Manhattan New School in New York City, which spans grades one through five, takes an unusual approach to early childhood education. Rather than exclusively focusing on the traditional "three Rs," schoolwork centers on furthering Passion. Director Shelly Harwayne explains, "Sure we teach the basics, but we want to help children develop a passion for learning. So we teach by following our students' obsessions and interests."

For example, if a boy loves baseball, his teachers give him as many books on baseball as he can devour, thus teaching him reading. For math, he computes baseball statistics. To teach him the history and culture of his neighborhood, they have him interview parks managers and sports organizers.

"Instead of stifling a child's passions," says Harwayne, "we try to use them as an asset and a natural source of energy for learning."

Reading this, some parents might wonder, "Absent the traditional curriculum, how *well* do these kids really do?" Wonder no more: Passion obviously stimulates intense learning. Children who attend this school go on to the best middle schools in New York. Not surprisingly, enrollment has exploded since the school was founded.

Child Skills: Learning How to Sustain Passion

A child who can't deal with disappointment, frustration, and competition—each of which inevitably occurs when one pursues an interest—is rarely able to sustain Passion. I remember Steve Henderson, a boy I went to camp with. Steve truly loved football and baseball. Unfortunately, after he lost a game, no one could talk to him for hours. Once a bunkmate forgot to give Steve enough space after a bad loss. Steve became so upset he lashed out until that poor kid started crying.

I've seen the same behavior in adults. Judy, an accountant who came to me because she felt her life was "missing something," confided that she had always wanted to do stand-up comedy. Finally, at my urging and after a lot of practice, she went to an open-mike night at a comedy club. Judy was an instant hit her first time out. She was flying high with excitement about her debut; I'd never seen her so happy. Next, she entered a Tri-State "Funniest Accountants" contest—and tied for *first* place. But Judy was so disappointed about not winning outright that she never entered another contest. Being unable to get past feelings of failure and disappointment, Judy lost her Passion. Why? As a child, Judy was never shown how to deal with the inevitable setbacks. If long ago she had been taught that developing a Passion means handling disappointment, she might not have quit. Steve's and Judy's fates are more dramatic examples of what we all face.

Passion means persistence. A child must learn how to get over the unavoidable rough spots by soothing himself. And as Lillian Katz points out, "Learning to deal with setbacks, and maintaining the persistence and optimism necessary for childhood's long road to mastery, are the real foundations of lasting self-esteem." To that end, here are a number of skills that will help your child savor, not lose, the spirit.

Understanding his own feelings

Mood Mastery and Expressiveness help facilitate Passion. As I stated in chapter 1, children as young as three can start to learn how to self-soothe. However, since a young child's capacity to *identify* feelings hasn't yet developed, you may have to first help her come up with a word or words that describe the experience of having trouble learning something new, or feeling threatened in her first efforts. Multiple choice often works well, as in "Do you feel mad, sad, or glad?" Or you can validate by saying something like "I see that you feel disappointed" or "That must have hurt." When a child learns to identify and express what he is feeling, it's easier to deal with any kind of disappointment or frustration.

Four-year-old Adam was downcast after his enthusiasm had been dashed by an irritable coach at his preschool athletics group. Mom asked, "Do you feel mad or sad about Coach Rick?" Hearing the word that described his feelings, Adam yelled out, "Mad!" and then elaborated: "I don't like when he yells." Realizing that Adam, sensitive to begin with, was taking the coach's moods personally, his mom was then able to offer a soothing counterthought: "Adam, when he yells, try to tell yourself, 'It's not about me, he's in a bad mood.' "

In time, children learn to identify their own feelings and to incorporate parents' counterthoughts into their own repertoire. The next week, when Adam's overbearing coach let loose a tirade on the field, his mother, sitting on the sidelines, heard him saying to his friends, "Coach Rick . . . he's just in a bad mood."

Soothing disappointment with tender truisms

Offer your child compassionate clichés—popular, self-soothing sayings that have been handed down for generations. When the going gets rough, a child can reach back into his reserve and repeat them to himself. According to several surveys, the most-used bromides— decades-old sayings that help people through difficult times—include "This too shall pass," "Tomorrow is another day," and "One day at a time." Add to your repertoire others that may be part of your own family lore. If none of those work with your child, try to identify any kind of unique one-liner or a series of phrases that will.

For example, whenever Kyra is down in the dumps after a soccer practice or game in which she didn't do as well as she'd have liked, her dad asks, "Did you give it a good try?" Most times, this simple question seems to take the edge off Kyra's disappointment. Kyra's sister, Katelin, has a much more sensitive temperament. To her ears, that question would feel like additional pressure or criticism. Following any defeat or disappointment, she needs reassurance and extra love. After some trial and error, they found that this line works wonders: "We love you, Katelin. Maybe tomorrow will be better."

As I've said repeatedly, children quickly begin to parrot the counter-thoughts and soothing phrases we suggest. Kyra often says to herself, "I tried my best." Katelin mutters, "Tomorrow will be better," after a defeat. And then there's Jack. His mother found that her five-year-old felt better about losing a race when she reminded him, "It's okay— most of the other kids didn't come in first either." Now Jack can be heard calming himself by saying, "Ronnie didn't win either!"

Practicing the art of realistic prediction

As Martin Seligman suggests in *The Optimistic Child,* we need to give children regular doses of reality about the world. What he calls "realistic pessimism" is far better than general enthusiasm, because children have a hard time believing anything not grounded in fact. I would add that this is particularly vital when it comes to helping them develop Passion. In this age of instant celebrity, which promotes the idea that everyone is "special," many kids actually believe that simply showing up is good enough. Kids need to be warned that they may not be great the first time out and that their efforts may not always be recognized.

What parent isn't tempted to say to a child on the way to an audition or a tryout, "I have faith in you, I love you, and I know you're going to get this part [make the team]"? Your child, in fact, knows that no matter how much you love her, you have no way of knowing whether that's true. We think we're protecting our children, and we say such things out of caring, but what happens when she doesn't get the part or make the team? She's not as prepared for reality. It can be a cruel, competitive world at times, and you don't help a child by forever shielding her.

Moreover, today's kids, weaned on video games that allow them to set their own level of achievement and frustration, are not always prepared to hit a beginner's wall—that moment when an activity feels so hard that he might be tempted to give up. If your child is forewarned, though, and learns to anticipate frustration, he will be better able to push past his fears and stick with an interest.

For example, on the day that seven-year-old Annie's school was casting a big production, her mother, Bea, reminded Annie as they were driving to class, "You know, Annie, a lot of other kids will be trying out for the lead, too." Bea then took a deep breath and told her daughter what the *realistic* possibilities were. "There's a good chance that you won't get the part. Maybe you'll get another role, or maybe you'll be asked to help backstage."

Negative, destructive thinking? No, children in this era of hype desperately *need* gentle but honest feedback. In fact, Annie was fortified by this dose of reality. She felt solid at the audition and was chosen to understudy the lead. This made her very happy. Had Bea not prepared her, Annie might have been intimidated and disappointed with the results.

Seeking adult mentors

In order to develop Passion, children must be able to identify *when* they need help and know *whom* to turn to. They have to get past the feeling that it's "uncool" to seek assistance from adults. As you read in chapter 2, many kids live in a world slightly apart from grown-ups; they tend to feel more distance from adults than is good for a developing core. As a result, children are increasingly guided not by parents or teachers, but by the second family. This can have bad consequences in all realms of a child's life, but particularly when it comes to developing Passion. After all, the best mentors are usually grown-ups. If a child is not at ease approaching anyone other than peers, he will have trouble accessing appropriate adult support and expertise.

For example, when Craig's teacher, Mrs. Brown, saw his interest in math, she gave him a more advanced workbook. Still, it was inevitable that Craig would get stumped and need help. But because Mrs. Brown was a teacher, and Craig worried about his "image," he couldn't envision asking her for special help. Hearing this, I encouraged a little role-playing at home. Mom pretended she was baffled by a tough math problem. What should she do? Craig, playing "teacher," said, "Oh, let me talk to you after class, and I'll show you how to do that." That brief interaction allowed Craig to gain a new perspective on his situation and come up with a way to ask without looking "nerdy" to his friends—he approached Mrs. Brown when other students weren't around.

Some predicaments are harder. In junior high, Ava had a tough-as-nails, testosterone-driven soccer coach. When one of his players fell or crashed into a fence, Coach Meyers would always yell, "Get up or get out. I have no room for wimps on my team." As a result, when Ava turned her ankle one day, she was understandably afraid to approach him. With some assistance from her parents, they came up with an alternative plan: to confide in Coach Gray, the younger assistant whom Ava thought seemed more approachable. As it turned out, she was right. Coach Gray was willing to act as a liaison, and he suggested to Coach Meyers that since Ava wasn't her usual spunky self, maybe she needed a day or two of rest.

Unlike so many adult-unfriendly kids I meet, Ava (with her parents' help) knew how to look for the *right* adult to approach. Had she not, she might have seriously injured herself by playing through the pain, or, sadly, she might have slowly withdrawn from the game altogether. But because her parents had always stressed the importance of mentors, Ava was open to the possibility of getting support from grown-ups. She not only trusted her instincts about which coach to talk to, she also felt confident that she *deserved* help.

Part and parcel of this is helping your child learn from very early on *how* to ask for help in ways that aren't negative and don't push adults' buttons. Margie, an only child, expected all grown-ups to drop whatever they were doing when she needed them—much the way her doting parents did. At home, Margie often whined when she didn't get what she wanted, and this behavior carried over to school. She repeatedly accused her kindergarten teacher of being "unfair." And she tended to treat all adults like servants; her tone implied, "You owe me." Margie only became more demanding as she got older. Not surprisingly, her entitled attitude almost always backfired—teachers and coaches rarely liked her. Of course, being able to ask for help, in and of itself, doesn't guarantee that a child won't have a hard time. However, I've observed over the years that children who are respectful—polite, who understand the give-and-take of good conversation, and who are mindful of the fact that they're not the only ones in the room—are better taken care of by grown-ups than children like Margie.

Finding a Passion buddy

With rare exceptions, most children hate feeling isolated. That can be a deterrent to Passion. An abiding interest in a subject or an activity often involves hours of alone time devoted to study and/or practice. Therefore, it's a good idea to encourage what I call a "Passion buddy"—another child who shares the same interest. Mitch and Ernie became fast friends around hockey. They met at age five in an after-school program, pursued their mutual interest together, while creating one of those special childhood friendships. The camaraderie offered them an early chance at being great elementary school pals while becoming really good at a sport they both loved.

Children often do this naturally—join forces with kids they meet in classes or on teams—but some may also need a little encouraging. Jake, our young dinosaur expert, spent hours in his room poring over books and pictures, and his mother, Sue, was worried about Jake's lack of socialization. So, she enrolled him in a museum study group for "dino-boys," where he found others who were equally captivated by dinosaurs. Several of them stayed friendly and shared other important interests long after the eight-week program ended.

Thanks to the miracle of Internet technology, kids nowadays can have Passion buddies all over the world. (With supervision) they can join chat rooms devoted to a particular subject. And for a child like Brenda who is impassioned about writing, her like-minded E-mail buddies are a lifesaver against isolation.

Keep your eye on Passion. Every child needs you to nurture and

IT'S LONELY AT THE TOP: WHAT YOU CAN DO TO HELP YOUR CHILD BUDDY-UP

• Go with your child to the activity—the rink, the field, the classroom—see whom he's drawn to and focus on that child.

• Be a bridge. Most young children are clueless about initiating a friendship. Speak with the other parent and help your child make play dates.

• Build other activities around the shared interest. For example, have a post-game pizza party, or rent a video about the subject and invite other interested kids.

• As commitment to an activity deepens, get involved with the adult responsible for the group. This helps you keep another "eye" out for potential new friendships or potential problems.

protect this vital core-builder. All children feel better about themselves when they're interested in and good at something—besides the endless products of the pop culture. It's especially meaningful when they've worked hard and gotten through the inevitable hurdles it takes to get there.

CHAPTER 5

PEER SMARTS

Basic Skill #5: Guide your child in her relationships with playmates and friends.

Every Parent's Concern

My friends Jackie and William are admired by everyone because of their ability to cope with their young daughter Carrie's chronic medical problems—congenital, and pretty serious, vision difficulties. But if you ask Jackie what concerns her *most* about child-rearing, her daughter's physical condition is surprisingly beside the point. Here's a mother whose child has had to go through health challenges, numerous operations, and what is Jackie most anxious about? How her child deals with everyday social issues—whether she'll pick good friends who, as Jackie puts it, "have solid values."

Jackie is especially disturbed when she observes how certain children at Carrie's school treat each other. They're harshly critical, often fickle in their friendships, and frequently they exclude other kids. The idea of Carrie hooking up with those kinds of kids, or being hurt by them, Jackie says, is in fact a harder issue—more intense and problematic—than coping with Carrie's illness.

This sensitive, caring mother is representative of many parents I meet nowadays. At all of the talks I give, I find even preschoolers' parents are deeply concerned about their children making and keeping good friends and understanding what friendship is all about. They know that these skills are critical to development.

There's a growing adult awareness that the nature of kids' friendships will, in significant measure, determine whether their children will get into drugs or be tempted by other high-risk preteen and adolescent behaviors. More than ever before, parents feel this challenge in the earliest years. But they often haven't got the foggiest notion of what to do about it.

My response is that children need to develop what I call "Peer Smarts"—which enable them to cope with other kids, make good choices, as well as keep and be a good friend.

Why Peer Smarts Is Important to Your Child's Core

Without a doubt, this is an incredibly difficult issue—for Jackie and so many other parents and, most of all, for children who come to me with problems related to friendship. The truth is, peer relationships have become increasingly important as an anchor and a place of reference for today's kids. Whether it's in day care, pre-K, or nursery school, children are interacting with other children at younger ages, and social issues are coming up earlier and earlier. The fact that so many mothers work nowadays has "fueled an enormous day-care industry," reported the *Wall Street Journal* in 1996, noting that some 10 million American preschoolers need child care—twice as many as twenty-five years ago. Currently, about half of all three- to five-year-olds are enrolled in Head Start and other pre-K programs, nursery schools, and, especially, organized child care facilities. Hence, even our youngest children are asked to make difficult decisions about peers: whom to befriend and at what cost to their personal sense of integrity.

That such statistics were barely tracked twenty years ago is in itself a statement of our times. But I've also seen this progression firsthand. In my early career, some twenty-odd years ago, when I first consulted to various schools, freshmen and sophomores in high school were referred for so-called peer issues. Around ten years ago, I began to get calls from parents who had children in junior high—grades seven and eight. By the mid-eighties, complaints about ostracism, bullying, and cruel taunting had trickled down to middle school, which in most areas of the country starts at grade five or six. And today, believe it or not, I'm called in to talk about peer issues in second- and third-grade classrooms—and even by some nursery school administrators. In short, the exact same issues are coming up, but they're happening to younger children who are not developed to handle them well.

Children today need Peer Smarts more than ever. This important core-builder enables a child to make friends wisely, to manage friendships when they're working and to know how to leave them when they're not. If your child is Peer Smart, he will forge friendships with "good" kids and, therefore, will be less likely to be exposed to—and be enticed by—potentially damaging, even dangerous, activities. Hence our fifth Basic Skill:

Basic Skill #5: Guide your child in her relationships with playmates and friends.

Peer Smarts enables children to be savvy about friendship: to redirect or break off from relationships in which they are being treated badly. It allows kids to say what they mean and mean what they say. In other words, Peer Smart children are able to benefit from the richness of these relationships without losing their core selves.

Core Threats: Why It's So Hard to Teach Peer Smarts to Our Kids

Children want to belong—to have a peer setting in which they feel heard and held, to have a group of buddies and even a best friend to whom they feel connected. Unfortunately, many children—and the parents who are trying to guide them—are floundering in this arena. As I see it, there are three key reasons for this crisis on the friendship front.

Because neighborhood life in America has changed, the fabric of friendship is less visible now. It used to be that children grew up amidst an ever-present extended family and close-knit community, with a best buddy living next door and lots of friends on the same street. When I grew up—during the "Wonder Years" of the late fifties and early sixties life was far from perfect. But I did feel anchored in my neighborhood. Not coincidentally, all of my mother's and father's best friends happened to be the parents of my friends. I saw the adults in their friendships. I saw them take care of each other, fight with each other, and get together again. In other words, I saw their social behaviors and values in action.

I observed my parents and their friends deal with the mundane and the significant. When one got sick, the others were there, bringing chicken soup, minding the children. In those rare instances when a couple threatened to divorce, friends stepped in, trying to help them be aware of the grave move they were contemplating. In their organizations, their churches and synagogues, their bowling leagues, their kitchens—that's where I saw my parents be good friends, and that's how I learned the elements of "friendship."

In contrast, children today live in communities based on economics, not built on shared historical values or common ethnicity. Ever since the seventies, when tremendous mobility and divorce began to change the American landscape, children may not know members of their extended families, or see them very often. They have less of a sense of "community" than generations past.

At the same time, their parents often don't have the same *kind* of friendships. They make friends at work or socialize at the health club instead of with their neighbors, whom they often don't even know. This point was suggested rather dramatically by sociologist Arlie Hochschild in her most recent book, *The Time Bind: When Work Becomes Home and Home Becomes Work.* From her studies and other researchers' work, Hochschild concluded that the workplace has become a kind of "surrogate family" and a place where friendships are forged. In fact, in one survey, nearly half of the sampling (47 percent) said they had "the most friends" at work.

This is especially true of parents born between 1946 and 1964, as author Terry Galway observes in a rather stinging indictment of his peers that appeared in *America Press* (July 1997): "Baby Boomers are a generation of emotional army brats, moving from stage to stage in their lives without putting down roots. Friends change with each move and each new stage. Childhood friends give way to high school classmates, then to college roommates, then to first-time colleagues, and so on. The notion of lifelong friends with a shared history and a common place has become such a rarity that it's almost quaint."

As a result of this shift, our children are growing up in neighborhoods where they rarely witness adults modeling friendship. Think about it: How often do your children actually *see* you at close range with your friends? Sure, you may talk to other parents on the phone or at the sidelines of Gymboree, but it takes concrete experience to get across what an abstract concept like *friendship* really is. How, then, do kids learn?

Most kids learn about friendship from the second family. When a child doesn't see friendship modeled at home or in the neighborhood, there is a void, an emptiness that is filled by the values of the second family, whose rules about friendship come from the pop culture. The irony is that children today are never really "alone"—in fact, they're more indirectly connected to each other than in any previous generation, thanks to television, videos, computer games, and the Internet. They're part of an instant and endless "community" of peers. As I have witnessed so many times, even two children who've never met can immediately relate to one another because of their common media experiences. Whether it's Barney or the Spice Girls that capture their interest, kids are all part of the same community—after all, American TV is beamed into some 230 million households. This means that children everywhere hear and absorb the same messages and see the same twenty thousand commercials no matter where they live.

So what's the problem? I believe that kids today have a "virtual" sense of belonging. They sometimes relate less to real peers than to the omnipresent kiddie culture. And the messages they digest—central ideas disseminated in advertisements and commercials, on TV, and in movies—are probably not the values *you* want to teach:

"I'm number one."

"What can you do for me?"

"What have you done for me lately?"

"Let me have it all."

"Let me go first."

"My sneakers cost more than yours; my sneakers are better than yours."

Such "antivalues" spread from one child to another and affect the fabric of friendship. Because kids want so desperately to "belong," they're unwitting sponges, soaking up attitudes and behaviors they learn from the pop culture without knowing it. Most children under six don't even understand that the purpose of advertising is to sell a product, reports the Center for Media Education—they are unconsciously indoctrinated. Absorbing such attitudes certainly doesn't do much to strengthen a child's core nor does it encourage solid, meaningful friendships. This brings us to our third and perhaps most deadly threat to Peer Smarts.

Children are oppressed by the "tyranny of cool." I call the problem "nerdphobia"—the unrelenting childhood fear of not being "cool." As Haley, eleven, explained to me, someone who's "cool" has to be a little mean. "You have to make other people feel uncomfortable around you. You have to know how to be nasty by acting like you're better than other kids, like nothing bothers you." She then added, "And that's not me. But I want to be popular. What do I do?"

"Being cool" means that a child is pseudo-sophisticated—in dress and attitude—and it begins far earlier than the preteen years. Sometimes, in fact, I'm stunned at how early children become conscious of all this. Recently, I was in a shoe store with my kids, and while they were trying on sneakers, I heard a very young voice pipe up from behind us: "But, Mommy, I don't want *those*. They're not cool, they're too cute. I want them to be cool." I turned around, thinking I would see a preteen girl, but there in front of me was a precocious preschooler.

Nerdphobia terrorizes children, molds them, *and* informs their friendships. "Cool" is a product, sold on TV, in the movies, on computer screen. Even young children are uncomfortable with the idea that someone might think they're not cool. They *must* have at least something, some symbol, that proves they're cool—the clothes, the videos, the right sayings. Remember that old nightmare about being naked in public? For today's kids, being a nerd—being without your cool—is tantamount to being unclothed.

Sure, children have always eyed each other's clothing and possessions. But, now, the ante is so high that it's impossible for kids (no less their parents) to keep up. Children see the trappings of wealth and luxury on TV and movies every day; this affects how they see themselves *and* how they relate to other children. Therefore, in spite of your values, the symbols of what's in and what's out not only permeate, they help define, your child's world.

In one school, a group of third-grade girls had been so swept up by nerdphobia that they had divided the boys into "nerds" and "boy-boys." When I asked the girls what "boy-boys" were, they replied, "The *real* boys. They dress right, they walk and talk right—they're *cool*." Third graders!

Taking these cultural factors and second-family pulls into consideration, it's easy to see that a host of elements works against good friendship. Fortunately, there *are* steps you can take to help your child develop Peer Smarts.

Parent Skills:
What You Can Do to Foster Peer Smarts

The following parent skills are divided into four parts: The first sections involve understanding "peer styles"—how children relate to one another in their friendships; the second requires you to look carefully at how *you* relate to your child at home. The third section introduces the notion of parents developing their own "parenting peer groups," which connects them to their children's friends' parents and, most important, broadens their understanding of how their child interacts with peers. Finally, the fourth section below offers concrete steps you can take to make your house a home—strategies that will help your child stay connected to you and, in the process, develop Peer Smarts.

Understanding your child's peer style

I point out repeatedly in this book that I don't believe in one-size-fits-all solutions. Therefore, you need to look at who *your* child is—and to develop specific strategies that work with him. To help you, I turn to the latest information about "peer styles" emerging from the burgeoning field of relational psychology.

Through nearly a hundred different studies, researchers June Flesson and Alan Sroufe, professors of psychology at the University of Minnesota, have found that by looking at a child as young as one year old and observing how he or she relates to his or her parents, it's often possible to predict what kind of friends that child will make at age ten. That may sound like an amazing claim, but it is a finding that turns up consistently in Flesson and Sroufe's work.

In other words, the mode of relationship that predominates at home, and the child's experiences or "relationship" in his family, are internalized and utilized by that child in the outside world. If a parent is overbearing and strict, for example, and the child is frequently reprimanded, he will "absorb" both sides of that relationship. This isn't to say that he'll always be put upon by others; in some relationships, he may be a bully and in others a victim.

Thus, a child's peer style—how he relates to friends—is a combination of two primary factors: that child's basic temperament and how a child has been treated at home. Peer styles are *fluid*. For each style, there is a continuum, ranging from a healthy manifestation of that style to a more troublesome one. Children slide along that continuum, depending on mood, circumstances, and the other child. Therefore, some relationships might elicit more productive and positive behaviors than others.

Here are the four predominant peer styles:

A Leader can be a boss or a bully. At the basically healthy end of the continuum, this kind of child is assertive and generally exhibits a can-do spirit. He's often an all-around kid who everyone wants on the team or at the party. At the negative end, we see the bully—a child who lacks empathy, finds it difficult to share, and is critical of others. He doesn't feel okay if he's not the boss.

A Star can shine or grab the spotlight from everyone else. At the positive end of the continuum, she isn't anxious about taking a risk. She's outgoing, loves performing and being front and center. She's also the kind of child who helps other kids try new things. She's popular, of course, but not because she works at it, brags, or curries favor. At the troublesome end, we find the kind of child who *must* occupy the entire stage. She avoids equals, for fear of being upstaged and, therefore, prefers to surround herself with gofers and wannabes.

A Loner can be a free spirit or an outsider. At the healthy end of the continuum, he's an original who thinks for himself. He can amuse himself for hours, is interested in his peers, but doesn't need positive feedback from them. At the other end, we see a child who can't connect to others and is always on the outside looking in. He may be ostracized as well—a perpetual mismatch who never quite fits in.

A Joiner can be a voice of reason or a victim. In the healthy version, she's a kid who exhibits empathy and understanding and is content to join in and be a part of the tribe. She doesn't make policy decisions—and that's fine; she's happy to cooperate. Going toward the unhealthy range—the victim—she abides by decisions in order to be liked. She's not in touch with her own passion or wishes of her core self; rather, she takes on those of others. At worst, she compromises her core completely, allowing other kids to encroach upon her personal boundaries—all in the name of being accepted.

I should also point out that while temperament is a factor, it is not synonymous with peer style. True, one can look like the other and the two are often related. Leaders at either end of the continuum are usually Intense/Aggressive types, and Loners tend to be Intense/Sensitive types. However, the important difference is that peer styles are fluid and temperament is not. And peer styles can change in a particular relationship with another child because of the chemistry between them; temperament for the most part does not change dramatically.

How you can maximize your child's peer potential

You probably recognize your child in the above peer styles. She may evidence the more visible attributes of a particular style, in some cases sliding toward the healthy end of the continuum, in other cases not. It depends on who she's with and the circumstances. However, here's the good news: As I stated above, while you can't magically change your child's basic temperament (see chapter 1), you *can* influence his peer style by changing your own behavior and focusing on the parent/child and sibling relationships at home.

It's particularly important to take stock of family dynamics when you see your child moving toward the negative end of the continuum— if he's a Leader who is inordinately critical of other kids, a Star who demands center stage, a Loner who *can't* relate to his peers, or a Joiner who goes along with the crowd at the expense of his own feelings. Say to yourself, "Well, if my child is continually in relationships that don't work for him, where does that come from—what's going on at home?"

Parents can change their children's peer styles. This may come as a surprise—after all, most of us have been taught that peer relationships are about our children's friends and "outside influences." If Johnny's in trouble with kids at school, it's because of what's happening there. Not completely. While peers can have a negative impact, *your behavior* determines the kinds of friends your child gravitates toward in the first place. In fact, Flesson and Sroufe's research confirms what I've seen over the last twenty-five years in my practice:

The single most important factor in the development of Peer Smarts is the way children are treated at home. If we're accepting or critical, inclusive or exclusive, demanding or giving, relaxed or anxious, if we encourage siblings to be loving or allow them to mistreat one another at home—all of these behaviors can affect the kinds of friends our children choose.

I hasten to point out that the most heartening conclusion of this research is that if the basic patterns of interaction change at home and children are open to possibilities of change, they are able to shift their patterns of friendship. Therefore, whenever parents come to me troubled by their child's peer relationships, I say, "Tell me a little about what goes on around the house."

In Frankie's case, his parents feared that he was turning into a perennial victim. A Loner, at times, he was able to talk to peers about his interest in science and computers; some of his classmates were even impressed with his knowledge and inventiveness. But he also seemed to attract kids who picked on him, stole his lunch, and played pranks on him. Their antics were starting to make Frankie dread school despite his good grades. I asked, "What's Frankie like at home? How do you two interact with him?" Before long, the picture was clearer.

In his family, Frankie was often criticized. He wasn't the athlete his father wanted him to be; his room was always filled with what his mother called "meaningless clutter"; and he wasn't socially adroit like his older sister. His parents certainly didn't *mean* to hurt their son; they simply weren't aware that they were trying to turn Frankie into someone he couldn't be. But until they began to monitor their own behavior, Frankie would continue to find himself in hurtful relationships.

Another child, Emmy, was a Joiner, often sliding toward the negative end of the continuum. She was the consummate people-pleaser, fearing that if she didn't do what her friends wanted or didn't echo their opinions, they wouldn't like her. As I found out, her mother, Anne, was a bit of a spotlight-stealer. Being a former model whose life revolved around vanity, Anne still had great visibility as an admired socialite. She expected her children to revere her, too, and adapt to *her* needs. Is it any wonder, then, that Emmy gravitated toward kids more popular than she was—and that she was willing to cater to them, losing her core self in the bargain? Emmy's friendship choices could not be different until Anne became aware of her impact on her daughter.

In the cases above, when parents resolved to pay attention to what was happening at home and (as much as humanly possible) to be honest with themselves, amazing changes occurred in their children's friendships. For example, Frankie's parents got on top of their own criticism by toning down their harshness and realistically praising their son instead of constantly pointing out his faults. After several months of feeling more accepted in his family, Frankie made friends with a boy who had similar interests and temperament; he no longer felt "at home" with kids who bullied him.

And Emmy's mom, Anne, became more aware of how she steered

family conversations toward herself. After just a month of trying to turn the tables—listening to Emmy as often as she expected Emmy to listen to her—her daughter's compliance with school mates abated. Her teacher reported that Emmy was "finding her own voice" and, not surprisingly, a couple of new friends as well.

The lesson here is that children will be able to seek better types of friendship when the relationships with us, their parents, change. This potential for transformation is true well into the teenage years.

Bear in mind, too, that although children go through different developmental phases, generally the same peer style predominates at each stage, even if the behavior *looks* different. For example, a child who is bullied at home may have trouble sharing as a young child and later, as a teenager, may become the kind of kid who ostracizes other children, excluding them from "his crowd." The same basic underlying dynamic propels different behavior at different stages.

That said, there is one exception: While problems at home can precipitate problems with friends, unexpected or dramatic shifts in peer relationships are not usually caused by the parent/child relationship. In other words, if your child suddenly becomes a victim, or, out of nowhere, starts isolating himself from his peers, it may be a situational challenge—for example, a different teacher, a charismatic new friend, a bossy kid joining the class. Such changes may also indicate that your child has reached a particular developmental plateau, and has to make a leap to the next level—for example, the switch from kindergarten to first grade, which can be very stressful.

Learning about your child through *parent* peer groups

One of the most important keys to helping your child develop Peer Smarts is to know her friends' parents—well. Next to looking for the reasons for your child's peer style in your own backyard, it's most important to look in her friends' backyards, and to develop "peer groups for parents."

First of all, parent networks are essential in postmodern America. In the absence of a nearby extended family, these groups help your child see how adult friends negotiate with each other. Second, during the workweek many children are supervised by care-givers; parents may not set their children's schedules, much less oversee them—all the more reason for them to get to know other parents. Being part of such a network helps you hear what goes on when your child is away from you and know how he's interacting with other kids. In turn, this

ASK YOURSELF . . .

It may sound simple, but it's true: Who your child is at home and how he is treated will be mirrored in his peer relationships. But you can't change what you don't see. Therefore, the first step is to look at what goes on in your family. Below are questions about your own behavior as well as what your child witnesses and experiences at home.

• If my child is hypercritical in his relationships, do I criticize too much?
• If my child has to be the star, do we too often give him the limelight or do we not give him enough attention?
• If my child is too bossy with friends, am I bossy with her or do I let her boss me around?
• If my child is a bully or a victim, does he see my spouse or me bullying each other or him?
• If my child is picked on by other kids, do I too often criticize?
• If my child is a "caretaker," do I tend to look after others and not give anything to myself or do I expect my child to take care of me/another member of the family in the same way?
• If other children take advantage of my child, do I allow or encourage such behavior at home? Do his siblings push him around too much?
• If my child has trouble playing with others, do I too often ask him to amuse himself?
• If my child is an outsider, is he the "odd man out" in our family, or are we a family that isolates from others?

knowledge allows you to have some insight and control over what's happening. When there are problems with the children, you're able to intervene with his friends' parents—quickly and appropriately. Here are two important points to keep in mind.

Start early. The best time to start networking with other parents is when your child goes to that first play group or Gymboree session. It is not just the play group (or other peer activity) that counts; it's the information-swapping among adults that can matter most to your child's friendships. For example, Malcolm, three and a half, was a sociable and commanding kind of child, a Leader whose mother, Paula, an attorney, had been arranging play dates with other parents from the time Malcolm was one and a half. At one point, though, Paula began hearing from the other mothers that Malcolm had begun to slide toward the negative end of the continuum, becoming somewhat of a bully. Paula knew that nothing different was happening at home. This was an instance in which an abrupt difference in peer style reflected a developmental problem or a change in Malcolm's environment. By listening to other mothers, Paula realized that Malcolm seemed to get upset when a third child "intruded,"especially if the interloper was a bit aggressive. It was hard for him to share; he'd feel left out and reacted with anger—verbal and physical. Obviously, this began to affect Malcolm's friendships—the other kids were becoming reluctant to play with him.

Because of Paula's connection with *her* peer group of other mothers, she was able to shape Malcolm's play dates to keep his tantrum opportunities to a minimum. At first, she arranged get-togethers with only one other child; and then as she began including a third, she made sure it was a nonaggressive child. Hearing about specific interactions from the mothers also enabled Paula to talk about the issue with Malcolm during calm moments between play dates.

Amy, a marketing consultant who worked part-time out of her home, witnessed her five-year-old Jessica get upset when her friend Sara, wanting more time at Jessie's new computer than Jessie was giving her, announced, "I'm never coming over to play with you again." The two had developed a nice give-and-take since meeting as three-year-olds, and Jessica usually called Sara "my best friend in the whole wide world." In spite of their history, Jessica, a bit of a Joiner, believed Sara's threat and was extremely disturbed. There was no time for Amy to mediate. The minute Sara heard her mother's car horn outside in the driveway, she ran out the door. Unaware of the drama that had just unfolded, Ellen, Sara's mom, simply drove her daughter home.

Later that evening, though, Amy called to tell Ellen what had happened. By being able to compare notes, the two mothers concluded that the girls needed to bring their own toys and comics, rather than relying on what was at one house or the other; and the moms had to help them with guidelines about the new computer. Predictably, the girls quickly forgot about their tussle and were eager to make another date.

Continue networking through your child's high school years. Knowing other parents becomes even more critical as your children get older. When I was a kid, if I so much as crossed against the light with my friends, one of their parents inevitably saw it and reported the event to my mom and dad. Today, without those extra eyes in the neighborhood, being in touch with other parents is not just a benefit—it can be a lifesaver.

Good friends of mine, Eileen and David, are beginning to see the wisdom of this as their daughter, Marci, approaches her eleventh birthday. Eileen and her husband face an array of tricky decisions that go with junior high territory, and tell me they can't imagine going through this phase if they were not deeply connected to other parents. How in the world could they know whether Marci's use of public transportation to and from school is safe, whether the pizza shop after school is an okay place to go with her buddies, how much money is really needed for snacks, which parties are supervised? All of these questions can be answered appropriately because Eileen and David talk about them, and strategize, with Marci's friends' parents.

One time, for instance, a party was being organized to celebrate the end of fifth grade. Marci *expected* to go to it. "Just because . . . Well, because everyone else is going," she told them, adding, "If you don't let me go, I'll be the only one!"

At first, Eileen and David didn't know at whose house it was going to happen, what activities were planned, or who'd be there to chaperon. They said they'd have to find out more of the details. "If you talk to the other parents, I'll die," Marci pleaded. "Mom and Dad, pleeeeese, everyone will think I'm a baby."

David and Eileen held their ground—and so should you, even if your child seems vehemently upset or angry. "I simply can't agree to that," Eileen said firmly. "It's just not right. In fact, I'm *never* going to stop talking to other parents."

The irony is that Marci felt relieved. Looking at the expression on her face, Eileen told me that she could see that Marci felt reassured by her mom's insistence. And though Marci only admitted this later, the party itself was less important than being chauffeured there in the brand-new mini-van one of the families had just bought. Next thing Eileen knew, Marci voluntarily gave her several phone numbers of other friends' parents "just in case" she needed them.

Another benefit of having your own peer group is that your child gets to see *you* negotiate relationships. There is no doubt in my mind that when you let your child see you dealing with issues of friendship, he will benefit immensely as he moves into adulthood. I've known Aaron since he was eight, and he is now in college. Walter, his father, was interested in and involved with most of Aaron's friends and his friends' parents as well. Through the years, Aaron saw Walter talk to them. He saw him disagree, even get angry, with other parents for granting privileges too early. He later saw his dad make peace with those same parents. Moreover, Aaron saw his father live and act according to his belief that people should be treated with honesty and respect.

Naturally, father and son had more than a few battles along the way. But in spite of their fights, Aaron is turning out to be just like his dad— sincere and thoughtful—a person with good judgment, *and* a good friend. That's what he saw when Walter interacted with his friends' parents—and that's what he has become.

Making your house a "home" to hang out in

Certain houses become known as "homes"—places where children like to hang out. Obviously, children feel protected and safe when they live in welcoming homes that offer food, humor, recreation, boundaries, and predictability. But this sense of protection extends to the child's peer group. Even in a worst-case scenario—say, another kid wants your child to experiment with drugs, she's more likely than not to come home and discuss it with her parents.

Another obvious advantage of creating a home for your child and his friends is that you get to see and hear what kids are into. It allows you to keep tabs without being intrusive. You will learn things that help decode your own child's behavior—fashions, the latest lingo, references to pop culture phenomena. And, as we all know, information is power.

What are the common attributes of these homes that so consistently attract young people? I've provided an at-a-glance answer in the box on page 148. But here are the five skills that parents of all children need to develop in order to make their homes kid-friendly.

Offer children goodies to eat. This may seem inconsequential, but according to a Yankelovich Youth Monitor study, which asked children what parents should do or have to make their homes more hospitable to kids, almost 80 percent responded, "Buy the right snack foods." (That answer, incidentally, was way above activities, such as

"Take me to the movies.") Granted, parents who make "homes" for children often complain that the kids are "eating their way through our refrigerator," as one mom put it. All the same, in these houses, children find not only refuge, but also a full assortment of junk and healthy food on hand. Since most of the time, of course, kids go for the junk, you may need to make some rules about how much they can consume during any visit. It's a good idea to talk with other parents about this. Some kids have restricted diets; and their parents definitely should be consulted.

For example, Connie's mother, Margaret, was worried about her five-year-old's sweet tooth, which made Connie pudgy, and therefore unhappy. When she went to Sally's house, Connie saw it as an opportunity to ask for as many sweets as possible. Therefore, it was really helpful for the Smiths, Sally's parents, to understand that they had permission from Margaret to put reasonable limits on the sweets Connie could have at their home.

Know how to talk with your children's friends. For your house to be a home—and to keep tabs on what's happening—you need to learn the language of "the natives." Remember, kids are sometimes more likely to talk to parents other than their own, so there's a good chance that another child will spill the beans when yours won't. And if your child sees his best friend talking to you, he's more likely to view you as child-friendly and savvy. Just as important, these kinds of exchanges will enhance your standing in your child's eyes. One six-year-old whose mother accompanied the class on a trip, remarked, "Wow. The kids really like my mom."

In a similar vein, nine-year-old Ryan's mother, Gail, made it her business to talk to her son's best friends if he got into a worrisome genre of comics or violent computer games. It allowed her to get a better grasp of what was interesting to all children, not just her son, and to determine whether it was a phase or a genuine obsession that she ought to take seriously.

Another mother, Dorothy, loved to talk about what was going on in school with seven-year-old Liana's friends. Unlike Liana, whose one-word answers gave Dorothy no clues as to what was really happening, her friends embellished their responses with details about fights ("Erica insulted J. B.") and gossip ("Mark is sad because his parents are separating, and he doesn't know where he's going to live"). Not surprisingly, talking to her mom about school with her friends around

A KID-TESTED GUIDE TO
ADULT/CHILD CONVERSATION

The children I talk with are very clear about how they'd like parents to engage their friends. Thus, if you want other kids to open up—without embarrassing your own—you need to follow certain guidelines. These apply from preschool through high school.

- Hang out and be available. *But don't hover.*
- Bring up general topics, as opposed to particular subjects. If they're picked up, great. If they're not, *don't push.*
- Don't ask *pointed questions* about topics that are touchy to your child. Friends will sense your child's discomfort and withdraw.
- Don't just focus on the kids; talk about *yourself,* too.
- *Don't be phony*—kids of all ages pick it up and feel disdain.

became a social event, rather than a parent "grilling." In this way, Dorothy was not only able to learn what was going on in Liana's relationships, it also gave her deeper insight into how Liana's peer group was affecting her moods and reactions at home.

Have a sense of humor. This is, of course, part and parcel of being able to talk with kids. But, clearly, the best-liked parents seem to be able to laugh at themselves as well as at what kids say or do. Current research trends indicate that elementary-school-age and older kids especially enjoy lighthearted verbal repartee—dishing it out and taking it in. In surveys and in my own experience in parenting workshops, we are beginning to see that children admire a good sense of humor in adults. This same attitude was validated in my own interviews with children. A majority of the 150 kids I spoke with brought up "being funny" as one of the traits they loved most about their "favorite adults." Actually, I don't think that's mysterious at all. After watching hundreds of teachers in their classrooms, it's obvious that humor helps smooth the journey over rough spots. This is particularly critical as your child moves into the preteen and teen years, when it's not only important to talk with your child's friends but also to approach potential negotiations with a light heart and a great sense of humor.

For example, when Nan was playing at eleven-year-old Sasha's house, she knocked on Sasha's dad's studio door. She asked Mark, an artist who worked at home, whether it was all right for Sasha and her to rent *The Saint*. "I saw it on a plane this summer, and I think it's completely appropriate," Nan announced to Mark. "There's nothing objectionable about it."

Mark didn't want to embarrass either of the girls, so he laughingly said, "Since when does Sasha need a lawyer to get what she wants?" Nan laughed. He also wanted to be respectful to Nan, who obviously had given the matter a lot of thought before she knocked, so he added, "I'm sure you've looked at the movie very carefully, but I don't know that you two extending your date an extra two hours will work out in terms of our plans."

Mark ended the conversation by telling Nan, "I think that Sasha and I will have to talk about that together." In getting Nan out of the middle, he had observed a cardinal rule: It's okay to *talk* with your child's friends, and to joke with them, but never negotiate with another child. As soon as you do, you create a triangle. Instead, arbitrate with your child privately and, if necessary, with another parent.

Don't be afraid to set limits. In welcoming homes, children don't feel "bossed around," but they also understand that they can't get out of control. They know they aren't allowed to destroy property or to take things, and that they must honor the family's standards as well—for example, to be kind, not be rude or fresh to parents.

Many of us are afraid of setting limits with other people's kids. For one reason, we have a hard-enough time laying down the law with our own children. We also fear that our rules might go against another parent's values, or that kids will see us as ogres. However, none of those are good reasons not to set limits. In your home, on your property, you have a right—and a responsibility—to create safe, respectful boundaries. As I pointed out in earlier chapters, the children I interview say they want us to set rules; it makes them feel safe. They particularly want limits when other children are around. One four-year-old girl said it all: "I want someone to watch over me, especially when I'm on a play date."

Will you be seen as the Village Ogre if you lay out guidelines? Will the other children no longer talk to your child if you do anything that "betrays" the second family? I'm not promising that setting boundaries never results in a child being ostracized or parents being criticized, but that's the exception. Far more typical is what happened with Tom and Joyce Brown, who live in a middle-class suburb in Ohio. One day, Tom found cigarette butts in the garage, where their fifteen-year-old son, David, and his friends had been hanging out. The Browns came to me for help. Like most parents, they were worried about drawing a line in the sand that might alienate David and make him look bad in front of his friends. So, we practiced how to talk in a nonblaming way and to make it clear they wouldn't condone that kind of behavior.

The key was to transmit respect. When the Browns spoke to the other kids, they put the onus on themselves by saying, "We don't feel comfortable having anyone smoking in our garage, because we don't have permission from all your parents. We also worry that someone will get hurt, and it's hard for us to sleep at night knowing that might happen. So, we're going to go through the garage from time to time to make sure you're staying within these limits. And the garage will be closed after ten."

Far from getting furious, the kids had the more typical reaction: They heard it and tested it. When Tom and Joyce found cigarette butts in their garage again a few weeks later, they kept their word; the building was off limits for a month. Then, being reasonable, they gave the kids another chance.

The amazing thing was that David's friends not only continued to be friendly with him, they also began to spend more time *inside* the house. Far from resenting Tom and Joyce for the stand they took, the kids began to open up. Sixteen-year-old Cynthia, for instance, who never seemed to want to go home to her own house, finally talked about how upset she was; lately, her parents had been arguing a lot and Cynthia feared an impending divorce. It turned out that Kurt, another regular, also came from a troubled family in which he felt powerless; he told the Browns how much he wished his father would stop drinking.

Without actually meddling in the other families' lives, Joyce and Tom were able to help these kids by giving them an adult ear and by steering them in a constructive direction. They suggested that Cynthia consult the school psychologist who might, in turn, let Cynthia's parents know what she was feeling. And they helped Kurt find out where the local Alateen meetings were held.

Include friends in family rituals. A Friday-night supper, a regular walk, a trip to the playground, and other everyday events are dependable anchors in a child's life. In chapter 2, I discussed the importance of such rituals to help children stay connected with their families and to practice talking with adults. But now I go a step further: When you include a friend in family rituals, it also allows your child to see you interacting with her peers.

To be sure, one reason Mark could so easily talk with Nan without Sasha's getting upset or feeling that Dad was treading on her turf is that Nan has attended countless Friday-night dinners since the girls first became friends in nursery school. Similarly, as the Browns began inviting David's friends to Sunday brunch and holiday meals, they cemented their connection with his peer group—and with him. Even after he went away to college, David continued to bring various and sundry kids home on vacation—which helped Tom and Joyce stay in touch with his rapidly changing young-adult life.

Child Skills: The Three Ts and Other Tools

We need to give children concrete tools that will help them navigate the rough and muddy social waters of childhood. In the first section below, I introduce one such tool, "the Three Ts"—a strategy for your child to apply when peer problems get him down. Following that are three additional skills that your child needs in order to develop Peer Smarts: how to walk away, how to realistically question rather than automatically believe another child, and how to battle the tyranny of "cool."

Learning the Three Ts
This first child skill—the "Three Ts"—will help your child learn to rely on her core reactions to her peers and to make wise decisions regarding her friendships. The Three Ts are:
Trust
Take stock
Try to handle it

TOP TEN WAYS TO CREATE A WELCOMING HOME

Interviews with hundreds of kids and parents from nursery school through high school suggest you should keep these principles in mind:

1. Be an adult presence—in the background but *there*. Give kids space but pop in every now and then.
2. Have respectful rules, firm but flexible, that protect property and feelings.
3. Avoid embarrassing your child. Try not to deliver a list of "Don'ts" in front of her friends.
4. Don't ask pointed questions.
5. Have lots of food—some junk, some healthy.
6. Ask kids to help with projects, painting, gardening, and especially cooking and baking.
7. Remember, hanging out is about having fun. Kids think humor is essential.
8. If certain areas of the house are off limits, make sure your child and his friends know it—but also be sure that there's ample kid-friendly space for them to hang out in.
9. Decorate areas where kids hang out with practicality and whimsy; within reason, get your children's input.
10. If you expect respect from kids, be respectful toward them.

The Three Ts encourage children to trust their instincts and act on them. Sounds simple enough, but here's the aspect of this strategy that many "fair-minded" parents will find most difficult: *This skill gives your child the right not to like certain kids.* We parents tend to think that children, especially younger ones, should not be judgmental about other people. However, if kids don't learn to trust their core feelings, they will forever find themselves in unhealthy relationships and disconnected from their own needs. Therefore, I'm against a soft, fuzzy philosophy that promotes the idea that all people are fun to be with and that you must like everyone.

Teach the Three Ts at an early age; it is one of the best gifts you can give your child. Some children as young as two and a half or three are able to grasp the simple principles. You can arm her with a "Friendship Meter"—an internal monitor that guides her as she determines whether another child is a good friend or not. In time, your child will begin, on her own, to appraise her peers, to take concrete actions, and, as the old song goes, know when to hold and when to fold.

Let me detail each step:

Trust teaches children to have faith in their own feelings—their "gut" reactions to other kids. It's critical for a child to learn that it's okay to develop strong opinions by tuning into herself and trusting what her core says is right for her. But most children will not learn to trust themselves in this way unless we parents validate their feelings and encourage their self-monitoring. Often, we do just the opposite.

For example, just mention a play date with Austin, and Gary's face takes on a tentative look. This is typical; Alice, his mother, had noticed her four-year-old's reaction before, but she either ignored the subtle signal or preached acceptance. Confused, Gary said to me in private, "How come I don't like Austin? Mommy says he's nice, right?"

This is not unusual. Often, when a child doesn't have a good time, he may not know why. Or he does know why but his parents aren't paying attention to what he thinks. Either way, if a parent minimizes a child's feelings or tries to "fix" the situation, it doesn't engender core trust. Consider this exchange between Gary and Alice following one of his play dates with Austin:

Gary:	Austin didn't want to share.
Mom:	Did you give him a turn?
Gary:	Yeah, but, Mom, he's bad. I hate him.
Mom:	Gary, that's not true. You've known him since you were babies. He's really very nice.
Gary:	(Looking discouraged)
Mom:	I'm sure it will be better next time.

Like many parents, Gary's mother doesn't want him sounding so mean and using the word "hate." I'm not crazy about the word either. But perhaps Alice could substitute a more acceptable phrase, such as "don't like" or "can't stand." In any case, she must try to accept, not stifle, Gary's genuine core reaction. Rather than ameliorating his feelings, she must allow him to express them.

Parents need to take children's interpretations of their experiences seriously and affirm them—a child's reaction is usually an accurate indication of what's happening. Immediately after a play date, when the experience is still fresh, or later on as a follow-up to spontaneous remarks you make, your child may simply volunteer how she feels. If not, ask a series of concrete "judgment questions," such as those in the box above. Over time, she will learn to ask herself those kinds of questions and will do it without your help.

Taking stock helps children make evaluations about other kids. By listening to their own reactions, children can begin to understand their feelings in a variety of social situations. Even if your child says that he had an okay time with a particular friend, if he seems out of sorts, get specific. Always ask what happened. Sometimes, "fun" is what he thinks you want to hear. Or, in some cases, "having fun" may be destructive. Maybe the two buddies told secrets or had fun at someone else's expense.

Remember, the goal is not to "fix" or to make pious statements about how your child should feel. Instead, it is to connect your child with his own core responses. This helps him see that what happened made him feel a particular way. It also allows him to become more aware of his own role in the relationship.

After I talked with Gary's mother, she was able to have a very different kind of conversation with him after his next disappointing play date with Austin.

Mom:	I can see how upset and mad you are.
Gary:	Uh huh.
Mom:	Maybe there's a reason. Did Austin call you names?
Gary:	No.
Mom:	Did you take turns?
Gary:	No.
Mom:	Well, what happened?
Gary:	Austin wouldn't let me play with his *Star Wars* X-Wing Fighter.
Mom:	And you were mad about this.
Gary:	Yeah, and he also took my Han Solo and wouldn't give it back.
Mom:	So you really didn't have a good time.
Gary:	No, Austin's no fun.
Mom:	He certainly wasn't today, and that's why you're upset. It feels bad when you don't share with each other.

Gary sat on his mom's lap for a while. A few minutes later, she said, "Let's see what we can do to make it better next time."

Try to handle it reminds your child that friendship is about try-ing, rather than being passive. And this often means taking a con-crete action. Once she understands a problem, she needs to know she has choices. She can try new behaviors, different approaches. Realiz-ing she feels bad around a friend, your child might talk to the adult in charge, ask the other child to stop doing whatever it is that bothers her, or walk away. The point is, children must know that they have options.

Again, you will need to do most of the problem-solving at first, espe-cially with a young child. Suggest that there's almost always some-thing that can be done, and ask your child to come up with some ideas. Effective how-to questions are validating, specific, and framed in a positive way. For example:

• I know you're upset [validation]. How could you take turns [spe-cific] during your next play date so that you both have a good time [positive frame]?
• I see how excited you are [validation]. Can you think of a way to find out now [specific] whether you've been invited [positive frame] to Alexandria's party?

And if your child can't come up with a solution on her own, offer to step in. The key here is to take responsibility for initiating the action.

Tell your child what you're about to do, so she doesn't harbor the illusion that situations magically improve. Also, make sure the action doesn't blame anyone—another child or parent. Your options might include:

"I'll make arrangements with her mother to make another play date for you."

"I could call and find out if she's still angry."

"Next time you two play we'll help you take turns better."

The action plan that you create together will help your child feel better in the friendship. She will eventually learn the core-saving notion that she doesn't have to tolerate an unkind or ungenerous friend.

I've helped many parents teach the Three Ts to their children and have taught many of the children who come to me how to cut through their peer problems. It works because it gives children a new way to think about their friends—and permission to trust their own instincts.

Knowing it's okay to walk away

It's incredibly important for children to know that ending a friendship is a viable option. The truth is, your child won't like everyone, nor will everyone like her. It's important to validate this core-protecting precept: Sometimes walking away is natural and okay. Remember that a child's core is his essence; we protect it by helping him stay true to himself. Sum it up for your child: "If you don't feel good with a friend, and you know what's the matter, first try to make it better. But if you can't, it's okay to walk away."

I remember one child, Jack, who in first grade was "best friends" with Kevin, a terrible braggart. Kevin was a Star at the negative end of the continuum; he always had to be admired. He surrounded himself with kids who had less of everything—and he never let them forget it. Jack, a Joiner, on his better days acted as the "glue" among his peers by making good suggestions; over time, though, he seemed to slide toward the victim end of the continuum. Whatever Jack did, whatever he said, Kevin always had done more, knew more; he'd been there and done that. And, the longer Jack hung around Kevin, the worse Jack felt about himself.

Of course, Kevin's behavior was rooted in his interactions at home. I once overheard his mother, Jean, respond to a woman who mentioned how much her son had grown that summer: "You think that's a lot? Why, my Kevin shot up more—three inches in just two months."

Jack's mother tried to talk with Kevin's mom, but her concern fell on deaf ears. The boys' teachers, who also noticed Kevin's incessant bragging, had a class discussion about the importance of modesty. Finally, Jack's mom ran him through the Three Ts. Thanks to her preparation, the next time Jack felt put down (or less than), he got up the nerve to say, "Kevin, you shouldn't be so braggy!"

But Kevin didn't change very much. In time, Jack decided—on his own—that maybe Kevin would never change. Jack's parents confirmed his experience by saying, "You have the right not to be his friend." They stopped making play dates, and the relationship eventually withered away. However, the entire process gave Jack an important message about relationships: *If it can't be fixed, you don't have to stay forever.*

What a gift that was for Jack! What a life skill! Think of adults you know—maybe even yourself—who can't walk away from bad relationships. In fact, a healthy core includes knowing when to leave and having the strength to do it. In contrast, one of the hallmarks of troubled children and adults is that they keep going back for more. They think they can change a bad situation or that it will magically get better if they just hang in a little longer.

Also, remember that kids' relationships are fluid. Leaving a friendship today doesn't mean necessarily that next year, or maybe even sooner, two children might not be a more appropriate fit.

Thinking before believing

Learning how not to be gullible is a surprisingly important Peer Smart skill for children—one that speaks directly to protecting their core. Some children who are immersed in the pop culture have

---

WHY KIDS AND PARENTS HAVE TROUBLE LEAVING
- We think children need to put up with uncomfortable situations.
- We've been taught to "turn the other cheek."
- We believe it's our responsibility to take care of others.
- We're afraid we or our children will be left out.
- We think the other parents will blame us or think us intrusive.
- We believe the rift will last forever—and that there's nothing that can ever be done.

---

learned to be astonishing salespeople. Other kids, usually Joiners, are incredibly vulnerable to their "pitches."

Shy Ivy, for example, was an open mark for Caroline, a fast-talking eight-year-old in her class. Just for sport, Caroline repeatedly tried to convince Ivy of something unbelievable—and she often succeeded. On one such occasion, when Caroline told her that she *knew* Ivy's parents were going to get divorced, Ivy became so upset that she went to her teacher. She was barely able to get the words out and couldn't calm herself down once she did.

Ken, a sensitive four-year-old Asian boy, was told by Sean, a child in his class, that his eyes were really ugly. For extra effect, Sean added that other kids agreed: "Everyone says so!" he exclaimed with an air of authority. And this was *pre-K,* mind you. Ken was devastated when he saw his mother that afternoon: "Everyone hates me . . . my eyes are ugly."

Why would children believe these claims? Sometimes it's because they are *concrete thinkers.* Such kids haven't yet made the developmental leap that enables them to think more critically and "get" the abstract idea that someone may be putting one over on them.

There's another factor as well: *Empathy*—seeing that someone's motivation can be different from one's own—also affects children's gullibility. While the latest research shows that children under a year are capable of primitive empathy, it doesn't really kick in as a friendship skill until a child is between three and five years old. With many kids, though, it happens even later and more gradually. For a child who hasn't gotten to that point developmentally, it can be difficult to understand that although she is well intentioned, another child might not be.

Finally, there is often an additional component at work: *social anxiety.* Especially when the perpetrator is a popular child decked to the nines in the latest pop culture gear, and his status lends an air of credibility to whatever he says. One such boy, Byron, a student at a suburban middle school, is good-looking, articulate, and the star of several athletic teams. This eleven-year-old actually told me without any embarrassment, "I can sell anyone on *any* idea." Children who are socially insecure and eager for acceptance are easy targets for a boy like Byron.

Being gullible also may be a sign of a learning difficulty that can affect a child's perceptions and self-esteem. Gene, for example, was having trouble keeping up in learning to identify the letters of the alphabet. He felt slightly inferior to other kids and was, therefore, more easily taken in; he assumed everybody knew better than he.

In any situations like these, it's essential to help your child make judgments of other children—their motives *and* the possibility that they may be downright mean. Remind him of the Three Ts: Trust the feelings that come up, take stock, so he knows what the feelings mean, and try to handle the situation by taking reasonable action.

In addition, your child can begin to learn how to ask himself a series of questions that will gauge his gullibility and help him gain a new perspective. They are designated to clarify distinctions between truth and lies, between one's own motivation and that of others:

Could she really know that?

Does he know better than I do?

What's the worst that could happen if that were really true?

Has she ever tried to fool me in the past?

Is he just trying to act important or show off?

Such questions literally help your child to think more clearly and be less reactive. They also give her a "stock" answer to have on hand that calls the huckster child's bluff. For example, it usually stops a kid in his tracks when a formerly gullible Joiner says, "I don't believe what you say—you make things up!"

Battling the "tyranny of cool"

Regardless of a child's individual peer style, accepting one's "nerdiness" is an important child skill, and we must help. Part of the solution is to praise your child for behavior that is usually thought of as uncool. To see what falls in this category, refer to the "Nerd Bill of Rights" in the box on the following page.

Granted, those are difficult rights to hold on to, even for the most loving, sensitive child. As we've seen, *kindergarten* children are already being labeled by the kids in power as "geeky" and "nerdy." However, with parental encouragement, some children *can* take a stand against the tyranny of cool.

Developing Empathy and Courage. The key to this skill involves two traits that are vital to any child's core—empathy and courage. I've seen parents elicit courageous action when they teach their child to view schoolmates through more empathic eyes. For example, Leslea came to me when her son, Zachary, was in kindergarten, because she

THE NERD BILL OF RIGHTS

The following applies to all ages, because the definition of a nerd stays reasonably stable throughout childhood.

- To openly care about how well one does in school.
- To not be exclusive.
- To care about what responsible adults think.
- To talk to kids who don't have all the "right stuff."
- To have Passion and not be embarrassed by it.
- To not go along with hurting or scapegoating another child.

And, most difficult of all,

- To come to an unpopular kid's rescue, especially by telling a parent or teacher about his being picked on.

was concerned about the values Zack was picking up at school. Leslea had good reason to worry. One of his classmates, Luke, started wearing thick glasses, and Zack along with several other of the cooler kids in the class—a.k.a. the "boy-boys"—were making fun of Luke. I suggested that Leslea ask Zack a few questions in a non-blaming tone of voice:

"How do you suppose Luke feels when people make fun of him?"

"Why do you think he began to wear glasses? Take a guess."

"Do you believe that teasing makes it easier or harder for him to like school?"

Such questions made Zack think. He discussed his ideas, and Leslea interjected her own. Zack didn't immediately undergo a magical transformation, but over time it began to sink in. His mother's questions allowed Zack to see Luke as a complete person, rather than a nerd who had no feelings. And what made this conversation possible was the absence of a preachy tone in Leslea's voice.

Equally important, thinking about Luke in this new way made Zack less afraid to talk to him. In fact, he became a little curious, and finally asked Luke why he was wearing glasses and what it was like to wear them. He even tried them on.

Eventually, Zack began to refrain when the other boys teased Luke. Then, because he was able to identify with Luke's feelings, he did a really "nerdy" thing: Zack stood up to the group. "Leave Luke alone!" he shot back at his buddies, fearfully imagining they'd now start picking on him. Zack was partly correct. For several days, he *was* laughed at by some of the boys. But kids being kids, they soon forgot.

And remember Haley, whom you met earlier in this chapter? She didn't want to be mean to other kids but desperately wanted to be popular and didn't know how to resolve her dilemma. This situation came to a head when Debbie—a Loner in a class full of Leaders and Stars—was ostracized by the in-clique. Debbie "dressed down like a sixties hippie," some of the other girls mocked. Haley knew in her heart that it was wrong to tease Debbie. Her family didn't have a lot of money, and maybe Debbie wore secondhand clothes because she *had* to. Her core self was telling her a truth that was hard to hear, but even harder to act on. Haley hated herself for jumping on the bandwagon.

Finally, Haley confided to me what was happening. I encouraged her to take a chance—to experiment with behavior that the other kids might think was not cool but which was consistent with her core feelings. We ran through the Three Ts, focusing on what she really felt and thought about the situation, and on what her core was telling her to do. The truth was, Haley didn't want to be "so snooty and so critical" of others. So, I said, "Okay, you might have to take a risk here. What can you do?"

She thought for a moment and said, "I can sit with Debbie one day, when she's alone. Maybe *all* the other girls won't hate me. I think Joanna will still talk to me."

She was right. Haley sat with the nerdiest girl in class and discovered that her world didn't cave in. She wasn't labeled a nerd for life. Not only Joanna, but several other girls, stood by her. Sure, a few kids turned up their noses at Haley that morning, but she decided those who laughed weren't worth caring about.

I want to point out here that Haley didn't become best friends with Debbie. Haley is a kid, a good kid perhaps, but no saint. She didn't turn Debbie into a project, and take on the job of transforming her. But she continued to talk to her every now and then and, most significantly, she felt better about herself. Haley maintained her core *and* sustained her friendships.

When the school year came to a close, Haley told me, "You know, if I'm a little nerdy, it's not the end of the world." By defining how she felt about her friends, what she wanted, and being able to take risks, Haley strengthened her core immeasurably. She started dressing in a style *she* liked rather than the way the other girls expected; and she was nice to other kids. By year's end, a whole new group began to form around Haley—the self-described "Nerd Pack." Those children were actually beginning to take pride in what we used to think of as square behavior—doing their schoolwork, having interests, dressing uniquely, and being nice to others.

Finally, I could say I knew a group of kids who didn't subscribe to the tyranny of cool.

CHAPTER 6

FOCUS

Basic Skill #6: *Help your child to pay attention*
and to love learning.

A Nation Out of Focus

The very first time I popped the rerelease of *Star Wars* into our VCR
for my kids, I thought to myself, "This is going to be a major treat for
them." I was almost wrong. They complained throughout the two-
and-a-half-hour movie, "It's too slow. It takes too long. When's the action coming?" By the end, of course, they were drawn into the story
and even asked to sit through it again. Going through it with them,
though, I realized that the scenes *did* seem long—compared with the
fast-paced, chopped-up movies we see nowadays. Yet, just twenty
years ago, this was *the* movie that exhibited the height of technological
wizardry and superstimulation.

We have become a nation of the "attentionally challenged"—people
who just can't focus. Sadly, our children are the greatest casualties.
Mind you, I'm not talking about the millions of adults and children
who have been accurately diagnosed as having attention deficit disorder (ADD), a syndrome the mental health community characterizes as
an inability to concentrate and control impulses.

Granted, ADD is the diagnosis of the decade—a catchall classifica-
tion for any child who can't sit still or who continually acts out in class.
Ten years ago, we never heard the term; today, the acronym "ADD" is
regularly emblazoned on magazine and book covers, our TV screens,
and the Internet. For many children, the diagnosis has been a lifesaver, helping them get the attention and remediation they need.
However, some children are also *mis*diagnosed, given a label that can
become an excuse for not being responsible, not living up to one's po-

• *159*

tential. All the same, neither of those groups of children is what I have in mind. What I am talking about are the many more millions of children (and adults) who have what I would call an ordinary attention span but who seem to be experiencing an increasingly difficult time maintaining Focus on everyday tasks. Indeed, something has happened to ordinary attention—to our ability to withstand frustration and to be amused—something that's growing exponentially and can be seen everywhere you look. I certainly see it in my family, in friends' families, and in my meetings with children and parents.

• When I picked my son up from a play date recently, I noticed Becca, the little sister who couldn't be more than three. She was lying on the living room rug, a doll tucked under her arm, having a bottle while she watched TV. The minute her mother appeared, Becca also wanted to be held. In other words, this tiny toddler needed simultaneous stimulation through almost every sensory channel.

• I watched five-year-old Lydia, the daughter of a good friend, in her room with the TV on and her Lego set spread out in front of her. She was wearing a headset, listening to the *Anastasia* soundtrack, eating Sour Powers, holding a Beanie Baby, and drawing a picture *all at the same time.* She is, I marveled to myself, the more "grown-up" version of Becca.

• Doug is in fourth grade—a nice kid who is popular, plays sports, and does okay in school. Unfortunately, he never picks up a book for his own pleasure. His parents, who are avid readers, are beside themselves. Why is Doug so resistant to reading? "There's too much detail. It's boring," he explains.

• When eleven-year-old Alvin does a task that requires "figuring out," if he doesn't get it immediately or can't execute a project the way he wants, he slams down his pencil and walks away. Where does he go? Nintendo 64 or Super Mario Brothers Kart, where he can totally control the level of difficulty—and his own frustration.

All of these kids are basically normal and, I believe, are going to be okay. They certainly don't need remediation or medication. The question is, do they sound familiar?

Of course, they do. While none has a certifiable "disorder," each is a victim of a cultural malady—overstimulation—that has eaten away at our ability to focus. In frighteningly escalating numbers, children today—and not only those who have ADD—can't concentrate without becoming easily bored or easily discouraged. They need action, action, and more action—arousal that heightens every sense. And they need praise from and engagement with their parents to a degree unparalleled in the past. No wonder just about every parent nowadays expresses the same type of frustration with their kids. We're all smack in the middle of a crisis of focus.

Why Focus Is Important

To paraphrase the late Gilda Radner's character, Emily Litella, "What's the big deal about Focus?" The answer is that this core-building trait is a necessity *and* a gift—a primary skill. First and foremost, having Focus enables your child to direct and sustain her attention. This clearly influences how she learns and what she retains. Focus is the key to academic success. It enables your child to attend to what the teacher says in class, to do homework without falling prey to the many distractions at home, and to slog through the learning process. The ability to concentrate enables your child to take in new information. Through Focus, a youngster can furnish her internal computer with images and data that, ultimately, help her mediate and manage her world.

A child who has this primary skill can stay with a subject or an activity. This deepens his understanding, and enables him to truly immerse himself in learning. Focus, of course, goes hand in hand with most of the other core-builders, because it is the trait that enables a child to apply himself. This is particularly obvious with Passion. Your child might be deeply interested in a sport or activity, but if he lacks Focus, it's unlikely that he'll stay with it. Focus also compliments Caution, which you'll read about in chapter 8. Without Focus, it's difficult for a child to reflect, to exercise good judgment, and to make sound decisions.

Focus also helps a child pick up social cues, so that little Harry knows when he's being too loud or standing too close to another child. Focus helps him zero in on his listeners: While relating a story, he can tell whether or not he's losing his audience.

Focus enables a child to pick up all kinds of "rules"—of socialization, of conversation, of games. If she can tune in, she'll know what's expected. This, in turn, helps her build healthy relationships, which, as I explained in chapter 5, leads to a strong sense of self and deeply held self-confidence. Hence, our next Basic Skill:

> Basic Skill #6: Help your child to pay attention
> and to love learning.

Let me illustrate how Focus can save a child's psychological well-being by telling you about five-year-old Adam. In preschool, his speech lagged behind the other kids and he had trouble understanding games that his peers found easy. Yet, when Adam's teacher gave him a box of crayons and a blank piece of paper, he could sit there for untold lengths of time, and draw pictures that exhibited great precision and imagination.

It wasn't long before his classmates began to notice. They'd say to him, "I wish I could draw like you, Adam." By midyear, whenever there was a class project that involved drawing, everyone invariably wanted to work with Adam. And whenever one of them finished a picture, he or she would ask Adam, "What do you think of this?"

Not surprisingly, Adam relished art and the positive attention it brought; and he just kept getting better at it. Thanks to his Focus, he also developed his Passion, which led to finding a niche in school and among his peers. He also started to participate in class and was more eager to learn reading. In short, the confidence Adam gained from this core skill spread to other academic, emotional, and social realms.

Focus affects every aspect of identity—the ability to take in information and express it appropriately, to mingle with one's peers, to be in the flow of life. Focus enables a child to be an integral part of what is going on at any given moment. It empowers a child to derive the benefits of specialization: competence, confidence, and the ability to get what he needs. Not surprisingly, children with Focus tend to develop a network of friends who are more or less like them—and other children with good Focus are usually kids on whom they can depend.

The problem, however, is that living in our culture, it's hard to sustain this vital skill. Virtually everything in the kids' world works against Focus.

Core Threats: Why It's So Easy for Children to Lose Focus

As I explained in the beginning of this chapter, I believe we've become an attentionally challenged culture. I don't make this point to be glib; I'm genuinely concerned about the widespread, culturally reinforced lack of Focus that permeates our own and our children's worlds. I'm not alone in this observation; the popular press frequently reports that so many of us are "addicted to speed," that time gets away from us, or that, as one magazine put it, we are living in "the age of interruption."

Addicted to speed. Thanks to modern technology, we can receive a fax from the office while we're diapering the baby, or check in with a client via cell phone as we're driving the kids to school. And it's not just that we have more gadgets. Each device loads us up with more options—and more interruptions: call waiting, call forwarding; beepers intruding anywhere, anytime. Television, which once had three major networks, now has literally hundreds of channels, and we, with remote controls in hand, have become savage consumers. Studies find that "grazers" change channels twenty-two times a minute—ten or twenty empty seconds feels like an eternity.

Fighting back, television programmers take their cue from MTV, which pioneered the fast-paced style so prevalent in the media. One- or two- minute scenes have been supplanted by frenetic, strobelike images; and programmers have all but done away with "blacks"—the barely perceptible instants when a show fades to black and then cuts to a commercial. They know that a blank screen makes the average channel surfer's finger start itching. "Every station looks at every second of air time," admits an executive vice president at one of the networks. Isn't it telling that the Nielsens, which record audience taste, now use a *minute-by-minute* measure rather than the old program by program readings it tracked until 1973?

Then there are computers. Where there once were a few shelves devoted to PC products, entire stores are now devoted to programs and games. In most ways, this is a great, almost wondrous, development in the history of humankind. The magical electronic speedway, the Internet, expands almost daily with a mind-boggling array of sites and sounds. Yet, for all the promise of our high-tech revolution, is it any wonder it's hard for the average person—adult *or* child—to focus?

In fact, the general consensus is that not only has the landscape changed, but so have our brains. There's ample evidence that we crave speed and avoid boredom at all costs. We want answering machines with a fast-playback feature. TV programmers and filmmakers feed our appetite for action over suspense, and speed over story line.

Barry Levinson, director of *Diner* and the hyperkinetic TV series *Homicide,* observes, "Our rhythms are radically different. We're constantly accelerating the visual to keep the viewer in his seat."

A normal fast-talker—excluding an extraordinary speed-talker like Robin Williams—delivers up to 150 words a minute, noted *New York Times* columnist James Gleick in a 1997 piece entitled, "Addicted to Speed." But, Gleick added, "listeners can process speech at three or four times that rate. Can, and these days, want to." It wasn't always this way. Politicians and preachers once orated for two or three hours at a time, an unthinkably long stretch and slow pace compared with today's radio and TV announcers, which explains why so few of us have the patience to listen to an hour-long State of the Union address. And forget about reading books, which actually requires your total concentration. Do we wonder why 6 million videos are rented yearly, compared with 3 million books taken out of the library?

Given our overstimulated and overscheduled lives, we can barely focus on each other! The typical working couple in America spends only twenty minutes a day in meaningful interaction. And the time spent with our children is often stressful—rushing from one activity to the next, caught in traffic, sandwiched between multiple responsibilities. As I pointed out in chapter 2, the research indicates that while we occupy the same space as other members of the family, we are often each doing our own thing.

It's not hard to see how this state of the nation threatens a child's ability to develop Focus. As Levinson puts it, "You cannot put a child in front of a television set where he is bombarded by images and not ultimately have an adult who is born and bred to see things differently." I agree. Moreover, I've observed three related trends in today's children that pose a threat to Focus:

The do-it-now mentality. Our children hear urgency from us, see it in our example. Children also listen as we regularly bemoan our demands and our deadlines; we work on "time management" and hope to increase "efficiency" in our workday lives and in our family lives. The old-fashioned notions of process and patience have been replaced by instant gratification—which, given technology, is easy for kids to come by. The do-it-now mentality, not surprisingly, is taking a toll on children's academic performance. Schoolwork—reading, writing, studying—is simply too slow for our speed-addicted children, which is probably why only 27 percent of seventh graders read for pleasure, compared with the 47 percent who watch more than three hours of TV a day. It also may be the reason that increasing numbers of children don't do enough homework and require remedial work in math or English when they get to college.

Future focus. Even worse than the message of instant gratification is that children now are taught to spend much of their Focus in anticipation of what's to come, rather than enjoying what's in front of them. For example, I call a friend's house, and their three-year-old answers. To make conversation, I say, "So what's new, Gregory?" Without missing a beat he says, "I'm watching TV. *Muppet Babies* is up next." Rather than focusing exclusively on the current show, he's already thinking about what's up next. In a similar vein, the day after her fifth birthday party, an extravaganza with a clown entertainer, Isabella said to her mother, "Who will we have for fun at my *next* birthday?"

The future-focus mentality in children is, of course, not entirely new. What is new is that it's constantly fostered by the media. TV specials are advertised a month in advance, but even worse are movies, which are beginning to be touted a full year before they open. For example, the *Rugrats* movie, due out in 1998, was already being advertised in 1997. Children everywhere, including my own, take notice and immediately start lobbying before its release. Obviously, the studios know what they're doing. I am among the millions of parents nagged by their kids as stores are blanketed with future-focused products.

Self-scheduling and self-regulation. Several decades ago, we began to feed babies "on demand," instead of adhering to strict, unbending schedules. This progressive development in child-rearing has evolved into a kind of unprecedented self-scheduling. Children today expect to be able to continually feed their own demands. And it's not just us. The computer revolution, with all its benefits, is unfortunately a major factor. Every program and video game lets a child set a comfortable level of difficulty and speed, thus allowing him to control his level of frustration. If it's "too hard," he simply ratchets down a notch. As I mentioned in chapter 1, researchers Debra Buchman and Jeanne Funk, who examined the video-game-playing habits of nine hundred fourth through eighth graders, found that the highly exciting, immediately rewarding entertainment was preferred over more leisurely, less exciting (and less violent) educational videos.

The freedom to self-schedule has literally changed the way children play. In chapter 2, I discussed the burgeoning phenomenon of child-centered play facilities. But as the recent bankruptcy reorganization of one of the giant chains in that field, Discovery Zone, demonstrates, relegating adults to the sidelines and letting kids loose in a world of their own is not enough. Discovery Zone found out that in order to keep kids coming back, they had to trade in their colorful jungle gyms and trampolines and bouncing balls for razzle-dazzle high-tech games. In other words, no matter how much fun the setting, old-fashioned play just doesn't cut it anymore.

It's not that every computer game is inherently bad. In fact, Buchman and Funk concluded that the powerful combination of demonstration, immediate reward, and painless practice makes electronic games an ideal instructional tool. Unfortunately, the lessons are not always what we want kids to learn. Self-regulating games and gadgets not only vie for children's attention, but also these activities undermine the kind of Focus a child must develop in order to practice perseverance.

Watch Joseph, for example, an Intense/Sensitive four-and-a-half-year-old who has a low frustration level. When he's asked to participate in a game, a puzzle, or an interaction in which he's expected to share, and he doesn't immediately get what he wants, he's apt to go into a meltdown. Not so with Nintendo, where he simply sticks to one of the easier "worlds" (levels). When a child is able to self-regulate to this extent—from the nature of his stimulation to the pace at which he has to absorb material, to the type of reward—it's almost intolerable for him to focus on things that don't have immediate feedback or require even a moderate degree of problem-solving.

Clearly, our children are bombarded from all directions. Even rereading this section makes me exhausted! While much has improved with the introduction of high-tech advances, we've also paid a price: The speed of daily life, the intrusion of lightning-quick media, and the cultural premium placed on instant gratification—all work against a child's ability to sustain Focus. We parents, of course, are subject to the same overstimulation. Still, we are our children's primary hope. To bring out the best and make the most of the information age, we must know how to teach Focus.

Parent Skills: Fostering Focus

The parent skills below are divided into two sections. The first will help you understand your child's way of focusing; in it, I explain the four focusing styles I've most frequently observed. The next section enumerates what you can do to make the best of your child's focusing style. What I've done here, as in some of the other chapters, is to adapt the research inspired by children in a clinical population—in this case, kids who have mild attention deficit disorder—to show how various insights and strategies can benefit children who have the ordinary kinds of focusing difficulties that are so often a by-product of our culture.

Understanding your child's type of focusing style

Your child is biologically predisposed toward a predominant mode of focusing. As I explained earlier, the most current research indicates that differing abilities to focus are mostly a matter of basic wiring. In other words, Focus, like temperament (chapter 1), is part of the package your child comes in with. Not surprisingly, temperament and Focus are often linked, as I demonstrate in the following descriptions of each style.

It's interesting to note that psychologists once believed that focusing difficulties were directly linked to anxiety. Certainly, a child who is under pressure—having a difficult life transition, or caught in the middle of a family crisis—often has trouble focusing, but some kids can sustain this ability better than others. We now know why: There's a *constitutional* component to Focus. Children are born with different focusing styles that determine how they will attend to whatever they encounter. Therefore, even if a child's environment is stressful, the degree to which a child is affected is a function of his focusing style. That's why it's not uncommon to see a child like Jeremy. He lives in the inner city, surrounded by a big family full of constant hubbub and crises; yet he is able to sustain his Focus on a task longer than Erin, who is the only child of two college professors.

It's critical that you as a parent recognize and bridge your child's type of focusing style—how she attends to her world and everything in it. Here are four fundamental types.

The Procrastinator. This child is okay once he begins to focus, but getting him started on anything feels like a lifetime occupation. His temperament is typically either Intense/Sensitive or Reserved/Clingy. He's the five-year-old who, every morning, has to be reminded to put on his shoes. He's the seven-year-old who needs to be endlessly prodded to feed *his* hamster, the nine-year-old who stalls before beginning his homework, the teen who waits until the last minute to tackle any project. This child has trouble settling down when the rest of the group—other kids at a play date, classmates, family members—are called to do something together. He's the last to get to the dinner table, the last to put away the toys in school, the one who loses more things than you'd like and is often considered "irresponsible."

The Laser. This child lives in the extreme. Like a laser, when she's on she can pierce through just about anything; when she's off, nothing's there. Therefore, once she engages in the act of focusing, she can't stop; in fact, the act itself seems to make her focus even more. Conversely, when she isn't turned on, she's out to lunch. And once she's in either of her modes, it's really hard moving her into another. Not surprisingly, the Laser child is usually an Intense type—Aggressive or Sensitive. She has trouble with transitions and letting go. She's the toddler who can't bear to end a game or doesn't like to leave a play date, the middle-school child who can't get ready for school if she has started writing in her diary, the teen who doesn't hear an alarm go off because she's so engrossed in a book. Parents of such kids often remark, "She gets so involved, the house could be burning down, and she wouldn't notice!" When she's not focused, though, she may daydream, not hearing questions, requests, or assignments. In other words, she's as intense in her nonfocus as she is when she directs her laserlike attention.

The Barometer. The Barometer child, as his name implies, has a sensitive and variable focusing style, largely dependent on his inner as well as outer environment. The Barometer child is greatly affected by physiology and mood—fatigue, or anger, for example—as well as what's happening in his environment. True, many children fit this picture, because almost every child's ability to focus is somewhat variable. However, the true Barometer type, who typically has an Intense/Sensitive temperament, is less resilient when something interrupts his Focus. At particular times of the day, it's almost a waste of energy to ask the Barometer child to focus. It may be that as long as an activity is interesting and user-friendly, and he's not feeling anxious, or as long as he's working with children he likes and he isn't too tired, he'll stick with it. However, the minute an activity starts being boring or hard, or when something more compelling distracts him, he walks away. There's no internal regulator to tell him, "Get back to the task at hand," whether it's schoolwork or feeding the dog. As a young child, the Barometer type may waver when he's learning something new or at a slow point in a game. As he gets older, he's likely to be like ten-year-old Lyle, who explained, "When a teacher is boring or when it takes her a long time to explain something, I space out." Or he may be like fourteen year old Maggie, who dutifully begins to clean her parrot's cage, and then, when the phone rings, walks into another room and "forgets" to finish the job she started.

The Rock. This child evidences a certain variability—ranging from a fairly intense Focus to some degree of distractibility. However, for the most part, she is steady, staying in the center range. She usually can attend to what's in front of her. We might also think of her as having normal powers of concentration. She is most likely an Easy/Balanced type of child, who is well within the average, if not superior, range of ability to do just about anything she attempts.

Once you begin to recognize your child's focusing style, you will see that your child is not "bad" because she loses things, or "stupid" when she forgets her lunch, or "irresponsible" if she leaves her baseball mitt on the field. If you look back, you'll probably recall that she's been doing such things since she was a toddler. And once you *accept* your child's focusing style for what it is, instead of feeling disappointed, you can help her build on her strengths and accommodate her weaknesses.

Working *with* your child's focusing style— not against it

Let me stress at the outset what *not* to do to get your child to develop Focus. Never aggressively try to "break through." I've seen mothers and fathers who try every bit of cajoling, berating, punishing, lecturing, to make their children listen when they're young and to make them learn when they get older. *It almost never works.* One reason these strategies fail is that there's no way of knowing what's getting in. You could be yelling, explaining, or begging. It won't matter, he's somewhere in the stratosphere! And you're left standing there, stuck in a frustrating "dance"—a routine that's so familiar you know all the steps. You've done it with your child a thousand times before.

So, what can you do instead? Know who your child is—and find the approaches that work best. The following will help you tailor strategies to your particular child.

Learn the signs that indicate when your child is capable of focusing.
Get to know what your child looks like when he *is* attentive. A child's
ability is at its lowest ebb before he eats or during transitions—for example, when he is just waking up, when you're leaving the house or
just getting home. These are not good moments to get through to most
children, especially a Barometer type who has particular trouble focusing at such physiologically or psychologically sensitive times. Instead, try to get to them when they'll be more receptive. If your child is
a Laser, notice when he's more likely to be "on." If she's a Procrastinator, when are the easiest times to get her motivated? Even if he's a
Rock, he is probably more focused during certain parts of the day or
certain activities than others.

Go with your child's mode of focusing. Some researchers and learning experts recommend reducing stimulation for all kinds of children
who are easily distracted. While I respect their view, I do not agree.
After all, the theme of this book is to tailor your strategies specifically
to your child. I have found that some children focus better moving

---

GREEN LIGHT: WHEN YOUR CHILD IS OPEN

Every child is different, but the following are some universal indicators of times and situations in which all children, regardless
of specific focusing styles, are best able to concentrate—and
hear you. You've probably got a green light when your child . . .

- Is not hungry, worn down, or tired.
- Is not in the middle of an exciting activity that's competing for
or drawing in his attention.
- Is in a good mood, because of something she's about to do or
get.
- Has just finished eating.
- Wants something specific from you at that moment.
- Is temperamentally/biologically steady.
- Is not just about to begin or complete a transition.
- Is alone and not hanging out with siblings.
- Doesn't have a friend (or friends) watching.
- Is proud of an accomplishment.

---

around, others sitting still; some can concentrate better when they're alone, others when they're with a whole bunch of people.

Furthermore, it's not a good idea to assume that the way *you* focus will also work for your child. Ritchie, a Barometer type, fought with his parents because he insisted that he could focus best when he sat in a particular room with a wall on one side and the TV on the other. For another child—perhaps even another Barometer type requiring a *different* environment for optimal focus—that setup might be too distracting, but to Ritchie it felt, as he put it, "cozy." Mom and Dad didn't pay attention; they repeatedly sent him back to his room to work at his desk. So, we tried an experiment. They agreed to let Ritchie study that way for a month. To their surprise, his grades got better, and he also began to be less defensive around homework. I don't recommend this for all kids, but it may be right for your child.

For Samantha, a Procrastinator, it was hard to sit still, and even harder to get started on a task. She was like a jumping bean, dancing and doing cartwheels. Luckily, her mom recognized this and helped her by making an active game out of memorizing the multiplication tables. Every time she jumped from the coffee table, Mom would ask her another question, "Seven times nine?" and Sam, sounding like a cheerleader, would yell out the answer, "Sixty-three!" Mom accepted that her daughter focused best when she had a physical outlet for her energy, and Samantha happily learned her math.

Find out your child's focusing channels. With what sense does he process best—his eyes? His ears? His sense of touch? Remember, don't try to beat 'em, join 'em. One father found that his Barometer child was most attentive to life lessons during storytelling; she reacted well to the soft, gentle tone of his voice. Likewise, Anna, the mother of an Intense/Aggressive Barometer child, needed some way to calm him down; words and reminders were not getting through. After discussing it with me, she realized that activities involving tactile stimulation, like finger-painting or doing a jigsaw puzzle, actually soothed her child and made him more open.

Divide tasks into smaller chunks. If your child has difficulty sticking with a task, set aside short blocks of time for chunks of activity. Through observation, you can determine the longest amount of time your child is capable of paying attention to a task. At first, that's all you should expect from him. Although you won't change his focusing style, which is mostly inborn, you will help him develop a greater capacity for focusing. For example, when you teach Go Fish to your four-year-old Barometer who tires easily, play for only five minutes at first; maybe he can last for ten minutes next time. When helping a Procrastinator child with a task, you might set two timers, one to let him know when it's time to start, another to let him see how much time he has to spend on it. Of course, if your child is the Laser type, you might have to limit his time at certain activities—and tell him how long you're willing to play a game with her before she becomes engrossed.

Create success scenarios. Stack the deck for your child: Create situations that allow your child to work well and make it through the process. Take into account the circumstances that motivate him, those that will promote learning. These include the type of project and time of day, the child's mood, his interests. The object is to enable your child to have small experiences of success—which, in turn, lead to bigger successes. For example, somewhat reserved five-year-old Bart was hesitant to work with Legos, because it involved manipulation of small pieces—he lost patience easily when they didn't immediately fit together. So his parents encouraged him to try to connect just two pieces, rather than have a particular construction in mind. At first, Bart didn't want to try, but his parents were patient. Eventually, Bart got so much better that when his mom and dad suggested he make a little Lego bed for one of his action figures, he was eager to try. He then became interested in the pictures on the Lego box that showed more elaborate projects and started asking his dad to help him figure out how to make some of them. His parents had obviously accomplished the mission of creating success for their reluctant builder, not frustration.

Remember what you're up against: a culture that offers success on demand. If a child plays pinball at an arcade, for example, he gets millions of points just for trying. Naturally, he wants to keep playing. Arcades and video games (even adult games in Las Vegas) are all based on the same principle of variable reinforcement: Give people a little success, and they'll keep coming back for more. It's a very effective learning tool, and since we really can't compete with it, we ought to borrow from it.

Watch your tone—don't lecture and don't berate. In this golden age of psychotherapy, some of us turn into teachers or even therapists when we talk to our children. We fall into a certain preachy tone, use too many words, repeat the same point over and over. We don't notice whether our kids are paying attention—and guess what? They're not. You've seen the signs: Your child's eyes glaze over, he's no longer looking at you but rather at a spot on the wall, and his facial expression is screaming, "I'm not hearing anything." That's a sure sign to *stop* talking—you're not getting through.

Many children who have trouble focusing are also sensitive to tone, particularly Barometer types. Five-year-old Ritchie, for example, continually said to his mother, Anne, "Stop yelling at me." She was perplexed and insisted to me that she "wasn't a screamer." I asked her to recall precisely the kinds of situations that triggered Ritchie's accusation. "It's usually when I want him to do something, or stop doing something. I just say it a little more forcefully, and he thinks I'm 'screaming.' " As with the study scenario I described above, I helped Mom believe Ritchie. To Anne, what felt like raising her voice slightly sounded to Ritchie like screaming. Once that happened, he couldn't hear the words she was saying—he only could *feel* her tone. She was losing him every time. However, once Anne learned to take a deep breath so she could recognize how her tone affected Ritchie, she was able to come up with an attention-grabbing phrase said in a gentler way.

Watch out for negative labels. Take care not to call your child "spacey" or "irresponsible" when he loses focus. This is particularly important if you have more than one child. We tend to polarize our kids' focusing styles. For example, if one sibling is a Laser and another a Procrastinator, parents can inadvertently fall into the comparison trap: "Matthew [the Laser] could spend hours doing puzzles when he was David's age." It starts innocently, and within a few years, David, the Barometer child, is seen as unfocused. The label sticks and becomes self-predicting. David eventually believes he can't focus at all when, in fact, he focuses in a different way and has different talents from his brother Matthew.

The idea is to avoid battles. When you find yourself covering the same old territory with a child, it's a pretty good bet that you're basing your reaction on what you think your child usually does. You're not making room for him to approach a problem in a new way, a way that's right for him. And instead of making a positive connection, you end up in a repetitive dance that has a life of its own. Your child isn't listening and certainly isn't doing what you ask. It takes up more of your time and, after a while, makes your child become the labels: bad, destructive, and unsuccessful.

Praise your child's Focus rather than his performance. As I've already mentioned in the chapters on Expressiveness and Passion, it's important to notice *how* we praise our children. Whenever a child works well, acknowledge her Focus. You don't even have to speak directly to her. As Alice, the mother of three elementary schoolers suggests, if you really want kids to listen, just start *whispering* to your spouse or friend. Children are inveterate eavesdroppers. Mention your child's accomplishment on the phone or to Dad or Grandma when the child is in earshot: "Boy, Karen was able to stick with jump rope, and she didn't give up, even when it was hard for her. You should see her jump now." Overhearing you on that occasion and others, Karen will internalize the message that she's able to persevere and be successful. She'll be able to say to herself, "I can stick with things." And her concentration will become more resilient.

Help your child see the connection between having Focus and achieving the results he wants. If a child remarks "I hate it" or "I did a lousy job" during or after executing a project—for example, a picture—that probably means he lost Focus. Point out the problem *as it relates to Focus:* He needs to give his work more attention or time or both. You might say, "Well, when I draw something I don't like, I try to figure out what went wrong. I try to concentrate harder next time so that I'll do a better job." That way, you're modeling perseverance and, at the same time, allowing him to critique himself. If he tries again and does it differently next time, it will be because he has learned the importance of Focus.

Take the same approach with an older child. Say it's Sunday evening and your thirteen-year-old son—a Procrastinator—has a lot of math homework. You might ask a question like "If you have sixteen problems to do, what do you think tonight will be like if you don't start soon?" This helps him focus on the problem. Then, step back and let *him* figure out that it would be a good idea to map out a plan.

Reward your child effectively. Parents often unwittingly feed into both the "What's in it for me?" and the "What's next" mentality sold by the pop culture and bought by the second family. We bribe kids to get them to cooperate and reward them when they do. Now I'm not against bribes—we adults call them "incentives," and "rewards." As I pointed out in my first book, *Parenting by Heart*, there's nothing wrong with them. The problem is that we offer excessive rewards. If a child cleans his room, he gets ice cream; if he sits still for a while to do his homework, he gets an hour of computer games. This pattern is destructive to a child's core because he develops the habit of rewarding himself in ways that are not appropriate to the task ("I did half my chores, so now I can watch TV").

Instead, try to acknowledge his achievement in ways that "feed" your child's core. For example, one mother asked her four-year-old son, David, "Do you think you can water these two plants?" After he finished, she didn't give him anything or promise him a new toy; his reward was her response: "That was terrific, David—the way you were able to water those plants. That took a long time [which it did, to a four-year-old]. Do you see how they perked up?" David walked away saying to himself, "Wow, I did a good job." His "reward" was his own feeling of accomplishment.

Healthy rewards include praise ("You're getting much better at this"), time together ("Clean your room and we'll play spaceship with this empty carton"), or even a small quota of second-family treats ("If you do your homework, you can play Nintendo for fifteen minutes"). Or offer a reward when the child doesn't expect one. For example, when she feeds her cat without prompting, you might surprise her with a new book about pets.

Yes, it's okay to use television and computer games as a reward—but on a limited basis. Let's be honest: It's impossible to keep children away from television and computers—and we don't necessarily want to. Besides, the media can be used as leverage; it means a lot to kids nowadays. What could be worse than missing the TV show everyone else will be talking about tomorrow at school? Problems only occur when we go overboard—when we trade fifteen minutes of cleanup for a two-hour program or let computer games dominate a child's play.

Be aware of how scattered and divided *you* might be. We parents can model concentration like many other core-builders in our own lives. Do you read with the radio and TV on? Do several things at once? Rush constantly and try to crowd in as many activities as possible? All of it sends a message to your children. Ask yourself, what type of focusing style do you favor? Your child isn't necessarily like you, but your example will surely make an impression. It may even cause you and your child to lock horns.

For example, Evelyn, an editor, whose focusing style is Laser, says, "I remember a cousin accusing me of ignoring him when we were kids because he'd jump on the bed next to mine while I was reading a comic, and I never noticed." Evelyn's intense Focus has been a boon to her career as an editor, but her focusing style has had its drawbacks at home. "A bomb could go off and Mom wouldn't hear it," said Sue, thirteen, a Barometer child, who took her mother's behavior personally. "I hate it when she ignores me," she confided.

I helped Evelyn see that her ability to focus so intently was off-putting to her daughter, whose own Focus was tenuous at best. But once Evelyn became more self-aware and could anticipate times when she'd be lost in concentration, she could do things differently. Evelyn began to plan her most intense work—for example, editing a manuscript—when Sue wasn't around. However, when it became necessary to bring work home, Evelyn also could warn her daughter, "I'm about to read these papers, so I'll be preoccupied for the next twenty minutes." These easy changes helped both mother and daughter avoid further clashes over their different styles of Focus.

Child Skills: Improving Focus

The skills that help children develop Focus empower in two areas: the ability to monitor their own attention and to combat whatever threatens their concentration. Let me explain: While it's true to some degree that people are born with particular focusing styles, Focus is a skill that can be improved. Children can be taught to strengthen their concentration, even though the external world distracts, diffuses, and sabotages their concentration every step of the way. We need to help kids create an internal structure that will help them stay focused in spite of the frenzy. To that end, use the "Three S's:"

Seeing it
Saying it
Switching strategies

Learning the "Three S's"

Seeing it. This part of the process promotes self-awareness. A child must learn to pay attention to body signals that tell him—on a visceral level—when he's losing Focus. Such signals include fidgeting, feeling

A PARENT'S FOCUSING CHECKLIST

It's important to look at what *we* do with and to our children that can impede their ability to focus. When your child seems to be losing Focus, ask yourself:

- Am I moving or talking too fast?
- Am I complicating the task (asking him to do the whole room instead of suggesting a portion, giving him too many directions at once)?
- Am I allowing too much stimulation (TV, computer, video games, phone time)?
- Do I reward excessively and inappropriately (a lot of TV in return for brushing her teeth)?
- Do I interrupt my child's Focus (while he puts away his toys, reminding him of something else he has to do)?
- Am I clear about what's most important (letting her know that in the morning, she has to get dressed before she feeds the hamster)?
- Are my instructions too vague ("Be good at Grandma's" instead of "Say hello to everyone when we first get there")?
- Am *I* multifocused—doing six things at once that divert my attention from my child?

tired, daydreaming, yawning, looking around the room, staring aimlessly at nothing. With help from a parent, a child can begin to recognize these signs. For example, when Buddy, four, has trouble sitting still during storytime, his teacher says, "Buddy, I think you've lost focus. Maybe you need to get up for a few minutes." Likewise, when eight-year-old Dale starts yawning over math homework, her mom says, "You look like you're having trouble staying focused. Go outside for a while—take a break to refresh yourself." And when Mom is telling twelve-year-old Miranda about weekend plans with Dad, she notices that Miranda has a faraway look. Instead of getting angry or continuing to try to get through, she says, "I can see that it's hard for you to focus right now. Maybe this isn't a good time to discuss this. We'll talk about it later."

Saying it. Kids not only have to recognize their focusing problem but also feel free enough to verbalize what's happening. Otherwise, their difficulty in sustaining Focus can activate a self-defeating spiral of events: A child repeatedly loses Focus, he's labeled "ditsy" or "irresponsible," and very quickly he feels like a failure, and gets defensive. If he can't admit at the outset that he's lost attention, he'll end up defending himself and making lame excuses ("The cat ate my homework"), even lying ("But I *did* finish it").

Sound familiar? It's important at such times to reassure your child: "Don't worry—everyone sometimes has trouble focusing." And give her specific phrases that she can use when she feels she's lost Focus—phrases that neither put the blame on herself or on another person:

"I stopped paying attention."

"Oops—my mind wandered."

"I'm thinking about other things."

"I'm too tired to concentrate."

"I keep losing my place."

"I don't understand."

It's wonderful when children are able to verbalize in this way. I remember the time I started telling a story to our next-door neighbor, who is ten. A few sentences into it, she said, "Ron, I can't listen now. I'm tired." It was such a crystal-clear message—especially when compared to a child who becomes defensive. Such a youngster is not only unable to connect with his own core but also is disconnected from the task *and* the people around him. He simply can't say out loud that he's having trouble.

Switching strategies. With awareness (seeing) and admission (saying), it's possible for your child to take the third step: switching strategies—in other words, doing something to regain Focus. Here are four important skills that can help.

• *Prioritizing.* Help your child figure out which task is most important to get done *now*. For example, when her mother noticed that Gretchen, five, was dawdling instead of cleaning her room, she said, "Gretch, I think you're losing Focus. Wouldn't it help if you decide what's more important? Maybe first you could just put away your more delicate toys." Or if your child is packing for summer camp, ask him to think in stages and take them one at a time—first, make a list; second, lay out the clothes; third, do the actual packing.

• *Breaking it down.* Children need to learn how to "chunk"—break tasks down into smaller pieces, and do a few at a time. This is particularly good when something is overwhelming. If your daughter is paralyzed by the twenty problems she has for math homework, suggest that she tackle five problems in groups of four instead of all at once.

• *Relocating.* Sometimes it's easier to focus in another place, or under different conditions—like Ritchie, who needed his cozy setup to concentrate. Or Brian, who needed a distraction-free setting to do things he didn't like. When asking members of the family to lower their voices didn't work, he moved to another room so that he could be alone.

Providing a quiet place is particularly important when helping children combat sensory overload. A lot of kids have trouble with this, though, because they're hooked on constant stimulation; being alone might feel lonely. Still, because noise and distraction prevent Focus, these kids should start with small chunks of time on their own.

• *Slowing down.* The ability to slow down and to "edit" oneself is critical to developing Focus—and it can be instilled in children as young as three. Recently, for example, I visited a Montessori preschool where children were playing with Cuisinaire rods. Whenever the teacher saw a child speeding up, she'd ask, "Are you taking your time?" And throughout the morning, she kept asking, "Have you stopped to check your work? Have you looked it over?" Words of wisdom that can be used by many parents at home.

As children learn these different techniques, they will learn how to slow themselves down and develop Focus. This key attribute engenders perseverance; and, over time, kids who focus can better take in whatever they need to strengthen their core.

CHAPTER 7

BODY COMFORT

Basic Skill #7: Help your child accept his physical appearance and feel comfortable in his body.

A National Obsession: Women and Children First

If the message of this book is "Accept the child you have," then fostering Body Comfort is your greatest challenge. I have talked thus far about recognizing your child's emotional and cognitive makeup. Now we must consider his *physical* reality—an equally vital part of his core being.

Having a healthy body image is particularly difficult in our culture, because we Americans are so obsessed with thinness and good looks. Naomi Wolf first labeled this phenomenon "the beauty myth" in 1991, but women's enslavement at the hands of advertisers and fashion designers has long been the subject of countless magazine articles and books. Mental health practitioners cite our equating attractiveness with thinness as a major factor in the proliferation of eating disorders, which currently affect some 7 million American women and girls.

However, there is a new, untold story about this preoccupation with the body beautiful: *Children* are becoming obsessed—not clinically ill (for the most part), but truly preoccupied with their bodies. And why not? The entire culture is—and the problem has trickled down. At younger and younger ages our children—including boys—are affected by the beauty myth. And though bookshelves are surprisingly bare on this topic, *all* children are at risk.

- Four-year-old Andy asks, "Am I fat, Mommy?" And before Mom has a chance to answer, he asks another question: "It's bad to be fat—right, Mommy?" (That's right, *four* years old.)

- Penny, who is eight, complains to her parents, "My legs have too many muscles, and they're too hairy." Already self-conscious, Penny tries to hide these alleged imperfections by wearing dark tights to cover her legs.
- A group of fifth-grade girls are beginning to apply pressure to their unwitting parents: They want to have second holes pierced in their ears. Why not? After all, most of their MTV favorites, as well as real-life adolescent neighbors, have multiple piercings.
- Delia, at five, is on the same dubious fashion track. She already knows who rules the teen-age roost. Playing dress-up, she comes out with a mock nose ring, stick-on tattoos, and a clip-on belly-button ring.
- Nine-year-old Jerry was referred to therapy because he had been fighting with other boys in school. "Why did my parents let me dress this way?" he asks, his slender body enveloped by jeans and a jacket six sizes too big. "Now the other boys think I'm tougher than I really am."
- At a summer camp I visited, many of the girls (and some boys) walked around with individual water bottles—the kind with the little spout on top that you pull up. Quite a few had refilled their bottles with diet soda. It was hard to remember that these were nine-year-olds. On one hand, they looked like toddlers, sucking on a bottle; on the other, they were like little women at a health club.

According to a 1998 *New York Times*/CBS News poll of American teenagers, when asked the one thing they'd like to change about themselves, the most frequent answer from girls *and* boys alike was "My looks" or "My body." In a recent *Parents* magazine survey, when asked to rank preference, children (and parents) put an "overweight child" on a lower level than a child in a wheelchair or one with any kind of deformity.

And here's another new twist: For many years, we saw this preoccupation only in our daughters. But like many other formerly "gendered" phenomena, we're beginning to see younger boys who dislike aspects of their bodies the way girls do. "Lots of data suggests that males increasingly worry about their bodies," says psychologist Judith Rodin, author of *The Body Trap*. "The pressure is on both sexes."

What is more, messages about being thin—and therefore attractive—don't only come from the outside. They come from within the family as well. Parents, often preoccupied with health and nutrition,

CHILDREN AND BODY IMAGE: WHAT RESEARCH TELLS US

Studies in the last decade have begun to show that preoccupation with body image appears in our children at younger and younger ages:

• In a Cincinnati study that surveyed third-grade boys *and* girls—nine-year-olds—29 percent of the boys and 39 percent of the girls had already dieted, and another 31 percent and 60 percent said they wanted to.

• A California study determined that 81 percent of ten-year-old girls were or already had been on a diet.

• In a national study of girls *and* boys in grades three to six, 45 percent said they want to be thinner, 37 percent had already dieted, and around 7 percent scored in the eating-disorder range.

• Sixty percent of girls between grades one and six develop distorted body images and overestimate their body weight.

• A national survey in the late eighties showed that 90 percent of American boys *and* girls were unhappy with their weight.

may be on diets themselves. Some actually encourage dieting because they want their child to have that competitive social edge in school. When I first began to practice over two decades ago, such concerns were practically unheard of. But now I regularly get calls from parents of preschoolers worried about children's weight, manner of dressing, and other appearance issues.

I see the alarming statistics (see the box above) come to life in my clinical practice—and so do colleagues who specialize in eating disorders. Margo Maine, Ph.D., is author of *Body Wars,* which chronicles the ways in which we all battle our bodies, and *Father Hunger,* about anorexia and bulimia. Dr. Maine points out that whereas ten years ago, eating disorders were primarily confined to affluent Caucasians—typically, adolescent girls—this is now an equal-opportunity condition that cuts across all races and socioeconomic groups. In fact, Maine reports seeing Third World immigrants come here to escape the poverty and hunger at home only to conform to our standards and purposely starve themselves.

What can we do? Clearly, we have to pay attention, because children need all the help they can get in order to withstand the cultural mandates concerning appearance.

Why Body Comfort Is Important

There is a direct correlation between acceptance of one's body and feeling self-confident; the world seems to open up for children who are not self-conscious about appearance. Relatively free from these obsessions, they have the energy to think and to engage spontaneously in activities. This state of being is what I call "Body Comfort."

Body Comfort enables a child to take for granted that her body is a vehicle to gain mastery and pleasure, rather than to make a statement or gain status. In turn, this promotes the likelihood of her being social—which is more consequential than merely being "popular." Body Comfort empowers a child to try out and challenge herself in sports and to engage in public speaking—small interactions (talking and hanging out with other kids), as well as those on a grander scale that involve leadership roles (being class or club president, serving on school committees).

Naturally, Body Comfort contributes to healthy sexuality. When children are taught how their bodies work, when they feel good about how their bodies look, and when they're allowed to touch their own bodies without shame, they learn to respect and protect themselves. They are capable of distinguishing loving from unwanted advances; and they can say no. Thus, Body Comfort lays the groundwork for them to experience a myriad of wonderful feelings.

In short, Body Comfort adds up to a base of confidence—physical confidence that, in turn, leads to sociability and mastery of skills. Hence, our seventh Basic Skill:

Basic Skill #7: Help your child accept his physical appearance and feel comfortable in his body.

I must stress that Body Comfort is not about being attractive by cultural standards—having a model figure or a perfectly sculpted physique—it's about *comfort*. The difference between a child who is at ease in his body and one who is not is like night and day—and it has little to do with looks or body type. For example, Sally always has been somewhat overweight since I met her when she was in early elementary school. Although she's slightly plump, she moves with grace, whether she's draping herself over a couch, or dancing through a room to the latest top-forty tune. She's uninhibited, acting out parts she sees on TV for her family and not afraid of being in the spotlight. She spends relatively little time dressing or primping, despite the fact that she's part of a looks-conscious crowd.

Compare this child with Trent, who since age three has also been a bit pudgy; at seven, he has become noticeably shier. He complains to his mother about the way he looks, the way his clothes fit him. He seems to put himself under the microscope, viewing his body with an ever-critical third eye. Although his natural instinct is to get involved, he holds himself back. For example, he loves acting, and is a good singer, but he didn't want to be in the school Christmas play. He doesn't go after anything that would make him the center of attention because he feels "funny about the way he looks."

Even though Sally and Trent have similar body types, their different perceptions set them apart. Sally is accepted by her peers because she *accepts herself*, while Trent grows more alone. It saddens me that I see more and more Trents in my practice; they don't have eating disorders and probably will never develop any extreme problems with food or their bodies. But such children may have a lifelong struggle to feel comfortable in themselves. Looking around us, it's not hard to see why.

Core Threats: Why Body *Dis*comfort Is So Prevalent

Everywhere you look, you can find threats to Body Comfort. Consider these major pitfalls:

Pop culture messages start to bombard children by the ages of two or three. Media and toys tell children, "Be pretty and handsome, thin and strong." All the Disney heroes and heroines—Mulan, Pocahontas and John Smith, Sleeping Beauty and her Prince—are lookers. Even the Beast, in the final scene of Beauty and the Beast, turns into a handsome man. Or look at Barbie and Ken, TV characters, and most of the kids who appear in commercials. A few rare "geeks" become popular, like Steve Urkel on *Family Matters*, but most mainstay media personalities have model-caliber looks.

It's not just about faces. Barbie, the girl's toy of choice for decades, has made generations of normal-bodied girls feel inferior. It's an impossible standard, as Aroen, a teenager I know, found out. She wrote a report on Barbie's body measurements and estimated that if Barbie were real person, she'd stand almost seven feet tall, have a forty-inch bust, and—the topper—a twelve-inch waistline!

It's not surprising, the editor of *Sassy* told a reporter from *People,* that her magazine, which is read by preteens and teens, gets "letters from girls who are five feet three inches and weigh a hundred pounds, who want help getting down to ninety-five." Surveying the content of that magazine, as well as *Seventeen, Teen, YM,* and several women's magazines, Jill Zimmerman, a psychologist who specializes in body issues, found that the pervasive message was "superthin equals sexy."

And guess what? Now our sons are confronted by the same impossible-to-emulate standards in their playthings. Recently, my son was given an original Han Solo action figure. The twenty-year-old "Han" has an average build, whereas the more recent incarnation is so pumped up and "buff"—PopSpeak for muscular—he could make Arnold Schwarzenegger envious!

Parents fall prey to the same influences. We can't just blame media. While buff images may dominate, there has been a real increase in childhood obesity, causing parents to become concerned about their children at earlier and earlier ages. Pediatricians expect infants to triple their weight and double their height in the first year—pound for pound, they need two to three times as many calories as obese adults. And, yet, we as a nation have such negative thoughts about fat that parents and some doctors often put babies on low-fat, sugar-free diets. In one study of fourteen hundred new parents, for example, many didn't know that babies *need* fat and cholesterol to grow.

Moreover, the problem is more than a misdirected health concern. We parents have been indoctrinated by the beauty myth, too. A 1994 *Glamour* magazine survey found that only 19 percent of the four thousand young women who responded reported having mothers who *liked* their bodies. Some of us were raised in households where our parents obsessed about their looks and dieted constantly. Such attitudes have a way of being handed down from generation to generation, leading some parents to even play favorites, doting on the most attractive, slimmest child. Thus, long before our children are exposed to outside influences, we unwittingly pass on our own conditioning. In one study of nine- to eleven-year-old children, eight out of ten of their parents (82 percent) admitted that they dieted "sometimes" or "very often." Nearly half of the children (46 percent) said exactly the same thing!

Consider Dee—Penny's mother—who, like her own mom, has spent the last many years like a yo-yo, always trying to lose that ten pounds. Is it any wonder that Penny has an obsession about how *she* looks? Dee has inadvertently transmitted to Penny her difficulties around accepting her own looks. Dee's older daughter, Kristin, who is fourteen, rebelled. She is obsessively sloppy and doesn't give a damn about how she looks. She vows privately, "I would die if I ended up like my mom."

Another mother, Drew, exercises every chance she gets. When she became a mother, she brought baby Alicia with her to the gym to sit on the sidelines while she worked out. The other women weren't even fazed at the sight, probably because they understood why exercise and toning were so important in Drew's life. That message wasn't lost on Alicia. At five, she already looks in the mirror and is consumed with the notion of having "pretty" dolls and clothes—and, of course, being pretty herself.

Schools inadvertently reinforce the problem. Children don't only get these messages at home. In some classrooms, teachers post weight or body fat analysis "scores," gym teachers display body measurements and various kids' "personal bests." All of this may be done innocently enough, but it adds to harmful social comparisons and only affirms the cultural messages—for girls, that thinner is better, and for boys, that bigger is better.

We've heard countless stories of casualties—typically, teenage girls suffering from anorexia or bulimia. One such twenty-three-year-old, Marya Hornbacher, who documented her struggle in her book, *Wasted,* admits that by *five* she was boasting to a friend, "I'm on a diet." But obvious victims of these pathologies are only the tip of the iceberg. We need to take a long, hard look at how this national obsession affects the average child, boy *or* girl, and how it potentially can hamper the development of a child's inner core. Therefore, we parents must learn the skills that will protect our children; it's up to us to teach them to respect, accept, and manage their bodies.

Parent Skills: How to Promote Body Comfort

Children *can* be helped to attain Body Comfort. But most of them can't develop Body Comfort without a parent's influence. The skills below are divided into two sections. The first involves learning how to look and listen for a body obsession in your child and taking steps to diminish it. The second offers concrete steps you can take at home to decrease the likelihood of your child's becoming preoccupied with her appearance—and that will prevent your own attitudes from affecting her. You will see that we cover a wide range of diverse areas—eating patterns, clothes-buying, exercise. This might feel overwhelming. But remember that your child's body goes everywhere with him; he's constantly moving it, looking at it, touching it, taking in nourishment to sustain it, dressing it. Indeed, more than any other core-builder in this book, Body Comfort impacts on virtually every area of your child's functioning.

Look and listen: learning how to spot trouble

I've pointed out for every core-builder in this book, the first step is always to recognize who your child is. This can be tricky when it comes to Body Comfort—first, because kids don't always verbalize these problems; second, because we're swimming in the same cultural sea, so it's often harder for us to recognize these issues. Still, helping your child develop Body Comfort requires paying attention. Remember, even if your child is not complaining about his appearance, he may be starting to worry about it. So, be on the lookout for nonverbal signs, behaviors that indicate he's indirectly asking for help (see box on the following page).

If your child does complain out loud that she doesn't like her body, listen carefully. By "listen," I don't just mean to the details about a play date or the day at school. What's important here is to listen for the obsession about appearance. By an "obsession," I mean persistent thoughts that simply won't quit—a preoccupation about body image or appearance that gets in the way of everyday life. The following steps are similar to those I suggest in chapter 4 when I talk about helping kids come up with counterthoughts to replace negative self-messages.

Recognize the difference between thinking and obsessing. Obsessive-compulsive behavior and eating disorders are relative newcomers to the field of mental health; only in the last decade have we begun to have new insights into these problems in adults. We now understand them to be part of a ruminative process—that is, the afflicted person can't stop thinking about the issue. Children are no different. Adding to the problem, ruminating about one's body is a culturally—

and socially—reinforced phenomenon. So, it's particularly hard for parents to tell when a child has a normal worry about his body or an inordinate concern—or an obsession. In any case, however, the research and treatment can be applied to children who spend time thinking about their bodies and to those who obsess.

The box on page 189 summarizes the difference between a thought and an obsession.

Let's look at two examples: Olive, an African-American girl, came home from preschool upset about her curly hair. "I want it to be like Dory's," she cried. Her mother explained that different people have different kinds of hair, skin, noses, eyes. A few minutes later, Olive was engrossed in her Lego set. Over the next few weeks, her mother had several other talks with Olive about body differences, so it was clear that Olive continued to think about her hair. But the emotion she dis-

A THOUGHT . . .	AN OBSESSION . . .
• Is fluid—it changes over time, as your child moves onto other concerns or interests.	• Is repetitive and rigid; it's an issue your child rarely seems to "forget" or get bored with.
• Affects your child's mood initially but not steadily.	• Produces consistently negative affect—sadness, anger, self-deprecation.
• Is often grounded in some reality—your child *is* a bit overweight or *does* have stringy hair.	• Seems at odds, is disconnected, or even the opposite of who your child physically is.
• Doesn't close your child to outside input and suggestions.	• Makes it impossible for your child to hear advice—she has an answer for anything you suggest.
• Can be changed when your child does something to make the situation different.	• Doesn't necessarily stop even if your child takes an action.
• Results in your feeling helpful because your suggestions make a difference.	• Results in your feeling frustrated and resentful.

played—her affect—changed from being upset to being curious. She was able to have several conversations about her hair with Mom, without blocking out new information or continually feeling bad about herself.

In contrast, Tom was a handsome kid, popular among his peers, but somehow got it into his head that he was "too thin." He was often sad about it and down on himself. Though his schoolwork and friendships were fine, Tom repeatedly brought up his skinniness and rarely seemed to tire of talking about it. His parents couldn't really have a conversation about this perceived problem without hearing a litany of rationales and yes-buts. In fact, nothing they did or said seemed to make any difference; when the topic came up, Tom had an answer for everything they suggested. For example, when Mom and Dad recommended that he eat more or do a little bodybuilding, he told them, "I know it won't work." When Dad asked Tom to join him on his morning run, "I won't be able to keep up" was Tom's answer. Life went on, but the obsession quietly continued in the background.

Obviously, when a child simply *thinks* about a body problem, it's easier to deal with it. You can talk, and she'll listen. When she *worries,* however, you need to be aware that it's going to be a lot harder to get through.

Don't fight it. Whatever you do, when you hear repetitive worry, don't argue. If you try to cleverly talk your child out of it, you're fighting a losing battle, and you won't be helping your child.

Child: I've got fat legs, Mom.
Mom: No, you don't.
Child: Yes, they always look so big.
Mom: You're beautiful, honey. Your legs are fine.
Child: No, they're not.

Instead of trying to change your child's mind, name her obsession in a way that validates feelings. You might say, "Oh, you're upset—I hear you're talking about your favorite worry," "I guess you're playing your theme song, because you're worrying again," or even "You're into your thing again. It must be hard." Say it in whatever way fits your family's style—without sounding like a therapist. The goal is simply to make your child aware of what he's doing. Without judgment, let him know he's singing the same old song.

Give kind, but honest, feedback. Often, parents are confused about this point. They think it's important to accept children for who they are, but, at the same time, when it comes to something as touchy as body image, they're afraid to be honest. However, as I pointed out in chapter 4, Martin Seligman's research deals with how children's thinking is related to their behavior. His work underscores the importance of forthright feedback. This is difficult for most of us—we desperately want to help children *feel* better, and we think positive statements are the answer. But it does no good to candy-coat a situation.

For example, five-year-old Elliott was upset because the kids at school made fun of his ears. His mother responded by saying, "There's nothing wrong with your ears, and, besides, I love you anyway." The problem is, Elliott's ears really do stick out, and he knows it. All he heard was Mom's well-intentioned lie; he tuned out after that part, too upset to hear that she loved him anyway. If Mom had continued to deny his feelings, in time, Elliott would have learned to dismiss her opinions altogether. Also, in this scenario, there is no way the two of them could come up with a constructive solution.

Instead, I suggested to Elliott's mother that she be gently honest: "Yes, your ears are a little bigger than most kids and [gulp!] they do stick out slightly." That at least could allow Elliott to feel as if he's not crazy. More important, he would then trust his mother and remain open to her suggestions.

It's also important to respond with emotion. Some parents think it's best not to encourage a child's preoccupation—it might become more "real." But if you think about it, nothing is worse when someone expresses worry than not having the listener react. So, indicate that you "get" the problem and be sincere about it: "That must feel horrible" or "I'm sorry—that's really hard."

"Unpackage" the obsession. Don't be satisfied with huge, vague statements like "I hate the way I look." Such a general complaint is too big to handle constructively. Break the big idea down into smaller parts for your child by asking questions that will help her bring out details—and, thereby, be better able to deal with them: "Where and when do you think this?" Ask her to be concrete ("Show me exactly what you don't like about your legs"), so that it narrows down the feeling. Talking with such specificity often makes a child feel less embarrassed and paralyzed.

Don't assume. Be sure that you understand what your child means. If he says he hates his nose, try to discern whether it's because his nose is too big or he doesn't like its shape—or another reason you hadn't even considered. To clarify and to indicate that you're listening, repeat what your child says: "So you're telling me you think that your nose has a funny bump in the middle?"

Asking questions sometimes also helps identify the real problem. For example, when eight-year-old Tyra complained about her "tush," her mom asked her a series of questions: "What exactly don't you like about it? Who are you comparing yourself to? Who has one you admire?" When Tyra mentioned her classmate Jamie, Mom asked, "What is it that Jamie does that makes her tush look better? Does she dress a different way?"

Tyra then said something unexpected: "Well, Jamie's popular. She's friends with Barbara, and they're both really good in gym." As it turns out, Tyra's problem wasn't just her "tush," but feelings about her athletic skill—which was something Mom could help her improve.

To be sure, there are times when it's important to support a child who wants to change something about her body, but try to get the child to focus on what her body *does*, rather than what it looks like. Talk in terms of qualities, such as strength, agility, flexibility, speed. Increasingly, even adult experts—for example, managers of health clubs and spas—are beginning to stress fitness, not weight.

Reframe the obsession. As I discussed in chapter 1, "reframing" is a way of presenting the same problem in a new light. This is a technique used by family practitioners and hypnotherapists—and parents can do it, too. One tack is to relocate the problem, as Tyra's mom did. By making Tyra's complaint interpersonal ("Who are you comparing yourself to?") and specific ("What is it that Jamie does that makes her tush look better?"), Mom made the problem manageable and changeable. It was no longer a huge, hopeless thing; rather, something Tyra could work with.

Another type of reframing is to subtly relabel an unkind description with less cutting language. Indeed, many parents do this intuitively, sensing what researchers have begun to document: Language influences children's perception about their bodies. Without directly challenging your child's feelings, you can substitute other everyday words that are far less destructive. For example, a child who thinks she's too "big" or "fat" can be called "solid" or "muscular." One who complains about being too "skinny" or "thin" might find a new perspective with the label "slender" or "slim." In addition to using different adjectives, remember that it's good to talk about what the child's negatively perceived body can *do* in real life. Reframe, but always base the new description on your child's real assets. For example, with a tall child, you might offhandedly mention what an asset height is in sports, for reaching the top shelf, or seeing above a crowd. A short child may be flexible and, therefore, good at dance or gymnastics or wrestling. Skinny children might be more agile.

Take a realistic action. If your child is stuck in an obsession, taking the above steps gives you a shot at getting through to her. The finale, however, should be a suggestion for some kind of concrete and realistic action. For example, in Elliott's case, his mother brought in a teenage consultant—a gentle, kindly boy who lived down the block. Hearing Elliott's "big ears" dilemma, the boy immediately had a great suggestion: "Why don't you just let your hair grow a little, Elliott?

TAKE A BODY TRIP

Ask any adult you know, including yourself, whether they enjoy looking in the mirror. Many of us don't, because we obsess about various body parts. Help your child develop more positive images by taking a little body trip with him or her. Stand in front of the mirror together, and slowly move your eyes from the top of your heads to your toes. As you take your journey . . .

Each of you will silently linger on the features you like and make a mental note of the ones you don't prefer.

Exchange thoughts out loud about your favorite and not-so-favorite spots.

Help her see good features she might have overlooked, like a great smile or a clear complexion.

Talk in a good-natured way about whatever features you don't like and encourage your child to do the same about his.

This exercise is to be used between bouts of negativity—to strengthen Body Comfort, or just to stay positively in touch with your bodies.

That way, people won't even see 'em." This simple, realistic action changed Elliott's experience dramatically.

It also illustrates two important points: First of all, camouflage is often a great solution for many perceived body issues. For example, certain styles, colors, and patterns can conceal extra pounds or other body differences that make a child self-conscious. Helen, a chubby girl who began to wear looser styles and more muted colors, felt slightly more comfortable in school. Also, carefully chosen older children can be great consultants because they understand other children's cruelty, and not so long ago many of them have "been there." They're more likely to see a workable solution than we are.

Even if you think a child's complaint is completely irrational, when you unpackage it as I've suggested above, you will invariably find some small aspect on which your child has based his or her feelings. If you can break his distress down to that small bit of truth, you can almost always find something to do. For example, remember Penny, whom you met at the beginning of this chapter? She was distraught about her legs, but her mom didn't see anything wrong with her daughter. Still, she didn't fight Penny when she complained about her "fat thighs." Instead, she allowed her to wear longer skirts and dark tights.

B. J., a child who was skinny, but not horribly so, thought he looked "weak" and, therefore, tried to hide his physique. His mother thought that the oversized shirts he constantly wore looked silly. She was particularly upset because even at the beach on a sweltering day, B. J. refused to take off his shirt. But instead of fighting with B. J., she let go of *her* need to have him look a certain way. She understood that when B. J. had to wear a tight shirt or, worse, walk around without a shirt, he felt bad about himself.

With all complaints about body image, whether they seem irrational or have a basis in fact, it's important to notice whether your child continues to ruminate. If allowing her to dress in clothes that help conceal the alleged problem doesn't help, and she seems to become increasingly obsessed, it's a good idea to take your child to a counselor who specializes in body issues.

What else you can do at home to promote Body Comfort

As I said earlier, because parents are also affected by the cultural preoccupation with looks, we tend to pass it on inadvertently to our children. Therefore, we need to keep an eye on how *we* feel about our own bodies and what *we* do at home. The following parent skills will help.

Praise your children for brains, abilities, and social competence as much as for the way they look. An article I wrote for *McCall's*, "Looks Matter," struck a chord with many people. One of the keys I stressed was to monitor your comments to children. Pay attention to a variety of interactions. For example, count how often you say, "You look great"—a comment formerly made to girls, but now more and more to the boys as well. Compare that with the number of times you compliment a smart observation your child makes or how imaginative he is in fantasy play.

If you can't keep a mental track of your patterns, keep a log to increase your own awareness. Start when your child is three or four.

Avoid repeatedly saying things like "Doesn't he look cute?" What he learns from such comments is that you value looks over more substantive qualities, which will do nothing to strengthen his core.

Associate food with nurturing and good times. So often we busy parents grab food on the fly. A recent survey reveals that only half of our teenagers eat dinner on a regular basis with their parents. Even worse, 66 percent of Americans watch television while eating dinner. Setting aside for a moment the fact that rushed or distracted dining doesn't do much to promote conversation or family togetherness, it also makes it difficult for children to really tune into themselves or to have a positive association with eating. When children shovel food in unconsciously, they don't sharpen their taste buds, and they don't know when they're full.

You may not be able to eat together every night, but at least turn off the TV during dinner, and try to create a relaxed atmosphere at mealtimes (see box on the following page). Avoid food battles; never force a child to eat. Also, plan meals with the kids, and discuss what kinds of food are nutritious. To expand his palate, expose your child to different types of foods: Cook with him—and, when he's old enough, give him a chance to prepare some of the family meals. Talk about delicious food combinations, even about presentation. Discuss the chemistry of food—how flavors and textures blend, how different methods of cooking produce different effects and tastes. Use cooking to reinforce other skills, like following directions, sequencing, and computing (amounts).

Having a healthy relationship with food will also nourish your child's core. Food, after all, is synonymous with nurturing—it isn't simply a collection of vitamins and nutrients that fuel her body. Unfortunately, eating disorders have given food a bad name, and some parents purposely shy away from food-focused activities. But I know many adults who relish their love of food, who see cooking as therapy—and who use both in very healthy ways to comfort themselves and to lift their spirits when the going gets rough. And I know children who have lasting connections with their parents around food. Candy, the divorced mother of two twentysomethings, religiously made mealtime a treat for her daughter and son when they were growing up. She told them how she concocted various dishes and encouraged them to cook with her. Adults now, her children are excellent cooks who regularly call home for recipes. Most important, because food has been a

A DOZEN IDEAS FOR MORE ENJOYABLE MEALS

Following are suggestions gleaned from a number of recent studies and from veteran parents whose children have healthy attitudes around food.

1. Help a child eat by sitting next to him, rather than opposite, which is too intense and watchful.
2. Offer surprising selections to finicky eaters—a pizza for breakfast; cereal for dinner.
3. Go for good snacks—fruits and vegetables; try to serve no later than two hours before lunch or dinner.
4. Offer a buffet with a half dozen healthy choices.
5. Serve unfamiliar foods cooked in different ways; if rejected by your child, wait a month or two before trying again.
6. Learn your child's eating pace—some graze; others devour. Moderate meals by setting limits on time.
7. Don't make a big issue of using silverware properly, especially with little ones; it's not worth the fight.
8. Serve small portions; children can then ask for more.
9. Go with reasonable food idiosyncrasies, such as "My mashed potatoes and peas can't touch."
10. Once a week have a "special" meal or a theme dinner. One mother declared "Pig Night," when everyone was allowed to eat without utensils.
11. Don't make dinner a time to remind, lecture, or constructively criticize.
12. Have family meals as often as you can manage without losing your patience.

thread of continuity and nurturing in that family, both children have grown up with very healthy attitudes toward eating.

Start early to educate your child about her body. We parents sometimes have difficulty discussing sexuality. However, all children have sexual feelings and interests, regardless of how we feel about it. It's not as if we put ideas into their heads! And the bottom line is that *not* discussing sexuality works against Body Comfort. Don't be surprised when your child exhibits erotic behavior—touching himself, showing interest in another person's body, even sex play is normal. In a recent study conducted by Dr. William Friedrich at the Mayo Clinic, researchers asked mothers to note common sexual behaviors in their children. Over 60 percent of boys aged two to five and nearly 43 percent of girls touched themselves, roughly 26 percent of both genders try to look at people when they're nude or undressing, and 42 percent try to touch their mothers' or other women's breasts. Predictably, these observable sexual behaviors—what mothers *see*—decreased after age five, when children become more modest and discreet. In any case, the researchers concluded that those are but a few examples of normal curiosity.

Every family has its own code of privacy, and parents have varying degrees of comfort around discussions of sexuality. It's important to assess your own values in this area. If you're uncomfortable about sexuality, take steps to put yourself more at ease. Read books; ask other parents how they handle questions such as "Why does my penis get big?" Psychologist Anne Bernstein, author of *Flight of the Stork,* also suggests role-playing with an adult, taking turns asking and answering different questions. Indeed, if you make these discussions seem routine, your child will not only feel more comfortable about her everchanging body, she will come to you with questions and problems as they arise.

As much as possible, avoid struggles at home about your child's appearance. Many times, children's obsessions with their own looks are rooted in an incessant struggle at home over matching clothes, appropriate outfits, and correct fit. Everyone holds Mom responsible for how her child looks, so it's understandable that many mothers feel some concern, even tension. Still, making ordinary, everyday comments such as "Let me flatten your hair down," "Those pants don't match your shirt," or "You can't go out looking like *that*" transmit a very powerful message about your own insecurities.

Take body slurs seriously—don't allow them in your home. Children can say cruel things to one another, but almost none sting like those that attack a child's appearance. If two siblings are playing together or if your child is hanging out with a friend, and one calls the other "fatso" or "four-eyes" or "shrimp," take it seriously. Treat it as you would a racial epithet. In our appearance-conscious culture, those kinds of words can really injure/harm a child's core.

RAISING SEXUALLY HEALTHY CHILDREN

A sexually healthy child is one who has learned enough at home not to have to rely on friends or the media for information. Here are the points most experts suggest you remember:

• Make discussions of sexuality a normal part of family talks and start early—children between ages four and six start developing sexual awareness and curiosity about gender, although some will begin asking questions earlier.

• Call body parts by their right names. It's better to say "vagina" and "penis," rather than "private parts."

• Listen carefully to see what your child is *really* asking about—and then answer only what she asks. It's always better to dole out the information in several mini-conversations.

• Teach her the difference between good touch and bad touch and let her know she has the right to say no to unwanted advances and ask for help when she can't.

• Don't fall prey to gender stereotypes, which limit children and can damage their emotional development. Remember that everything from your tone to the toys you buy help shape a child's attitudes.

• Don't react negatively to cross-gender play—a boy wanting to put on Mom's makeup, a girl trying to pee "like Daddy"—most outgrow it.

• Set limits without shaming: "I know you want to take your clothes off now, but when we're in the front yard, I want you to wear your shorts."

• At whatever age your child becomes sexually self-conscious and insists on privacy, allow it. And if *you* are sexually self-conscious, ask for *your* privacy.

If your child is the brunt of such an attack, explore the pain he's feeling. Ask him, "How did you feel when Stevie called you four-eyes?" Don't be afraid, as many parents are, of reiterating the hurtful words, and watch closely for your child's reaction. Remember that even if a child is of average build or looks, when a sibling or friend calls him "ugly," "fat," or "anorexic" (an increasingly common taunt nowadays), he *feels* the part—and the pain of the insult. If a particular child has been making repeated attacks, then you as the parent *must* act—by speaking with another parent, a school administrator, or anyone else who might have contact with the children.

Dress your child cute—not "cool"—for as long as you can. In the last decade, there has been an upsurge of designer clothes for kids. Magazine spreads dedicated to children's clothing feature kids who look like runway models—miniature adults sporting the latest in cool. Children and parents alike buy into what I described in chapter 5 as "the tyranny of cool." In fact, many parents opt for expensive labels that replicate those magazine images. Some fashion spreads also depict children in poses that make them look like pseudo-adults—the girls have a come-hither look, the boys sport a macho air. Unfortunately, David Elkind's the "hurried child" is also now both fashion-conscious *and* a child aping adult sexuality.

Stay in charge of what your children buy. We have to try to steer our children away from cool. One way not to get into battles with them is to begin early—as young as two or three—by giving them limited choices. In other words, take two shirts off the rack that you can live with, and let your child decide which one he wants to buy. This will give him a sense of independence and, at the same time, regulate his appearance.

Establish what you're willing to spend, and point out that he can either buy three cheaper pairs of jeans on this budget, or one expensive pair. A child might choose the expensive one but it will probably happen only once. Gail, for instance, blew her entire clothing allowance on an expensive designer outfit. After a day or two, when all the kids began making fun of her for never wearing anything else—suggesting, among other things, that she probably didn't take baths since she

---

MONITOR YOUR *OWN* COOL QUOTIENT

We often unconsciously wish for our children to be like us, or we live through them, wishing them to be like we wanted to be. So, watch out! If you're a fashion plate, or a wannabe, or even if you're just desperate to have your child fit in—maybe because you didn't as a kid—unwittingly, you may be exerting subtle pressure on your child to be "cool."

never seemed to change her clothes—Gail learned a hard and lasting lesson.

It's infinitely easier to have a cap on a child's clothing allowance if you shop once a season. Tell your child, "We're going to try to buy as much as we can for this school year/for the summer." When you're shopping, take time to offer some shopping tips; for example, point out the meaning and differences between prices, labels, fabrics, durability, and practicality. All these concepts are teachable and the sooner you begin, the sooner your child will become a savvy shopper—more interested in quality than cool.

It's not only important to limit spending but also to insist that children put some of their own money into clothing purchases. I overheard a girl in Kmart saying, "But, Mommy, it's so expensive. I don't want it." Shocked at such levelheadedness in a preteen, I remarked to her mother, who promptly told me a family secret: Her daughter had to pay for some clothing purchases out of her own allowance. Start around early elementary school, at which point your child can develop greater awareness about handling money and making decisions about allowance. This kind of responsibility encourages children to make more cautious and ultimately wiser choices.

Make moderate exercise a natural part of your family life. As the 1996 *Surgeon General's Report* on physical activity stressed, a sedentary lifestyle is unhealthful for any age person. On the other hand, we also know that overdoing exercise can lead to injuries or, if taken to an extreme, can indicate a body-image or eating disorder. Somewhere in the middle is the key to health and happiness—ours and our children's. The *Surgeon General's Report,* which recommends at least thirty minutes of moderate exercise per day, concluded that such a regimen enhances self-esteem, combats loneliness, reduces anxiety and depression, leads to better interpersonal relationships, and improves body image. In another study of two hundred women, 87 percent said exercise improved the way they felt about their bodies. In particular, those who had never exercised as kids realized for the first time that their bodies were valuable for what they can do. The same phenomenon happens with children: The more they use their bodies and see how, with practice, effort, and moderation, they can become faster, stronger, and more skillful, the less apt they will be to concentrate solely on appearance.

The trouble is, many of our children are couch potatoes. According to the *Surgeon General's Report,* among young people aged twelve to twenty-one, 50 percent are not vigorously active on a regular basis, females are even less active than males. High school enrollment in daily physical education classes dropped from 42 percent in 1991 to 25 percent in 1995. And one particularly alarming study found that 40 percent of children ages five to eight exhibit at least one risk factor for heart disease—everything from high cholesterol to high blood pressure to being overweight. In contrast, children who exercise regularly have fewer chronic health problems, they're able to meet the daily demands of physical activity, they do better in physical performance tests, and they have a stronger self-image—more confidence. So start young. The best way to get your child moving is to set a good example. Invite your child to play games, go running, join you on walks, go sledding, dance, bicycle, jump rope, hike, swim.

Remember to concentrate on the positive aspects of exercise—like family participation and fun. Avoid discipline and regimentation—make exercise enjoyable, not a chore or an arena in which children feel they must excel. Equally important, help your child figure out what kind of exercise suits her, based on her tastes, her talents, and her body type. As children get older, and become involved in specific sports or recreational activities, help them set realistic short-term and long-term goals. For example, if you have a child who has been sedentary, start by doing a few minutes of stretching to limber up. Then take a ten-minute walk with him, or go out and play catch for a few minutes. A longer-term goal might be that he'll be able to touch his toes and build up his endurance so that he'll be able to play a half hour of a sport.

Model nonobsessive attitudes. This is an ironic use of the word "modeling," but I obviously don't mean posing for a fashion layout. The truth is, what we say in passing has an extraordinary impact on our children. Thelma, a woman I work with, remembers her mother always calling her into her bedroom before parties or family get-togethers to ask, "How do I look? Are you sure I look okay?" These insecure questions left a tremendous impression on Thelma—and as a result made her much more self-conscious about her own appearance.

Another parent, Al, was stymied as to why his "boy-boy," six-year-old Dwayne, seemed obsessed with looking great. I helped Al become aware of his own behavior: He constantly beat himself up over his growing paunch and thinning hair and made self-deprecating wisecracks. "Don't you think that might be having an impact on Dwayne?"

HEALTHY EXERCISING

Your child is probably exercising for the right reason and will more likely stick with the program if he or she . . .

Exercises for health, not to have a "better" body.

Isn't criticized or lectured or embarrassed by an adult or an older sibling.

Chooses an exercise or sport she truly enjoys, rather than something other kids are doing or what you want them to do.

Understands what various types of exercises do to and for his body—lifting weights builds muscular strength, running builds cardiovascular endurance.

Sets realistic goals based on her body and what it can do.

Keeps changing the goals to reflect his ever-improving performance.

Doesn't get discouraged if one day her performance is under par or if she's not meeting a particular goal fast enough.

Is praised for trying and improving, rather than for attaining a particular goal.

Learns how to reward himself after exercising with a healthy snack or a hot bath.

Understands that exercising is not a chore, a punishment, or a necessary evil—but a lifelong joy.

I asked. When Al grasped this, he started to restrain himself around his son, keeping his own body concerns to himself. In addition, Al took ownership of his attitude by saying to his son, "I've been worrying about this gut, but I should be exercising instead of complaining." Thankfully, Dwayne was still young enough to be nudged away from his budding looks obsession.

Ask yourself: What do *you* typically say when you look in the mirror or get on the scale, when you try on a bathing suit or contemplate going to the beach? If you're down on your own appearance, it's un-

LOSE THESE COMMENTS

Keep a lid on . . .

Comments about your child. It's one thing to try to help a child look good and wear clothing that becomes her, but avoid comments like "Pull in your stomach" or "Wear darker colors so you'll look thinner." Such remarks clearly reinforce body *dis*comfort.

Comments about others. On Grandparents' Day, Marla's grandmother was introduced to her principal. Afterward, she whispered in the ten-year-old child's ear: "That woman is fat. There's got to be something wrong with her to be so overweight." Marla, who really loved her principal, was totally confused.

Comments about yourself. Maybe *you* can take self-deprecation in stride, but your child can't. Even absentminded comments leave their mark. A mother says, "I can't stand my thighs." A father complains, "I gotta do something about this gut." Before either parent realizes it, their children are hung up on their bodies, too.

Comparisons about yourself with other people. Even if they're not said directly to a child, seeming throwaway remarks have an impact: "Do you believe the way Julie looks? She hasn't gained weight in twenty years. I've put so much on, I look like I'm ten years older than she is."

fair—and potentially harmful—to worry aloud in front of your children. We know from clinical experience that when a hypochondriac goes on about her health in front of even young children, this behavior makes its way into the next generation as well. The same is true for preoccupations about body looks. Children end up having similar worries or more modern versions—like body piercing!

However, if you do have an obsession, it's important to be honest and admit the truth to your child. For example, dark-haired Liza, six, said to her mother, "I don't like my hair. I want *blond* hair." Her mother answered, "I understand that feeling. So many of the girls on TV are blondes. That's something that has bothered, me, too, since I was your age. And, lately, you've probably heard me talking about getting rid of this gray in my hair. Maybe I've been talking about it too much. The truth is, no matter what color my hair is, I'll be the same person inside."

Child Goals: Loving Their Bodies, Loving Themselves

During the writing of this book, I described the various core attributes to my then eleven-year-old daughter, Leah. She had no trouble understanding or agreeing with the importance of helping children develop Passion, Peer Smarts, or any of the other Basic Skills. But when I said the words "Body Comfort," her immediate reaction was "Yeah, like that's really possible." She speaks, I'm sure, for so many of her peers. Children today know that just about everyone has some degree of discomfort about their bodies, and the idea that you could master or get beyond those feelings is farfetched. And, to some degree, they're correct: Children are so vulnerable, they can't develop the skills that promote Body Comfort without our input and without our grasping that this is a constant, ongoing process—a battle against not only the culture but, as I've pointed out above, our own difficulties in this area as well. For that reason, I call the following child *goals*—they're not so much skills but attitudes that require parents to regularly check in. Many of them involve body acceptance and consumer savvy, but children can't master these goals without at least our indirect help.

Trusting their bodies

Nowhere is it more important for a child to trust his gut instinct than when it comes to knowing what his body needs. Children who diet or are food-phobic are often children who haven't learned to trust their own bodies, or they're walking around with a head full of misinformation. As I point out in chapter 8, when we let children think for themselves, they learn to trust their judgment. Encourage your child to see that feelings of hunger, thirst, fatigue, hot and cold, are ways our bodies "speak" to us.

Throughout the span of childhood, kids' appetites wax and wane. They eat more, for example, before a growth spurt. When a parent criticizes a child for too much of an appetite or forces her to eat when she's not hungry, that teaches her not to trust herself. In contrast, when parents pay attention to what children say about foods, their likes and dislikes, their pace of eating, the extent of their appetites, then kids learn to have confidence in their own judgment and taste. As

I discussed in chapter 1, children, even infants, can self-regulate—that is, they will give us an accurate report of what's going on in their bodies . . . if we let them.

Children can also get the wrong messages about food from parents and, sometimes, from school. Nutritionists repeatedly point out that there's no such thing as a "bad" food. Any food can be "good"—it's excess that's bad. Arm your child with information about good nutrition, and help him learn to eat a truly balanced diet. Children, especially girls, are more likely to resist food fads and dangerous diets if they understand how food really affects their bodies.

Dressing for themselves

Trusting their bodies also affects children's clothing choices. When shopping with your child, therefore, stress comfort as much as style— the fabric and the way it feels on her body. "We want to buy you clothes that make you feel good," Alvin's dad said to him when he was only four. An Intense/Sensitive child by nature, Alvin complained that certain materials were "itchy," so his parents helped him find materials that were comfortable. What started out as a function of his temperament blossomed into a confidence-building skill. Alvin, who is now nine, has developed a style of his own; he knows what he likes and what he doesn't. And he seems quite oblivious to fads or the latest in designer jeans.

It takes courage for a kid to dress for himself, rather than just follow the herd. I've observed, though, that behind every child with a "look" of her own is a parent who regularly praised her individuality. I asked Cassie, a girl in fifth grade and the only child who didn't opt for that gangsta-rap baggy pants look, "How is it you dress in such a unique way? You're different from most of the other kids, but you seem so comfortable anyway." She answered without missing a beat: "I kinda had my own ideas about what to wear, and my parents almost always said it was okay."

Some children, like Jeffrey, prefer certain colors. For whatever reason, he fell in love with a red polo shirt when he was two and cried if his mother tried to put anything else on him. Instead of burdening him with *her* response ("How could you want to wear the same thing everyday?"), his mother went with his taste and simply bought four of the same shirt! Jeff outgrew his obsession with red, and in its place was a growing confidence in his core taste.

At five years old, Michelle was very particular about mixing colors;

she clearly favored certain combinations. For example, she'd never wear brown pants with anything but a blue striped shirt. Her parents didn't necessarily agree with her taste, but they didn't battle over it. Instead, they went with it, increasing the likelihood that Michelle would become not necessarily a fashion plate, but at least self-assured in her ability to select clothes based on what felt right to her.

Making independent choices

So often, I hear kids in stores ask, "Which one do you like better, Mommy?" Parents usually answer immediately, *telling* a child what to do. But kids must slowly learn to make independent choices. Here's how:

Help your child exercise her judgment. Explain the principle: "Color and taste come from inside you. I can't tell you what will feel better on your body and what will look best through your eyes." On every shopping expedition, encourage your child to exercise this new "skill." Let her choose—on her own—at least *one* inexpensive outfit. It will make her a better consumer if she "owns" her purchases rather than depending on you.

Of course, kids go through stages of confusion about clothing, or they get stymied by a special kind of purchase—say, a party outfit. Sometimes, we have to help out more than others. But most times, within your budget, tell them to go with what they like. Besides shopping, use other opportunities as well. For example, when preschoolers Laura and Sandy were playing dress-up, Laura came to her mom and asked, "Which outfit looks better, Mom?" Without sounding too much like a therapist, Mom turned the tables: "Which one do *you* like, Laura?"

Though we sometimes want to impose our taste, it's important to help children around these issues without being too heavy-handed. Otherwise, they'll never learn to make their own decisions—not only about clothing and food, but also about what they can do with their bodies. For instance, your child might want to try a sport you don't think she has the athletic skill to handle. Unless it's dangerous, let her try—you might be surprised. Or if your child suddenly develops a taste for a spicy food he's eaten at a friend's house, perhaps you can both learn how to cook the new dish.

However, if you see that your child is about to make an unwise or impractical choice, step in gently and in ways that at least validate some of his thinking. The night before his first day of kindergarten, for example, Matthew was laying out his clothing with his mom. He wanted to wear a heavy sweater that his grandma had bought him. Not wanting to discourage him from selecting his own daily clothing, she told him, "What a good idea that will be in a few months when the weather gets colder. You look great in that color and I know you like the way it feels on you. How about picking a shirt or sweater that's not so warm for tomorrow?"

Being savvy about what they see

You can help your child appraise the media as a soapbox, instead of allowing unrealistic images to excessively influence him. Sit with your child and teach him to become a more critical viewer. For example, point out how large people are portrayed negatively and talk about the attributions we all make about size and shape. To that end, psychologist Mary Baures founded Boycott Anorexic Marketing, a group that takes aim at companies using superskinny models to hawk their wares. Dr. Baures advises parents to encourage kids to ask a different kind of question when they see images that are impossible (and undesirable) to emulate. Instead of their wondering, "What's wrong with me?" we need them to ask, "What's wrong with this ad [or TV show or movie image]?"

Help your child realize that not everything he sees on TV is true. Some progressive schools are beginning to design assembly programs around these themes—for example, inviting teen models to come in with before and after pictures, and talk about what they do; also, special-effects and makeup artists explain how they "fake" full-blown hair or use various kinds of makeup to transform people.

It's heartening to see that these programs aren't just geared for girls. Male models talk about how many hours it takes in a gym to develop buff bodies. And to the often-puny boys who hear these guys, it's a relief to learn that it requires the kind of narrow dedication and commitment unappealing to most youngsters. Those great bodies are not symbols of real manhood.

These lessons transform kids' views of what they see. After Erica heard such a program at her school, she responded quickly when her brother, Tim, exclaimed, "Whoa, baby, mama!" in response to a *Baywatch* babe on the TV screen. "Forget it, Chris," the savvy eleven-year-old said to her five-year-old brother, "Those aren't real!"

If your child's school doesn't offer such a dose of reality, do it yourself. Find books in the library on modeling and special effects. Encourage your child to talk to people in the beauty business to find out the inside scoop. And when you read magazines, watch TV, or go to the movies with your child, use the moment as a springboard to discussion: "Do you think that most girls [or boys] really look like this?" Get children to start talking about what matters to them. "Does any kid in your class really look like that?"

Always keep a sharp ear tuned to your child's comments about characters on TV. Like many other negative habits, obsessions about appearance are easier to prevent than cure. An Asian girl, Su Lee, at age four, said to her dad, "Jill looks like the Olsen twins on *Full House*. But I don't." Her dad, realizing that Su Lee was beginning to observe physical differences, wisely responded, "Jill looks like a lot of kids you see on TV. Many of them also have blond hair and blue eyes. And some have dark eyes and hair like yours. Both look good—so do you." Later, Dad noticed Su Lee staring at herself in the mirror, smiling.

Developing a passion

Although an entire chapter of this book is devoted to Passion, it bears mentioning here as well. The single most important *indirect* way of helping a child develop Body Comfort is for her to have a nonphysical interest, which has a tendency to crowd out preoccupation with appearance. The excitement, the involvement, and the thrill of having an enduring real-life pursuit is much more compelling than the latest fads and fashions. Also, as I explained, Passion is an esteem-builder. When a child feels good inside, his outside is less important. And it's often the children who feel good about themselves who also look best. It's not that they're necessarily good-looking by media standards, but their self-esteem communicates health.

Remember that Body Comfort is connected to virtually everything in our daily lives. Given the social pressures we live with, it is a major challenge to successfully promote this core trait. But it's well worth the effort. What a gift it is for a child to be comfortable in his or her own skin!

CHAPTER 8

CAUTION

———

Basic Skill #8: Encourage your child to think ahead and weigh the impact of her actions on self and others.

A Climate of Chaos: "Look Ma, No Hands!"

It starts innocently enough. A three-year-old boy, walking alongside his stroller, wants to cross the street all by himself for the first time. A four-year-old girl in a play group dares her friend to play a trick on a third girl: "Let's hide Mary's favorite teddy bear." A boy, age six, who has just mastered his two-wheeler cries out to his mother, "Look, Ma, no hands!" as he wobbles down the street.

In my work with schools and with families, I constantly come across situations in which children in everyday circumstances need to exercise Caution. Sadly, many kids lack this core strength. The three-year-old boy lets go of his mother's hand and bolts into the street. Luckily, no cars are coming. The two four-year-old girls put Mary's teddy bear under a bed, and when Mary can't find it, she is reduced to tears. Fortunately, one of the mothers steps in, soothing Mary and reprimanding the other girls. The six-year-old boy is so busy showing off on his bike, that he loses his balance. By the grace of God, he only ends up with a skinned knee and a wounded ego.

Throughout life, all children have to face first-time situations that require judgment and forethought. And let's not kid ourselves. We all talk about wanting our kids to be successful in school and good, tolerant human beings. But in our heart of hearts what we want most is for them to stay out of harm's way. This concern haunts us as parents. Will our children stay safe and have the good sense to avoid the numerous perils that life puts in their way? Indeed, if a young child doesn't learn how to exercise Caution, when he gets older, those not-so-serious everyday events can become dramatic, sometimes gravely dangerous circumstances. Here are some stories that often find their way into our local papers:

- As part of their celebration, a group of junior high graduates headed off to a steep cliff overhanging a stream and dared each other to jump in. One boy, who initially resisted because he thought it was too dangerous, broke his back.
- A twelve-year-old girl went to a no-parents party and, as part of showing how "cool" she was, drank ten shots of vodka and ended up in the emergency room, having her stomach pumped.
- A group of suburban boys cornered a handicapped child and raped her. Later, some of them claimed that the pressure of being in a group prevented them from either stopping the violence or walking away.

Granted, the above are dramatic and tragic incidents. But they are rooted in the same absence of Caution seen in more mundane occurrences: There is an inability to reflect on what's right or wrong, safe or dangerous. In fact, the last several years have seen a striking increase in Caution-related problems. Drug experimentation and binge drinking, after decreasing for a decade, since 1991, have shown double-digit increases every year. Kevin Dwyer, president elect of the National Association of School Psychologists, has observed increases in discipline problems and classroom disruptions. Therapists, too, note that they are seeing patients at younger and younger ages and that their problems have changed from self-contained neuroses, such as fear or anxiety, to behavior and conduct disorders that are marked by poor judgment, impulsivity, and acting out—in short, a lack of Caution. Indeed, the tragic and perplexing incidence of murder in junior high schools—four in 1998 alone—are indicative of a major problem with impulsivity.

At the same time, the pop culture conditions children and encourages them to react without thinking. By the time a child is twenty years old, he will have seen or heard 360,000 thirty-second TV commercials. As we've discussed throughout this book, these spots uniformly advise children to "Just do it," "Obey your thirst," "Consider no one," "Act now," and other messages that emphasize instant action and a minimum of meaningful contemplation. It's no accident that the late nineties ushered in a personality like Dr. Laura Schlessinger, whose book title, *How Could You Do That?* sums up the rampant problem of sliding scruples that enables people to justify any act. Ask young teenagers, thirteen to fifteen (as pollsters in Rockford, Illinois, did, see page 51), what their ethics are, and they reply, "If someone treats you well, then they deserve to be treated well back. If it doesn't hurt anyone else, it's fine." According to those teens, there are no absolutes.

As I asserted in chapter 6, we've become a "nation out of focus," the victims of cultural ADD. I would add here that we're also suffering from a related malady, cultural impulsivity, and we're seeing the repercussions in our children. Everything goes fast today and exhorts children to move quickly. They don't necessarily become "hyperactive"—chronically impulsive, constantly in motion, lacking in judgment. Still, this climate of chaos affects all children, hampering not only their ability to concentrate and pay attention but also to reflect, make judgments, and to look at big-picture issues.

Although Caution comes toward the end of this book, it's obvious that this core-builder is vital in today's increasingly dangerous world. Of course, if you foster the seven core qualities that you've read about thus far, your child will indirectly develop greater Caution. At the same time, thanks to new studies on the subject, we also know more about the way Caution specifically works—how kids think, how they approach new situations. And recent research proves beyond a doubt that there are specific strategies we can teach even young children to help them develop Caution. Moreover, this core skill is high on the list of parents I meet, who are concerned because kids seem to be growing up in a world where temptation and danger appear to lurk around every corner. Therefore, we need to look at what Caution involves and give our children the kinds of values and reasoning skills that will protect them.

Why Caution Is Important

Caution literally protects a child's physical, mental, and spiritual core. It provides your child with the ability to think and plan ahead, to consider consequences to oneself and effects of one's behavior on other people—that is, to have empathy.

Caution involves a delay of gratification. Caution means curbing the impulse to *do it now*. It also enables a child to come up with alternative solutions, which, we know from experience, reckless children cannot do. In fact, a 1994 review of seventy longitudinal studies, tracking children from preschool to their teen years, confirms this: The most consistent finding was that an extreme degree of impulsivity—a lack of Caution—predicted adolescent delinquency.

Caution is about handling first time situations. Caution, as I define it, relates specifically to the way children react and handle first-time, potentially damaging or dangerous situations. These include ordinary, everyday occurrences, as well as more extreme and difficult predicaments. Granted, children need to exercise Caution time and again, but here I talk primarily about unfamiliar, initial experiences because these are the formative moments/events. An uncomfortable or dangerous first-time situation may not get easier in subsequent encounters. But the way a child first copes with or approaches a new situation tends to set the tone for the future.

Thus, Caution is vital to a child's core. From the earliest years, you know you can't accompany your child at all times or help her deal with every "first" she has to conquer. You won't be there for every risk she's asked to take. In fact, some new situations can't even be anticipated. However, if your child is imbued with Caution, he will be safeguarded by remaining physically and psychologically intact. Caution also preserves your child's individuality, giving him the ability to defy a group impulse and still be with his peers.

Most important, when children develop this skill, they tend to gravitate toward other kids who exhibit a similar degree of judgment. You can see this in any situation in which children congregate. For example, as early as nursery school, risk-taking and impulsivity are organizing traits around which peer groups cluster. In every classroom in America—although teachers recognize that there are grays—they tend to identify children as being either "part of the wild group" or "one of the quiet ones."

Some are more cautious than others. What makes some youngsters more cautious than others? We actually have some surprising answers. With the rise of caution-related disorders over the last decade, "impulsivity" and "hyperactivity" have been much-studied conditions. We now have documentation suggesting that children are born with varying degrees of natural caution. The way a child approaches a new situation—a phenomenon researcher William Carrey calls "initial reaction"—is, like temperament, focus, or activity level, a matter of hard wiring.

It seems that some kids possess a tremendous amount of wariness. They look carefully at situations and don't move in until it feels safe. Some of these kids are vigilant to a fault. This too-cautious outlook often leads even young children into therapy, because they need to learn how to jump into life, rather than hang on the periphery.

At the other extreme, I see just as many children who seem to be predisposed to recklessness. Their parents inevitably report that they've been like this since they were babies. They're known for "getting into everything" as toddlers, jumping off high places, constantly taking risks, and using poor judgment. These kids get into accidents, trouble with teachers, and dangerous situations with peers. I've seen this in numerous nursery schools. In one, a band of three-and-a-half- and four-year-olds who called themselves "the pirates" delighted in hijacking and terrorizing their classmates. In another, the wilder boys were mimicking the movements and attitude of rap performers. Even at such young ages, the aggression and frustration are very close to the surface and tend to come out in dangerous ways.

Naturally, children at both extremes are at risk. When approaching a new situation, they need both a healthy dose of good judgment and forethought—not too much lest they end up paralyzed. But the truth is that *all* children—even those in the middle zone—need to develop good judgment. Particularly because so many kids today must handle new situations on their own and at earlier ages, we must equip them with Caution. Hence, our eighth Basic Skill.

Basic Skill #8: Encourage your child to think ahead and weigh the impact of her actions on self and others.

Whatever your child's *basic* predisposition, don't worry: Caution can be taught. We parents can arm ourselves with awareness and information and, in turn, give our children the tools to face these daily and constant challenges. Unfortunately, however, the climate of chaos will be working against us.

Core Threats: Mixed Messages from the Second Family

In the United States, impulsivity has become a widespread culturally reinforced state of mind, and it should come as no surprise that the second family brings the message home. Children from infancy on watch cartoons in which people routinely jump off cliffs and recklessly accomplish other feats of daring. In so many movies and television programs, children see conflict resolution based in fantasy and having nothing to do with real life—characters make snap judgments or come up with magical solutions. However, there are really two sides to this story—the second family and us.

The second family promotes cultural impulsivity. In the last decade, toys and games that inspire thinking or require delayed gratification have all but disappeared, supplanted by products that have little to do with judgment and more to do with reflexes. History professor Gary Cross observes in *Kids' Stuff,* an examination of this metamorphosis, that by the 1980s "play was divorced from the constraints of parents and their real worlds." He points out that toys which once prepared kids for life—or at least were rooted in America's past (cowboys) or present (space exploration)—now emphasize "unreal creatures, like dinosaurs equipped with laser beams."

Further describing this evolution, Cross writes, "Preschool play, once the realm of blocks, pull toys and teddy bears, now features junior versions of fashion and action play. Educational toys were increasingly marginalized. Even Lincoln Logs and Tinkertoys were edged off store shelves by fantasy playthings."

Of course, fantasy toys in and of themselves don't dampen judgment or conflict resolution, but they tend to distance children from the reality in their lives. An action figure may have an arsenal of options in tight situations, and allow a child to create his own story lines, but when it comes to judgment calls in the real world, a child needs to be able to reach for his own inner resources.

Add technology to this mix, and you see how this flight from reality can take an even greater toll on Caution. By the time an average child finishes elementary school, he has witnessed 8,000 murders on television, and by age eighteen 200,000 acts of violence. Television producers often rationalize such figures as "violence-counting," claiming that tallying up numbers of murders, beatings, and other vicious acts has no meaning. However, researchers at the University of California at Santa Barbara, who recently conducted a national study on violence in the media, say that the number of acts isn't the issue. They concluded that one of the main problems with violence as it's depicted on TV is that, 40 percent of the time, nothing happens to the perpetrator. Clearly, that's a wrong message to send kids who are impulsive.

Or just watch your child with a handheld video game or sitting in front of a computer. As I explained in chapter 1, researchers are just beginning to explore the effect of video games on kids' minds and behavior. We already suspect, however, that video games rev kids up, particularly children already prone to aggression. In fact, these modern-day playthings are virtually templates for impulsivity. They reward speed and quick reflexes—and, in the process, strengthen the purely reactive portion of your child's brain rather than his judgment or ability to reflect.

Taking off my clinician's and researcher's caps, I, like other parents, have witnessed firsthand the way video games juice kids up. In my own house, there's no question that as they start playing Supernintendo or Genesis games, my daughter and son may begin as loving buddies, but within half an hour, they start to fight.

Can I *prove* that this kind of transformation is caused by video games? No, but I certainly see it happen repeatedly, with friends as well as my own kids, and I hear it from other parents. Only recently, at a wonderful holiday party that could have come out of a storybook, I observed this phenomenon again. Because it wasn't a child-centered or theme party, the kids were slightly bored, although they were getting along well. Then, one of the kids unfolded his new "64" and said, "Let's play Nintendo!" Suddenly, the whole bunch were like horses at the starting gate, all pumped up and raring to go. And within fifteen minutes, they began to argue and one-up each other. Was this a coincidence? I don't think so.

In peer groups, rash thinking rules. Indeed, when I look at the level of impulsivity in the second family, I am reminded of master therapist Murray Bowen's description of a dysfunctional family as an "undifferentiated ego mass." That's a complex term for what is actually a very simple idea. In such families, Bowen observed, one sees high reactivity and "contagion"—feelings that dangerously and quickly spread—

as well as low numbers of clear-cut rules and a low degree of empathy. Members of such families tend to be intolerant of outsiders and exhibit little patience for and understanding of people beyond the tribe.

How different is that from the second family, particularly as kids get older—with its pack mentality, just-do-it ethos, and lack of concern for others? In a group of teenagers, for example, when a powerful member of the group reacts, it's hard for others to keep from mimicking him. Or if one child disagrees with a commonly held view, the other members get tremendously upset. Differences of opinion are seen as threats. It's as if the dissenter suddenly becomes an enemy.

But here's an important point—which may sound surprising, given the fact that for the last seven chapters of this book, I've issued repeated warnings about the second family. Though peer behavior and pop culture thrills work against Caution, in certain respects, the second family also has a number of resources that support this core skill. This leads me to a surprising core threat: us.

Parents abdicate, and no one is telling kids what's "right" or "wrong." Remember, as I discussed in the chapter on Respect, how much more parents and children need to speak with one another—but don't? Unfortunately, we're busy and rushed in our own worlds, and they're off in theirs. We certainly don't speak about the tough stuff, which, I'll have to concede, the second family does. In fact, the media tend to at least bring up morally questionable and dangerous behavior—certainly more frequently than we parents do! As a result, that's primarily how children today are getting their information about first-time issues and risky situations. Kid shows, like *Sesame Street*, talk about going to a new school, crossing the street for the first time, visiting new places. On numerous after-school specials and sitcoms—for example, *The Wonder Years, Full House, Saved By the Bell, Sabrina,* and *Boy Meets World,* to name a few—children are exposed to a catalog of first-time experiences that arise around friendship, dating, sex, and other social issues, as well as drugs, eating disorders, and divorce. The problem is that, in the name of good drama, the lion's share of the story lines on these shows is often devoted to portraying risky behavior as tempting. Only in the last few minutes does a character come to his senses and realize that his behavior is dangerous; only in the end does he find out alternative ways of coping.

Certain public-service announcements—most notably, the ad campaign underwritten by the Partnership for a Drug-Free America—exhort parents to pick up the ball: Start discussing—at home—drugs and other dangers. The unfortunate truth here is that they're right, parents still find it difficult to talk to their children about such issues. As one mother at a workshop admitted, "I *want* to talk to my daughter about how to handle that first make-out party, but I'm uncomfortable." Another said, "I don't want my son to think I don't trust him." And another, "I don't want to give her any new ideas." What's going on here?

We've lost our parental voice. A few decades ago, most parents simply *told* their children what they were allowed to do and what they weren't—and that was that. Parents rarely discussed these matters or explained how their children were supposed to meet their expectations. Then, the pendulum swung completely to the other side. Recently, I worked with a couple on a magazine piece. The ostensible "story" was about getting your child to bed. Their nighttime routine normally took the parents from two to three hours, which is probably why they volunteered for the article. The main issue, as it turned out, was not bedtime, but the couple's endless tolerance of their precocious three-year-old. In response to her somewhat Intense/Aggressive temperament, Mom and Dad allowed endless negotiation and wrangling over bedtime. The father explained his leniency with this rationale: "I want my daughter to grow up having her own thoughts and mind and to be able to speak up for herself."

This well-meaning philosophy, when taken to its extreme, is known as "moral relativism" or "situational ethics." It holds that there are no absolute rights or wrongs; every choice is determined in the moment based on each individual situation. In these last several decades, this position has become increasingly popular among parents who believe they shouldn't thrust their values onto children. Interestingly, our educational system takes a similar stance. In many schools, you'll find programs, under the umbrella of "values education," that teach children how to meet new situations through prudent thinking. However, some of these programs tend to arm children with conflict resolution skills without giving them actual content—values—as well. Because of the common assumption nowadays that it's "wrong" to teach absolutes or to impose beliefs, too many programs don't espouse concrete axioms about good and bad.

The problem with such a child-rearing philosophy is that it leaves kids at sea. Study after study shouts this message loud and clear: The

Johnson Institute in Minneapolis, which followed tens of thousands of children, found that kids of all ages "need clear guidance, absolute rules about impulsive behavior, such as drinking and drugs." In the *JAMA* study (see page 62) as well, researchers found that clear expectations protect kids from risky behaviors—drugs, early sexual behavior, and impulsive acting out. Certainly, the absence of a sense of absolute right and wrong in our adolescents indicates this guidance is precisely what's missing in our impulsive culture. Children of all ages need a strong parental voice to anchor them.

We help anchor children by dispensing home-grown wisdom and common-courtesy advice—it's not right to take toys from other kids; it's not good to tell secrets; it's wrong to hurt another child's feelings; it's not wise to always follow the pack. In the families I've known and worked with over the years, those children who fare best under pressure have carried a clear voice in their heads from the time they were very young. This voice is louder and more urgent than the competing forces of the moment—their peers, the influence of group dynamics, the various temptations of pop culture. What they hear, of course, is their parents.

In fact, children will describe this by saying something like "I was about to gang up on that kid, but I could just hear my mom saying, 'That's not right.'" At one time, the parental voice was echoed throughout one's community; parents' beliefs were reinforced by other adults and by the local church or synagogue, community center, even the grocery store, where children were known and looked after. In the absence of a neighborhood safety net for our kids, a parental voice is more important than ever. Therefore, no matter how self-conscious it makes us or how disconcerting it feels to address certain issues, we need to help our children develop Caution.

Parent Skills: Fostering Caution

As numerous longitudinal studies show, children who stay safe learn that their parents are not only there to support them, but also to provide a set of beliefs and views that they can use as reference points. The following parent skills will help you cultivate the kind of relationship with your child in which you can get across your beliefs while you talk about first-time and dangerous situations before they arise. They will help you and your child problem-solve together, discuss situations after they occur, and, when necessary, come up with consequences that will help him or her be less foolhardy should a similar situation arise in the future.

Find the channel of "imagining" that works best for your child. In order to develop Caution, a child needs to be able to anticipate, and see ahead. However, true to the theme of this book, I advise you to look at how your child thinks. Find the channel by which he processes information and, in his mind's eye, "sees" best. Some children can connect to an emotional image, others to a visual or verbal one. Ask the kind of questions to which *your* child will most easily respond. For example, let's say your child is going to be in a first-time situation and won't have you to turn to for help.

- *When a child can best access emotional images.* Before four-year-old Peter's play date with a new friend, his mother asked, "How do you think you'll feel if you have to share all your toys?"
- *When a child can best access images visually.* Cheryl's best friend was having her tenth birthday party—a boy-girl event and one of the first out of her mother's supervision. A few days preceding the party, her mother asked, "Can you picture what kids will be doing at the party—maybe playing kissing games?"
- *When a child can best access images verbally.* On the last night of winter vacation for eight-year-old Kevin, his mother remembered the trouble he had gotten into with a classmate, Darrell, before the holidays. Darrell and some other boys ganged up on one of the kids, and Kevin insisted that he really didn't want to take part in the scapegoating. So, Mom asked her son, "Do you think you will still have trouble with Darrell?" When Kevin said, "Yes," she asked, "Can you imagine what he'll say to you to get you to gang up on that new kid again? What might you say back to him?"

Help your child develop a language of choice. In researching children's problem-solving skills and behavior, cognitive therapist Myrna B. Shure, author of *Raising a Thinking Child,* found that most nursery school children could only come up with one or two ways to attack a problem; some didn't even understand the concept of "different." She discovered, however, that among other techniques, word games, which stress difference and alternatives, were extremely effective. Not only did children improve their problem-solving ability, they also showed a decrease in impulsive behavior. Shure uses the following six word pairs to stimulate a young child's capacity to reflect and problem-solve.

- is/is not ("Is playing this game a good idea, or is it not a good idea?")
- and/or ("Should we go to the store and Grandma's or should we go to the playground?")
- some/all ("Can you eat some of the oatmeal in this pot, or can you eat all of it?")
- before/after ("Do you want milk and cookies before or after your bath?")
- now/later ("Shall we read this story now or should we save it for later?")
- same/different ("Do you want to wear the same color shirt as mine, or a different color?")

Shure's research indicates that if you start using these word pairs when children are as young as three or four, and they become accustomed to thinking about choice and difference on a verbal level, it will help them become better at problem-solving later on.

Children (and adults) need a language that will help them understand conceptually the dilemmas they're facing. Given this "language of choice," as I call it, children can practice how to make decisions. And, as Shure's research and studies using other cognitive behavioral techniques prove, they then are less likely to get into the kind of trouble that arises when they fail to think situations through.

For example, Tessie was able to help her four-year-old son, Wayne, choose whether he wanted to write a thank-you note for a birthday present, or call. Five-year-old Rose always had trouble getting dressed in the morning, until her father, Brent, started giving her a choice of dress or pants the night before; this made the next morning go more smoothly and helped Rose understand difference. Finally, obstreperous and messy Clark, nine, was more amenable to cleaning his room when his parents said, "Do you want to get it over with now or after we eat dinner?"

Explicitly tell your children what you think is wrong. Preparing kids to meet the world, to be safe in it, and to think through new situations is virtually impossible without letting them know what *you* think is right and wrong. As both the *JAMA* and Johnson Institute studies (see pages 62 and 218) demonstrate, when parents are very clear about what they believe, their children have better judgment and are less likely to exhibit high-risk behavior. In other words, when parents say explicitly, "I don't want you to _____ [steal, drink, kiss on the first date—you fill in the blank]," children more often end up *not* doing such things or doing them at older ages. In fact, what is most disturbing about the results of that Rockport, Illinois, survey is not the fact that those teenagers have made up their own morality, but rather that they did so without reference to any adults—their world seemingly lacks a parental voice.

As I stressed earlier in this chapter, we parents need to address moral issues, not shy away from them. The toddler needs to know that his mother doesn't approve of hitting as a way of getting a toy. The nine-year-old on a group trip to the museum who acts rudely toward the guide, or the preteen who is offered his first marijuana joint, both need to know that their parents don't approve.

It's easy for parents to abdicate this role, especially when so many others seem to be doing just that. Recently, for instance, my friend Vic recounted an incident in his suburban community that, I know, is typical throughout the country. His ten-year-old, Tara, and a group of her friends, all between nine and eleven, wanted to be dropped off at the mall and spend the afternoon there alone for the first time.

The parents dutifully got together and discussed it. "We were all sort of pussyfooting around the issue, saying things like 'I guess it's safe,' 'How harmful could an hour be?' and 'It probably will teach them independence.' All along, we were actually considering it, and letting our kids demand this from us. Suddenly, one of the mothers yelled out, 'I don't think this is right. Kids this age shouldn't be walking around a mall alone!' That brought the rest of us up short, but we knew she was right."

Vic's story is an example of how parents can waffle and waver on important issues. They don't mean to; they're certainly not "bad" mothers and fathers. In fact, many mothers and fathers are afraid they will "oppress" their kids with the clarity of their convictions. But as the latest research confirms, children who hear parents' beliefs are neither burdened nor confused by them.

Discuss solutions to first-time situations before hand. "Discuss" doesn't mean lecturing or simply saying, "It's wrong." You also need to state *your* beliefs and, in addition, ask your child questions that will make her think.

For example, four-year-old Lydia, who has demonstrated in other situations that she's already aware of her and other people's emotions, was scheduled for a play date with Juan, a new friend. Lydia's mom, Eileen, was aware that her daughter was sometimes bossy on play dates. So, she employed a preemptive maneuver, talking about what *might* happen before it actually did:

Mom:	Can you imagine what you will do if Juan wants to play his game?
Lydia:	I won't play.
Mom:	I know it's hard, but I believe it's important to take turns. How do you think that would make Juan feel to only play *your* game?
Lydia:	He'd be mad.
Mom:	I think you're right. Can you think of anything else you could do?
Lydia:	Play one game his way . . . and then it'll be my turn.

As the guidelines above show, the process is similar even with an older child—only the issues change. For example, when Ann, a visually attuned twelve-year-old, was about to go to her first "teen" party, this is the talk her mother had with her beforehand:

Mom:	Can you picture what you would do if kids started smoking?

Ann:	I might want to try it.
Mom:	(Instead of waffling) I understand. But I don't want you to smoke.
Ann:	Aw, Mom. . . . just a little puff? What's the big deal.
Mom:	No, not even that. I think smoking is dangerous and wrong. Can you picture another solution?
Ann:	Well, I could hang out with my friend who I know won't try smoking. Or we could just say we're not allowed.

Sort it out later. Of course, there's no guarantee that things will go the way you want. So it's very important to be able to discuss what happened after an event. But beware: Almost all children, regardless of their temperament, tell me that when parents try to extract information about a play date or a party, tone matters. It's really hard for kids to sort out their feelings, and when parents yell, grill, cross-examine, get hysterical, or lecture, they inadvertently teach children to *not* talk about difficult experiences.

Discussing first-time situations afterward stretches a child's thinking. You can help her learn the language of sorting out by asking certain kinds of questions:

- What if you had . . . ?
- Do you think, instead, you could have . . . ?
- Do you suppose . . . ?

This allows a child to think about other options in a noncombative, nonadversarial way. He can come up with alternatives, such as five-year-old Ben did when he pondered out loud with his mom how he got into trouble in the play area at kindergarten. Being visually oriented, Ben remembered the scene and said, "I could have gone to the teacher before I broke Gabby's toy." Again, the process is similar with an older child. Eleven-year-old verbally precocious Maddy reevaluated the following incident: A group of her friends shoplifted packs of gum at the local Kmart—and got caught. After thinking about it, Maddy realized, "Maybe I could have walked away. And even if my friends got mad, they wouldn't have said anything *that* bad."

Phrase questions in ways that promote reflection. When children don't exercise caution or judgment, parents tend to ask rhetorical questions like "Didn't I tell you it was wrong to hit?" or "Why did you do that if you knew I'd be angry?" Such questions not only lead to fights, they're also pretty much unanswerable. A child who exhibits reckless or thoughtless behavior doesn't usually know why. (No more than we adults always know why we do the things we do!) What is more, such questions offer little to increase self-reflection.

In contrast, even when a child is *contemplating* an action, and we ask answerable questions, it helps her reflect and, in turn, hone her judgment. As I stated earlier, the work done by Shure and other cognitive researchers proves that this approach encourages thinking. For example, if you see your five-year-old daughter about to go out without a coat in thirty-degree weather, ask (in a noncritical way), "What do you think will happen if you don't wear your coat outside today?" Even if this works, don't expect her to say, "Oh, thanks for reminding me." But remember that children as young as three or four are capable of such reflection—and, in fact, that's the best time to begin practicing with kids. If your question gets your child to stand still for a minute, and you see a flicker of acknowledgment in her eyes, that means her mental computer is probably whirring. You know that at least you've gotten her to *think* about the issue at hand.

Use experience to teach thinking. Let's say that after pondering for a minute, your five-year-old decides to brave the cold without a coat. View it as an expedition. You might say, "Okay, go out and see what the air feels like. Then tell me whether it is too cold to be out there without a coat." Chances are, the first blast of arctic air will bring her back inside—and she'll have had the experience of thinking through the problem and figuring it out on her own. Obviously, if your child wants to see what fire feels like or decides to climb onto the roof, you won't allow *that* experiment! However, when the consequences aren't serious, it's almost always a good idea to let experience be the teacher. This encourages children to problem-solve on their own.

Many experts agree that, except in dangerous situations, we cannot shield children from negative experience. As educator Mary Leonhardt, author of *Parents Who Love Reading, Kids Who Don't*, points out, "Handling small problems gives [a child] the self-confidence and self-esteem to be a well-functioning adult later in life." Infant researcher Jerome Kagan posits a similar view. After all, the reflective part of a child's brain is a "muscle" she needs to practice using and condition. Therefore, taking *some* risk is healthy—physical acts as well as trying new mental challenges.

For example, when six-year-old Patty had a fight with her friend, instead of rushing in with a solution, her mother, Victoria, asked, "What do you think you could do to make up with Sally?" Without directing her, telling her what to do, Mom listened to Patty's solution, which was to wait and not *do* anything. As much as she was tempted, Victoria didn't direct her daughter to do something more; she wanted Patty to experience whether her own solution would result in a satisfactory resolution of the problem—or not. As it turned out, Patty was right; Sally forgot their misunderstanding by the time they saw each other in school again. Had Victoria barged in with advice, it would have short-circuited Patty's experiential learning.

In the same vein, eight-year-old John felt the teacher picked on him because she asked questions when his hand wasn't even raised. It was as if she wanted to "catch" him not knowing the right answer. He was getting a lot of attention, but in his mind, for the wrong reasons. His dad asked pointedly, "What do *you* want to do?"

"I'm going to complain to Mrs. Farber during class," said John, after thinking about the problem for a few seconds. Knowing Mrs. Farber, Dad suspected that John's idea wasn't going to work. Still, he let it be and allowed John to try his own solution. In fact, John came back feeling even more put off by his teacher, so Dad went through the drill again, asking him what else he might try. By talking it out, John realized that Mrs. Farber never spoke to individual students during class. He then decided that next time, he would say something after school, when she was alone and less likely to be preoccupied.

Create consequences to encourage caution. When children don't "get" that an idea is bad or wrong or dangerous, parents need to remind them that there are consequences. We simply can't allow kids to treat themselves or others badly, to take undue risks, or to go against parental beliefs. Creating consequences will help your child know where you stand, which is particularly important around first-time issues.

Consequences delineate the outside boundaries of our values and beliefs and, as such, create security. In essence, you're saying to your child, "This is what I expect from you, and if you cross the line, this is the price you'll pay." Consequences are a child's safety net. As thirteen-year-old Dawson told me of his parents, "I wish they'd have some rules around the house because without them, there's a lot of chaos. Too much—chaos. That's why we need rules." For years, children in treat-

WHAT KIDS SAY ABOUT RULES

Privately, kids are pretty blunt about the necessity for rules and consequences. Almost every one of the 150 children I interviewed—at every age level—agreed that they feel more secure when their parents are clear about the rules. Here's a sampling of their comments:

"Someone should watch over me."
—Four-year-old boy

"I definitely don't want my parents to negotiate too much."
—Eight-year-old girl

"I feel better when my parents tell me what they want me to do."
—Seven-year-old girl

"I like Ms. Dawes 'cause the kids can't be bossy."
—Five-year-old girl

"She's a good teacher. Everybody has to raise hands.
—Six-year-old boy.

"I don't like that house; there's no one in charge."
—Ten-year-old boy

"We need consequences or we'll just keep trying to get away with things."
—Most frequent comment in groups of early adolescent boys

ment have made similar statements, but I recently got exactly the same feedback from a sampling of 150 "normal" kids in grades K through six whom I asked, "What do your parents do that make you feel good?"

Consequences—punishment—should always be tied to the incident in question, and geared toward teaching your underlying beliefs. For example, it could be as simple as telling a three-and-a-half-year-old child who has fallen off the monkey bars, "I know all the kids were going to the top, but you never have, and you didn't ask my permission. So, no more monkey bars until we practice."

Or suppose a preteen disobeys an after-school curfew: "You were supposed to be home at five. When we tell you to be home at a certain time, that's what we expect you to do. Now you can't go to the mall for the next two weeks."

Because creating consequences seems to be a tricky proposition for so many parents, allow me to sum up the important points to remember:

- Be brief.
- Speak to the point.
- Don't throw in added lectures about other transgressions.
- Don't criticize or make character judgments.
- Create consequences that are enforceable and tied to the rule-breaking behavior.

Help children develop a greater threshold for boredom. One of the indirect ways parents can help mediate their children's seemingly unquenchable thirst for arousal is, quite simply, to help them learn to deal with boredom.

- Emphasize long-term projects that can keep expanding and aren't instantly gratifying. Instead of your child's working on a single drawing, for example, suggest that he do a book of drawings over time, or undertake an art project that requires research, other participants, and a longer time to execute.
- Demand that she sit through church or synagogue services, some adult gatherings—anything that's not child-centered. Being quiet and contemplative requires practice; this skill develops as a child's capacity for boredom expands.
- Don't allow your child to endlessly interrupt. In fact, pay attention to times when he does. For example, many children interrupt adult conversation during television commercials. Absent electronic stimulation, they expect you to stop talking and pay attention to them—immediately.
- Don't plan one activity after another. As I pointed out in chapter 4, we unwittingly play into this problem by rushing here and there to keep our kids busy. Children don't need to be constantly stimulated. What they also need is to learn how to manage downtime.
- Limit the amount of time your child is involved with nonreflective technology—computer games, TV, headsets—so that she doesn't solely define fun as those impulse-driven activities. Also, don't keep replacing old games with ever-more-stimulating offerings.

Establish "review rituals" as part of your family routine. With our own and our children's hectic schedules, we can't always wait for quiet moments to come along. Life is so chock-full of activity, it's best to schedule a time to help children review their actions. I've learned from families in my workshops that there are all sorts of ways to set aside a routine time when family members can go over incidents that happened during the day. That way, children learn to express their emotions as they come up and negative feelings don't linger. The "how" and "when" of your review ritual may be very different from another family's. Still, there are several variables to consider:

• It should be a relaxed moment—one associated with pleasure. At the Grays, dinner is extremely leisurely—a natural time to talk. Yet, at the Davises, the same meal is an intensely pressured time—everyone's coming home, parents and children are cranky. Find out what's good for your family. The best moments, naturally, are those in which your child is most likely to be receptive.

• You can do it one-on-one with each child separately, or in a whole-family context, such as a regular family meeting. Which you choose depends on the dynamics of your particular family and how much time your collective schedules permit. Also, this may change as children get older. Certainly, it would be nice to think that everyone could have an *Ozzie and Harriet* kind of scene around the fireplace every night, but that often doesn't work—perhaps because two of the kids are really into sibling spats, or maybe because the nature of the problem that needs to be discussed is private. In those and many other cases, the only way to get a child to reflect and rethink a situation is one-on-one.

• A review ritual should not be a time to bring up past transgressions. Even if whatever is being talked about reminds you of something similar that's been happening, don't bring it up. For example, if your child starts discussing an argument with a friend in school that ended in a fight, it's not a time to talk about other fights or remind him of a forgotten chore. In other words, don't "kitchen sink."

Remember that the purpose of a review ritual is to face matters as they come up. Eventually, your child will get in the habit of doing his own mental review of his behavior—a hallmark of a child who has learned Caution.

Child Skills: Helping Kids STOP

The skills a child needs in order to develop Caution conflict with our climate of chaos and second-family ethics—the demand for conformity, the love of immediacy, the lack of reflection, and the disregard for others' needs and feelings.

Learning to STOP

Because children so often go on automatic pilot in this environment, I felt it necessary to create a simple, easily accessible tool. Quite appropriately, this one is called "STOP." STOP means:

Stand still
Think
Observe
Proceed

The strength of this approach is that a child can do it himself—in the moment. Also, it helps your child see that Caution, just like any other skill, requires practice and, in time, can be mastered.

Stand still urges a child to pause—stop. It tells him to take a moment before he acts. Being engaged in movement makes it difficult for anyone to think. Why else would we say exercise "clears" our heads? And if you've ever seen a child running, or doing any kind of physical action, you know how hard it is to get them to listen, no less reflect. Teachers understand this—and when they want students to pay attention, they clap their hands or blow a whistle, signaling that it's time to "stop" moving. Children simply can't think if they're in motion.

This is what I explained to Orin's mother, Celia, who brought her highly active seven-year-old to me because he so often seemed to "rev up" and get out of control. He inevitably broke something or hit another child. To stop this cycle, I suggested that Celia try to get him to stand still before she attempted a conversation with him or gave him directions. The next time Orin began to get overexcited, she literally stopped him in his tracks by placing her hands gently but firmly on his shoulders. Only when Orin's physical momentum was interrupted could Celia get her son to think about what he was doing.

Think makes a child reflect and try to predict consequences. Teach your child to ask himself questions, such as:

- "Is this wrong?"
- "Can I get into trouble for this?"

- "How will the other kids feel?"
- "Is this safe?"
- "What could happen to me?"

Even a four-year-old can begin to question himself in this way. For example, Adam was the only boy in his play group. When the kids were left alone, the girls asked him to pull his pants down. At first, he went along with them. It was a natural response for a child his age. When Adam told his parents about it, they didn't get too upset. With my encouragement, Mom and Dad tried to get him to think and to ask himself the above kinds of questions. Since Adam was so young, they also needed to reinforce their parental voice by clearly reminding him, "That was wrong of the girls to ask you to pull down your pants. Some things are to be kept private." Adam needed to be able to carry his parents around with him. The next time his playmates suggested that game, Adam was able to stop himself and say, "No, I'm not allowed. I don't want to play."

Observe inspires empathy and encourages your child to look at what others might be feeling. When three-and-a-half-year-old Lorna looks at another child's face, she is beginning to learn to ask herself, "What is *he* feeling?" At the same time, she also checks out her own feelings—her "gut," as it were. Some children's powers of observation are naturally high, but others don't automatically see potential dangers. Carolyn Zahn-Wexler, a researcher at the National Institute of Mental Health, who has studied empathy in infants, confirms, "Some children seem to be born with more empathy than others."

In any case, children can strengthen their intuition—throughout this book, I've talked about the importance of listening to their "gut" feelings. But I also must stress again, they need our help. How often do we hear kids (and adults) say, "I thought that was a bad idea, but I didn't pay attention to myself." Kids who are good observers not only trust what they see, they can also spot approaching trouble or danger. What should they be observing?

- facial expressions
- tone of voice
- the other child's emotions
- the other child's body language

For example, Greg, eight, who was involved in fun wrestling with his older cousin, observed that it was about to get serious when Warren's expression changed. "He looked mad and mean," he told his mom. "I knew he was going to hit me."

Even a four-year-old, Jenny, caught on and learned to observe people in her environment. After Mom had coached her to physically stand still and *look* at her classmates and teacher, Jenny reported, "Mommy, I saw that Mrs. Grimble was mad at how noisy the kids were. I sat down . . . so she didn't yell at *me!*"

Proceed reminds children that every day and in almost every moment, they have to make choices. The first three letters of STOP slow a child down and make her think and look. The "P" forces her to take a stand.

The "P" is also important because situations are like sharks—they keep moving. Children need to understand that they're responsible for what they decide to do. If they don't get this all-important choice-making concept, they'll become inveterate excuse-makers, who disown their decisions and spout off rationalizations and lies:

- "My friend made me do it."
- "I couldn't help myself."
- "It was my sister's idea."
- "My hand did it."

The point is, even if a child *chooses* to do a wrong or dangerous thing, it's not about having an argument with him over whose fault it was. He has to learn to accept that *he* did it—*he* took the action. What is more, age is almost beside the point. The research on cognitive development shows that even with a child who has just begun to talk and doesn't seem to quite understand, it's helpful to at least get him to start thinking about choices. In order to do this, remember:

- Wait for a quiet time. You can't get a child to own up to his responsibility if he's too excited, feeling terrible, or overly defensive.
- Ask questions to help your child identify his responsibility. They are similar to the questions I suggest to help a child sort out what happened, but they specifically remind your child that there was a moment when she actually chose to do what she did:
"When did you decide to do it?"

"What made you go along?"

"At what point did you think about saying no?"

"What if you had remembered that it was wrong?"

The aim here is to find quiet time to stress the fact that your child is responsible for his own actions. Children need to realize that they make decisions every moment during the day; they don't just get pulled along.

I remind you, once again: Try not to lecture or to bring the point home; let it be. However, it's okay to leave an impression that a child's in trouble because somehow he violated your ethics. Just make sure you state your value briefly; create a consequence tied to what happened; and, later, after feelings have died down, sort it out. Remember that the important aspect of this strategy is to make it your *child's* act, not yours. Over time, instilling Caution helps children internalize the parental voice and, ultimately, distinguish between right and wrong on their own.

CHAPTER 9

TEAM INTELLIGENCE

Basic Skill #9: Inspire your child to develop her capacity to be part of a group without losing her individuality.

"I" Versus "We": Maintaining the Balance

Most of us today are aware of a sea change in our culture: Being a team player now competes heavily with the time-honored tradition of making it on your own. Since the seventies, there has been a growing recognition that we are all part of some larger whole—the family, the corporation, the community, and, of course, the global village. But despite this trend, the eternal quest for uniqueness hasn't disappeared. To paraphrase a *New York Times* report on February 22, 1998, the tension between group cooperation and boot strap individualism is not going to go away.

The opposition between the two predominant cultural messages—"You're number one" and "Be a good team player"—naturally affects our children as much as it does us. The question then is, how do we help our children learn to be part of the greater whole and, at the same time, not lose uniqueness? The answer is to help them develop what I call "Team Intelligence."

Teaching children to achieve a balance between the "I" and the "we" is clearly one of the most difficult parental challenges of our times. I see evidence of this tension in kids of all ages, who are sent to me with problems that can be described as Team Intelligence issues.

• Yvonne, four, complains to her mother, "Patty and Ann always play make-believe together, but they don't ever ask me. I have good ideas, too, Mommy."

- Peter, six, a first grader in a progressive school, where almost every assignment is a team project, is having trouble moving from one group to the next if his part of the project isn't done to his liking.
- Carla, nine, comes home crying after soccer practice because the team captain accuses her of not cooperating. In truth, she doesn't respond well to the coach's teaching methods.
- Tom, seven, is often reprimanded for disrupting the class when other kids are speaking; and they don't want him in their work groups or on their teams.
- Rick, ten, always angers his friends because he "bends" the rules of whatever game they're playing to fit *his* views of fairness.

The parents of these kids are worried about them, and so are their teachers, who in the last ten years have increasingly referred such children to guidance counselors. Recently, in cities around the country, a new cottage industry has blossomed as professionals have begun to see the profit potential in therapy groups for children with problems in peer socialization. One counselor in a major metropolitan area, who hung out a shingle a year ago, already has six weekly groups whose aim is helping kids learn to work together without losing themselves. And that's just the tip of the iceberg. I predict we're going to see a tremendous increase in these groups—and a greater awareness of the importance of Team Intelligence.

Given the way our social lives and our schools are organized, it's not surprising that the challenge of balancing self and group has begun to appear at earlier ages. The 1991 report of the U.S. Bureau of the Census noted that over half of four-year-olds and 27 percent of three-year-olds were enrolled in educational programs prior to kindergarten. This is compared to only 16 percent of four-year-olds and 5 percent of three-year-olds in 1965. And the U.S. Department of Education notes that preprimary enrollment of three- to five-year-olds in day care has almost doubled between 1970 and 1994.

Teachers and parents urge these tiny tots to cooperate and collaborate, to be part of "the team" the minute they begin to socialize. Whether they are on the playground or taking part in "circle time"—a staple in just about every nursery school—the guiding principle is to be aware of the group. Even before school begins, there's an emphasis on teamwork in nationally organized activities like Gymboree— everybody holding the parachute together, taking turns, helping your partner.

The spread of progressive education has added to the emphasis on group participation. Montessori and Waldorf schools, as well as those modeled on the Bank Street School, rely heavily on teamwork and have greatly influenced early education. The "cooperative learning" movement, as it is called, has gotten good press. One survey of more than eighty studies concluded, "Children who learn cooperatively learn better, feel better about themselves, and get along better with each other."

Fast disappearing is the old educational model of straight rows of chairs with kids working in isolation. Experiential learning, popular in nursery and pre-K, involves children in group projects. In many schools throughout the country, elementary teachers employ a concept called "cluster teaching." Gathered around tables, students collaborate on everything from spelling to dinosaur dioramas.

Although I have been using "team" here in its broadest sense, the number of traditional teams has exploded as well. In the past, typical junior and senior high schools had, perhaps, a half dozen highly visible teams. Being a member was a mark of somehow being special, and the very notion of "team player" was associated with an elite group. Today, all of this begins early; it's not uncommon to see teams in kindergarten continuing through eighth grade and on to junior varsity and varsity. There are girls' as well as boys' teams, even some co-ed, and many more types of teams as well (math, art, computer, chess, debating, even boosters—teams that cheer for other teams).

In fact, in interviews I've conducted, school principals throughout the country repeatedly point out that the number of teams has increased dramatically. They report this with a mixture of pride and concern. They are glad that kids are involved and active; at the same time, educators worry that some children can lose their sense of individuality. My own experience leads me to share the principals' views. I've seen the difficulty children have trying to balance collaboration with having enough faith in themselves and trust in their own beliefs to go up against the group.

There is no doubt that our children will need Team Intelligence when they go out into the world. We now take for granted phrases that weren't in use when we were kids a few decades ago, like "team management," "global communication," and "cultural diversity." By the year 2050, 75 percent of the workforce will include people of color, according to Derek and Darlene Hopson, coauthors of *Raising the Rainbow Generation*. For this reason, 40 percent of American corporations already have some sort of diversity training in place. In short, today's worker, whether she's on an assembly line or in a boardroom, has to have a mind of her own *and* be a team player.

Your child is faced with a similar reality. Team Intelligence will see him through his school years *and* prepare him to be a citizen of the global village of tomorrow.

Why Team Intelligence Is Important

Besides preparing children to function in this fast-changing culture, Team Intelligence protects a child's individuality—his core. On the one hand, this core-builder solidifies a child's sense of himself. He knows that while it's important to cooperate, one should never give up one's core beliefs. On the other hand, because Team Intelligence involves learning how to sustain himself while being part of a group, it also provides an antidote to the pack mentality of the second family. Children who possess Team Intelligence are able to put aside their selfish, immediate needs for the good of the group and for longer-term gains.

Team Intelligence strengthens empathy. Team Intelligence enhances a child's capacity for empathy. As she begins to play with other children and, increasingly, is called upon to manage herself in group settings, she needs to be able to tune into others as well as tuning into herself. And she must learn to remain true to her own convictions while recognizing another child's feelings.

Research indicates that children are capable of responding empathically to other children at astonishingly early ages. For example, researcher Carolyn Zahn-Wexler reports that within the first year of life, a baby is capable of distinguishing his own cry from that of another child or adult. And some one-year-olds are capable of offering comfort to adults who display hurt. Sibling research confirms these findings. Child-development expert Judy Dunn, at Pennsylvania State University, who has conducted numerous studies on siblings, notes that well before the age of three, children are "skillful at reading and responding to the feelings and plans of siblings." A survey of the sibling studies shows that children as young as four months can develop rapport with an older child; by ten to twelve months, many babies actually miss absent siblings and exhibit delight upon their return.

However, a child's fear of ridicule or criticism can impede his natural tendency to be sensitive and supportive. It is truly a sign of Team Intelligence—and a developmental milestone—when a child can maintain his empathy in the face of group pressure and act on his better instincts. For example, three-and-a-half-year-old Lester noticed the pained expression on a little girl's face and was able to stop himself from joining his playmates' taunting. And in a public school, when five-year-old Lauren realized that some kids were hiding and noticed the worried expression on her teacher's face, she was courageous enough to step forward.

That Lester was able to say to his buddies, "She's gonna cry . . . I think we should stop, because it's not nice," means he has the capacity to hold on to his own idea of what's right in the face of peer pressure. That Lauren didn't worry about the other children being mad or calling her tattletale was a similarly important accomplishment. In both of these cases, the children exhibited Team Intelligence, which included a growing social awareness and conscience.

Team Intelligence also pushes children to become empathetic about difference. They become more observant, noticing that some kids learn or run faster than others, that children from different cultural backgrounds may have different attitudes. They realize that their own view of the world is not necessarily the only perspective; other ideas must be taken into consideration as well. For example, working side by side with Asian students has inspired some Caucasian students to approach schoolwork with a different attitude—Asians typically study more and seem to have a higher threshold for boredom.

Team Intelligence furthers conflict resolution. Not surprisingly, Team Intelligence leads to the development of better conflict resolution. When John does a project on the rain forest with the other kids in his cluster, even though he comes with ideas of his own, he must cooperate and negotiate. He has to know when to speak, when to listen, when to take charge, and when to sit back and give someone else a chance to hold the reins.

Finally, the family itself is a kind of team. Children who have Team Intelligence know that their needs are not the only ones that must be met; they know that sometimes they have to work toward the greater good. Having empathy at home engenders harmony and cooperation. They carry this awareness into other arenas and into the future. Knowing how to create good support networks in a neighborhood setting is a potential lifesaver in an adult world without small kinship systems or neighborhoods. Parents of kids with Team Intelligence say that their children . . .

- Know how to follow rules that make sense and how to question those that don't.
- Know how to ask for what they need and pitch in to a collective effort.
- Know how to resolve conflict before it reaches crisis proportions.
- Know how to negotiate on their own behalf without being ruthless or unkind.

For all these reasons, this Basic Skill is obviously vital to a child's core.

> **Basic Skill #9:** Inspire your child to develop her capacity to be part of a group without losing her individuality.

However, because of the mixed messages of the culture, this is not always easy to do. Indeed, there are a number of factors that make it difficult even for adults—parents as well as teachers—to maintain this critical balance, no less help our children achieve and maintain it.

Core Threats: Why We Overlook Team Intelligence

Although schools increasingly emphasize group participation, this core-builder is largely neglected. Neither the mental health establishment nor parents seem to realize how valuable Team Intelligence is. One reason for this is the persistent cultural focus on the "self." As a society, we put a premium on "finding oneself" and "breaking out of codependency," but there has been little or no focus on helping people get along with one another. Even more to the point, there is an absence of attention on developing a healthy balance between "I" and "we."

Parents and pop culture emphasize "I". Taking their cues from our self-oriented society and the spate of how-to books that give tips on attaining autonomy, most parents tend to foster the "I" in their kids. They take pains to make sure a child knows she's "special" but are unaware that their doting behavior can affect a child's participation in collective activities. Also, most parents struggle in their own lives to maintain a strong sense of self within the powerful grip of the group. And because we walk the same tightrope as our children, we may be unmindful of the impact of group dynamics—the predictable forces and energies that develop among members during the lifetime of that group. Therefore, parents are often stumped by team problems, we don't always understand the complexity and importance of Team Intelligence, and we, understandably, have a hard time teaching it to our kids.

This leaves our children smack in the throes of the second family, which sends a mixed message. On the one hand, the second family insists on group membership rules—be part of the gang and keep grown-ups out. On the other, it focuses powerfully on the self, promoting the I-gotta-be-me at any cost mentality. Consequently, it's incredibly hard for children today to find the balance between self and others.

This tendency is evident in children of all ages, notes Paul Krouner, director of Camp Schodak, a summer camp near Albany, New York. Krouner, whose family has been in the camping business for generations, has observed "a definite trend" over the last thirty years: "The kids seem to be pulled in two directions now. Intellectually, they understand the importance of working on a team—a group that's bigger than themselves. Emotionally, though, many of the children seem to have an increasingly hard time not being at the center and putting aside their own immediate needs."

We all know children who have to be chief, are never content to be part of the tribe, and who have trouble cooperating to achieve a common goal. This attitude is terribly corrosive to a child's core. Such a child is consumed by envy and threatened by others' skills. She can't rest on her laurels or ever feel satisfied by her own accomplishments. She develops a kind of "show biz" mentality: "I'm only as good as my last performance." She fears that another's success compromises her own chances of excelling; consequently, she's always ready for a fall. Over time, such a child typically meets a sad fate: other kids stop wanting to include her.

The second family means "we" versus "them." I also see children stuck at the other extreme—in the "we" mode. Interestingly, this was once viewed as a "girl's issue"—the notion that one has to give up part of herself to the group, or lose her voice, as psychologist Carol Gilligan first described this cultural phenomenon. Today, however, I see it in many of the girls *and* boys who come to me with team problems. Given nerdphobia and the tyranny of cool, boys nowadays also run the risk of turning themselves inside out to conform to peer standards. They, too, study what's "in" on TV, are immersed in the "cool" culture, and disown parts of themselves in order to be one with the group.

This enslavement by the "we" has trickled down from adolescents and preteens to little kids of both genders. On a recent visit to a clothing store, I waited for my daughter, who was in the dressing room trying on jeans. A saleswoman in a suburban mall told me that over the last few years, younger and younger children are coming in with the specific goal of dressing to be part of the "in" crowd. Even first- and second-grade girls seemed to have a sense of what was cool. In another store, the manager said, "It used to be adolescents who wanted the right look to fit in. Now we're getting three- and four-year-olds who have to have a certain brand of clothing—to be just like everybody else." In fact, research has shown that children as young as eighteen months are capable of brand-name recognition. This comes as no shock to parents of young children, like mine, who often walk around humming the McDonald's or Burger King jingles.

Is it any wonder that by kindergarten or first grade, these same label-conscious kids have problems asserting themselves in groups? Indeed, many of them are already seeking help, making remarks about their teammates, such as:

- "They're always bossing me around."
- "If I don't do what they want, they say they won't like me."
- "Why are they all so mean?"
- "I didn't get a chance to do *my* ideas."
- "The same kids always get to go first."

Some of these children want to drop out of the fray; others put up with the pushiness because they want desperately to be a part of the team. They lose the "I"—and their core self—in the bargain.

In contrast, a child with Team Intelligence—a child who knows how to be part of a team without losing himself—evidences a healthy balance between "I" and "we." At times, he is assertive and puts himself and his judgment first; at times, he allows his needs and opinions to be second to the group. This isn't about leading or following; it's about honoring one's core self *and* still being a cooperative player who makes an individual contribution to the greater whole. Helping your child achieve such a balance is a gift that will benefit your child through life.

Parent Skills: Fostering Team Intelligence

In my many visits to early elementary school classrooms, I have seen—and teachers confirm—that by the time kids leave kindergarten, it's obvious some have already begun to develop Team Intelligence. They're able to cooperate and, at the same time, to sustain their individuality. However, that balance doesn't come naturally in our culture. Children need us to guide them.

As I stated above, we parents haven't had much training in Team Intelligence. We're not familiar with the intricacies of group dynamics, which create confusing dilemmas for our children. Participation on any kind of team—athletic, academic, or social—requires your child to interact with a conglomeration of diverse attitudes and feelings that make up the "personality" of every group. Often, the challenges and conflicts that arise have little to do with him as an individual and more to do with the group as a whole. Still, we need to help him hold onto the "I" in the midst of this powerful "we."

Before you can help your child develop Team Intelligence, though, you need to first educate yourself about group dynamics and the ways an individual assimilates—becomes part of the greater entity. To that end, I turn to the findings of the Tavistock Institute of England, which was inspired by the writing of psychologist Wilfred Bion. For the last several decades, clinicians and researchers in the field of organizational psychology, informed by Bion, have been studying how people behave in groups.

Bion's work illuminates why, without the proper skills of teamwork, a person can easily get lost in a group. Tavistock theory has been applied to real-life situations mostly in the last decade—typically, in the corporate world to understand the ways and means of large groups. Why shouldn't families benefit from these tools, as well?

Below, in the first section of parent skills, I offer what our profession has already learned from organizational psychology and how we can apply it to our children. By gaining insight into the way teams operate, you can effectively help your child swim in the often dangerous currents of group behavior. In the second section, I explain my "LAPS" technique (on page 247), which is a synthesis of the cognitive behavioral approach (changing thinking in order to change behavior) and the group dynamics aspect of organizational psychology. Doing LAPS will enable you to achieve similar results as those counselors running "peer socialization groups" and will help prepare your child to be a team player who can cope successfully with team problems.

The anatomy of a group:
what you and your child can expect

Bion and the organizational psychologists who succeeded him have taught us that the way people feel and act in a group is determined by certain predictable characteristics. Until now, most parents, and even some teachers, have not been taught about this complex phenomenon. They may notice that one child has trouble breaking in, another is being ostracized, someone else becomes a leader, another joins in, sometimes following blindly. They see that for some children being part of a group makes it hard to balance the "I" and "we," but they don't know why. In fact, all of those dilemmas are understandable when you are able to see how groups work.

The following ten fundamental laws will help. Each one is presented with its implications for your child and suggestions for what you as the parent can do. You won't like some of them; indeed, you might not even believe some of them. But decades of research bear them out. Whether you're talking about a school club, a basketball or chess team, a religious organization, or a bunch of kids that take the same route to school every day, this is what you can expect from a group—a word I use here synonymously with "team."

Law #1: *Groups tend to keep new people out.* Even if there's a coach or another adult leader, even when the children are very young, every group is an organism that doesn't like to take in other organisms.
Implication: *Your child will be an outsider at first.* Whether she is about to join a new play group, go into a new club, or attend a new school, she'll probably have to work her way into the group. She may even be actively excluded. Unfortunately, children—and we parents—tend to see this as a reflection on the individual when, in fact, it's a natural function of group dynamics.
What to Do: *Don't get mad; get involved.* Jordan's mom took a day off from work and went on his nursery school's trip to the zoo. She saw firsthand who might become friends with Jordan, and she decided to network with their parents.

Law #2: *A group has an unspoken personality.* In virtually every group, an ethos develops—a distinctive sensibility. It often combines the group's background of unresolved conflicts, collective victories and losses, unexpressed feelings, and unsubstantiated rumors.

Implication: *A group's history, its past and current reputation, may cause problems for your child.* Sometimes children try to join groups blindly and with false expectations of acceptance, or they see members' behavior as a personal reaction rather than simply part of who the group is.

What to Do: *Before your child joins a group, try to understand its unspoken personality.* Knowing a group's history and ethos makes it possible to avoid your child's getting set up. Because Noelle had to move midyear and send Gabriel to a new kindergarten, she made it a point to find out from parents and teachers everything she could about what went on during the first half of the school year, who was the class leader, what kind of cliques had formed, who had fights with whom, which parents were the most involved.

Law #3: *Every group has rigid—if unspoken—rules.* Group rules cannot be altered easily—they are much bigger than any one child.

Implication: *A child who doesn't recognize and follow the rules can't be in the group.* This is hard often for parents to accept—we think of our children as unique. But you simply cannot revise a group's rules to benefit, or better fit, your child.

What to Do: *Help your child live within reasonable rules of the group.* Arnold, a new fourth grader, tended to rush onto the school bus and take one of the most coveted seats in the back of the bus. Hearing that some sixth-grade boys had been hassling him, Arnold's parents discovered that an unwritten middle school "rule" was that older children got to sit in the back of the bus. They explained to their son that whether this was fair or not was beside the point; it was a rule he needed to respect.

Law #4: *Group reactions can be irrational.* The group can respond very powerfully, and sometimes even irrationally, when a member doesn't go by its rules. Such a response may be expressed by another child, or even by the adult in charge, but they speak for the group.

Implication: *Don't become irrational in return.* I've seen parents who get into terrible power struggles with groups, thinking somehow they can win for their child, but this is a mistake and only makes it worse for him. If you challenge a group's wisdom, you and your child will eventually lose or be ostracized.

What to Do: *In the face of conflict between your child and a group, maintain a reasonable attitude.* Wesley's mom, Anna, was rightfully infuriated by classmates taunting her somewhat shy son. When she told me what was going on, I said that if things didn't improve within a couple of weeks, she would have to intervene. But, in the meantime, I stressed that Anna needed to stop losing her cool. Even when Wesley reported an incident of insensitivity, she had to refrain from making comments that the other children should be more considerate. Although it's important for a parent to protect her child, in this case, it was more productive for Mom to bolster her son by listening carefully to him, rather than reacting too intensely. After a week, it became clear to both mother and son that Wesley's problem was with the leader, not the whole group. Wes stopped trying to approach the coolest kid and, instead, just hung out with the others. Gradually, tension lessened as he fit into the clique.

Law #5. *Groups are fiercely hierarchical.* Although it can change over time, there is always a clear pecking order of power.

Implication: *The popular, attractive kids decked out in the trappings of pop culture usually eclipse others.* This hierarchy is out of your control. Don't get insulted on your child's behalf, or angry that she's not on top.

What to Do: *Help your child find her own level in the pecking order.* Begin by making connections with lower-rung or mid-level children, as Hannah's parents did when she entered kindergarten. They got to know the parents, made play dates and dinner dates, and didn't try to get Hannah involved with the most popular children. In time—and on her own—Hannah became one of the most secure and sought-after children in the class.

Law #6: *Groups follow the most charismatic, and often the most troublesome, leader.* In some corporations, the slickest, silver-tongued talkers rise to the top. In some countries, very unstable leaders take over. In children's groups, it's often the cool ones who rule—sometimes, the most shallow and superficial kids.

Implication: *Questioning the wisdom of following such a leader is a losing proposition.* Whether your child is three or thirteen, avoid directly criticizing the leader. Your observation probably won't make a dent and might distance you from your child. Kids are initially drawn to this power and must come to terms with it. It's part and parcel of group dynamics.

What to Do: *Let your child learn from his own experience who is a worthy leader and who isn't.* Eight-year-old Robert wouldn't listen to his parents' heartfelt lecture about staying away from Matt, the class bully, whom they feared would ultimately get their son into trouble. They wisely stopped pushing and started listening, asking for details and letting Robert hear his own experience. In time, he began to remark about how "bossy" and "mean" Matt was to other kids. He realized he could be next on Matt's hit list and eventually started gravitating toward nicer children.

Law #7: *Group information is supposed to be private, but it never is.* From early on, kids learn that they're not supposed to tell grown-ups what goes on among them, but one child almost always spills the beans.

Implication: *Information that's important will leak out.* Therefore, it's vital to keep your eyes and ears open. The more you know, the better you will be able to guide your child.

What to Do: *Make friends with other parents of team members.* Whenever Marge wanted to know the "juicy stuff" that was happening in her daughter's fourth-grade network, she tapped into the mother's network. She called Lynn, a mother who volunteered as a teacher's aide during lunchtime. Lynn was a particularly knowledgeable source, since she eavesdropped on kids' conversations. As a result, without having to pump her daughter for information, Marge heard about the first spin-the-bottle game at a birthday party.

Law #8: *Groups punish revolutionaries.* Groups are basically conservative, and they can mercilessly punish members who try to overthrow leadership or speak out about members' dissatisfaction.

Implication: *It's hard for a child to maintain his individuality without getting locked into a power struggle.* If your child challenges the leader or is constantly out of step with the group, even if you run interference, other team members will resist. Most likely, everyone will stand by the group ethos and come to the aid of the established leader.

What to Do: *Show your child that being true to herself doesn't have to include criticizing someone who is different.* In other words, encourage a live-and-let-live attitude. Although Felicia was as disgusted as her twins, Jean and Daria, by the pervasive designer-clothes requirement in their group, she was careful not to provoke out-and-out rebellion in her daughters. "Follow your own style," she advised them, "but try not to pick on those who don't." In particular, she advised the girls not to openly defy Betsy, the class clotheshorse, and her sycophant, Randy. By concentrating on her daughters' (and her own) values and by encouraging their unique fashion sense, Felicia helped the girls fit in without losing their identities.

Law #9: *Groups almost always need a scapegoat.* At almost any given time in the life of a group, someone is on the outs, being dumped on. That's because aggression can't be directed against its leadership, so it is aimed at the group's weaker members, who are less likely to strike back.

Implication: *A parent must always be on the lookout for scapegoating.* Most of us can remember problems of this sort from our own childhoods, and it's often too painful to believe that our children have to endure it, too. But your child can't afford your being an ostrich. With scapegoating, momentum builds, the process takes on a life of its own, and it's very hard to stop.

What to Do: *Give your child a chance to stand up for herself—and then intervene if necessary.* From early childhood to mid-adolescence, you must advocate for your child—no matter what she says. When several boys began to make fun of five-year-old Jamie's stutter, his mother, Bertha, first suggested strategies to ameliorate the problem, such as ignoring the comments, walking away, or telling his teacher. After a few weeks, it was clear from Jamie's ongoing sadness and tears that he couldn't handle the situation on his own, so Bertha went to school. Politely but firmly, she insisted to her son's teacher that the offending children suffer some consequences for their nastiness. She refused to listen to code phrases, such as "shared responsibility," and "kids will be kids." In the end, her determination got the principal's attention, as it almost always will. The scapegoaters were told that they didn't have to be Jamie's friend, but that their insults would no longer be tolerated. After the ringleader's half-day suspension and a week's detention for all three boys, the teasing stopped. I've successfully used this hands-off-but-intervene-if-necessary guideline for children all the way though ninth grade.

Law #10: *Individuals can't negotiate with groups.* Group-think is so powerful that the group personality tends to drown out individual members' voices.

Implication: *Kids get into trouble when they take on a group.* There's no way a child, or even a parent, can negotiate with the group as a whole. Therefore, when your child is faced with a group problem, the only way to communicate is with *one* of its members.

What to Do: *Break the group down to its smallest parts—individuals.* Encourage your child to seek out either the most reasonable child in the group or another adult who can help. Henrietta, one of two sixth-grade girls in an after-school chess club, came home complaining because none of the boys were willing to play matches against her. Even the club's volunteer adviser, seemed to favor the boys. "It's like I'm not even there," she told her father, William, an ace player himself. William suspected that the advising dad was setting the tone of the club. Instead of making accusations, though, he offered to come to a few meetings and help out. With her dad on hand, Henrietta felt a little bolder, and took it upon herself to ask one of the friendlier boys if he'd play a match against her. That broke the ice and broke down the existing taboo as well. Henrietta was delighted when the other boys began to accept her as a full-fledged member.

• • •

Parents of children of all ages may have a hard time believing that the above organizational axioms hold true in their kids' lives. How often do we say, or hear it said, that "children are so cruel." The truth is, individual children are sometimes cruel; most often, though, you're seeing *group* behavior, and the kids are unconsciously acting out every one of the above precepts. However, once you're armed with awareness, you can take concrete steps to help your child avoid the humiliation and sadness that so often accompany team problems.

Doing LAPS

It is often extremely difficult for a child to discern her own feelings, no less what's really going on in the group and how her participation affects the greater whole. You'll need to help her.

Indeed, groups can be a hotbed of individual cognitive distortions—illogical bouts of thinking. A child plagued by such thoughts can't see clearly and, therefore, is unable to even contemplate changing a bad situation. However, cognitive distortions associated with *team* problems are decidedly different. Because of the power of the group, there is always at least a kernel of reality in an individual child's worst fears about her relationship with the other kids. It *is* hard to break in, judgments *are* being made, there *is* pressure to conform, to perform, to win.

Children need validation. They need to understand that the group has a personality and behavior all its own—and that it's not just the newcomer's problem. Your child can't do this alone. You need to help her develop group skills and hone her ability to come up with solutions that enable her to fit in—or to have the strength not to be part of a group. This is all part of fostering Team Intelligence.

To that end, I developed a four-step technique for dealing with teams, represented by the rather appropriate acronym, LAPS:

Listen
Advocate
Participate
Stay with it

Doing LAPS, together with a working knowledge of group laws, is the basic "parent skill" you need to help your son or daughter maintain a sense of self in the midst of the group dynamic. I've applied this strategy, or coached parents to apply it, to almost every child who comes to me with team issues.

Listen. Keep an ear tuned specifically for the emotional consequences of group pressure. The feelings that come up when children are faced with team problems are most often shame and self-doubt—issues that go directly to a child's core. For example, Yvonne, whom

---

LAPS IN A NUTSHELL

LAPS can guide you in helping your child become part of a group or team or club without compromising his core self. The plan of attack involves four parts, each of which is described more fully in the pages that follow.

Listen for the kernel of truth in your child's cognitive distortion.

Advocate by asking your child specific questions and coming up with small, doable strategies he can use.

Participate by being aware of your child's group activities, staying involved, as well as watching the group dynamics at home—and your role in it.

Stay with it by not allowing yourself to get burned out by the demands of your child's team participation.

---

you met at the beginning of this chapter, felt shame about not being included. Peter thought his contribution wasn't up to the other kids' and worried about being judged. Carla was humiliated when the team captain yelled at her. Tom was embarrassed by being singled out. These are all problems related to the I/we stresses created by group dynamics. In preschool, Yvonne came up against a clique's natural tendency to exclude. Tom bucked the rules. And Carla was probably a bit of a revolutionary.

How you listen can either thwart or encourage a child who is feeling bad about himself. So, pay close attention to your tone as you ask questions. Keep your voice kind, firm, and nonjudgmental. Be patient. It may take her a while to get out what happened—say, being excluded from a game—so don't crowd her; she may need to talk *at* you without looking at you, as I suggest on page 94. And try not to be invasive or to push her to tell the story faster. It's important to respect her pace— and just go with it. (Reread chapter 3 to refresh your memory about specific strategies based on the various expressive styles, to help your child talk.)

Finally, keep in mind this catchy phrase: "Before you advocate, you must validate." Remember that even if your child's thinking is somewhat distorted, a kernel of truth will emerge. For example, if she says, "They think I'm a geek," maybe there is something about the way your child presents herself that makes her an easy target. Don't ignore such issues in the name of protecting her. Instead, validate and try to ask concrete questions, such as "Maybe you're right. Why do you think they feel that way about you?"

Advocate. When it comes to team issues, it's often not enough for a parent to just be an empathetic listener. You may have to advocate for your child and, together, come up with small, realistic actions that your child can do to ameliorate the helplessness that both of you may feel. Again, specific questions that break the problem down into small, doable parts will help both of you feel less overwhelmed.

Even when you're able to listen carefully, it still may be tough to help your child if his difficulties replicate incidents that happened during *your* childhood—flubbed lines in a play, missed shots or goals. We all have memories of exclusion or excruciating social embarrassment. Who hasn't slammed up against at least one, if not many of the laws of group dynamics, when we couldn't fit in or vied with a leader? For example, Donna recently consulted me about her son Jeffrey. He was having enormous trouble fitting in and following first-grade rules that seemed to pose inordinate demands compared to kindergarten. As Donna was talking about an incident that left Jeff miserable, she became so emotional that it was no surprise when she blurted out, "This is *exactly* what happened to me when I was in first grade."

For most of us, those painful feelings are frozen in time, which makes it difficult to separate our experience from our children's. We assume we know our child's experience when, in fact, we may be projecting our feelings onto him. In that case, you won't be able to really hear your child, no less appropriately advocate on his behalf. Therefore, don't jump in immediately; sit with your feelings and sort them out—before coming up with a plan of action.

Participate. As much as possible, parents should be part of their child's involvement and thereby be able to witness her role within a group. In some instances, your participation may be mandatory. With the increasing numbers of cooperative nursery schools, for example, parents are required to act as a teacher's aide. Cluster teaching, which is also spreading throughout the country, requires a second adult in the classroom. And because so many schools are understaffed these days, parents may be called in to pinch-hit as teachers or coaches. The bottom line is that school is no longer a place just for kids. Parent involvement is the wave of the future.

In any event, your participation is a plus. It will help your child think more clearly and enable him to cut through the fuzziness of group dynamics. Your observations will aid both of you in understanding:

- his role as part of the group;
- how she interacts with others;
- how well he is able to hold on to his own ideas in the face of peer pressure;
- the general group personality and ethics;
- how the group treats other members;
- how the group handles outsiders;
- the group's leadership—the team captain as well as the adult authority—in action.

Your participation also can make your child really feel as if she's part of the team. So-called soccer moms (and dads) help their children become the insiders of the group—by chauffeuring, showing up for games, providing refreshments, going on outings, and opening their homes for socializing. This is particularly true for older children who have problems making friends. When thirteen-year-old Garth was having trouble forming stable relationships on his team, his father announced that there would be hot dogs for everybody at his house after the next game. Having teammates on *his* turf gave Garth an edge and made him feel more confident. Also, Dad had a better view of the group's dynamics and was a more knowledgeable listener when Garth talked about trying to make friends.

A word of warning, though: Don't get involved with an eye toward manipulating a child's status, or gaining favor with the leader. The goal of your participation should simply be to help your child settle into membership while maintaining her uniqueness. Erica's mom, for example, invited everyone out for pizza after many of their at-home games. It helped her child do something that felt like "her thing" with the team and, at the same time, built shared memories with her teammates off the playing field. Likewise, Matt's dad hosted a postseason party for his son's football buddies, and Claudia's mother offered their family room as a place where her daughter's art project group could work after school.

The "P" should also remind you to look at your participation at home. The family is a laboratory for group interaction. It influences a child's peer style, as I explained in chapter 5, and largely determines how your child will balance the "I" and "we." Whenever she participates in any group endeavor, be it a team or a set of peers, she can't help but replicate the behavior of your family—her first team. Therefore, if your child is having problems, pay attention to what goes on at home. How do you treat your child's interruptions and demands? What is your response to rule-breaking? The kind of cooperation and teamwork you require can either increase or decrease his or her capacity for Team Intelligence.

For example, eleven-year-old Ethan bulldozed ahead of other children; he always had to be first. If a classmate was talking, Ethan often interrupted by cracking a joke. He couldn't keep friends, because everyone thought of him as "pushy." Seen as a chronic rule-breaker, Ethan was ostracized from each of the everyday teams in his life— school projects and cluster work, hobby groups, even the gang on the school bus.

Discussing it with me, Ethan's parents realized that they stopped talking whenever Ethan had something to say—even in the middle of an important conversation. He was allowed to interrupt his brother, or finish stories the younger boy started to tell. He always had to try a new toy or piece of equipment first and never wanted to share. When reprimanded, he almost always talked back. Although Ethan's impudence was offensive, his parents were proud of his verbal jousting ability. Clearly, Ethan, who was becoming increasingly self-centered, wasn't developing Team Intelligence.

Over the next few weeks following our session, Ethan's parents changed their behavior and informed him, "We are going to help you learn to be more aware of others' feelings." They stopped giving in to his every interruption and demand. Upstaging his brother was no longer accepted. In all, they helped Ethan see that his behavior at home was affecting his behavior at school. "You're always going to find yourself on the outside, if you don't try harder to understand what's going on."

Within a couple of months, Ethan became much less pushy; he didn't break into other kids' conversations. He was beginning to grasp that rules didn't just apply to other kids. And out of this new persona, an accidental friendship occurred on the school bus. One day, Ethan sat down without his usual commotion and just started talking with another boy. When they discussed a mutual interest—baseball cards— Ethan refrained from his once-unquenchable need to upstage the other kid. Because of his parents' behind-the-scenes participation, he finally made a real friend. In time, one friend turned into a little group, and Ethan, beginning to develop Team Intelligence, was able to become one of the boys.

TEAM TROUBLE:
WHAT ARE YOU DOING AT HOME?

Parents of children who have trouble being part of a group need to ask themselves if they are in any way encouraging or condoning this behavior at home. Ask yourself . . .

* Do we give our child the spotlight whenever he demands it?
* Do we let her interrupt adult conversation?
* Do we hang on his every word?
* Is she the "favored" child?
* Do we bend the rules for him?
* Do we allow her to lord over her siblings?
* Do we subtly exclude him?

Stay with it. When a child participates in team sports, or has an intense passion, like acting, it can involve tremendous wear and tear on parents. Children might stay with the same group for six years or longer, thus, parental perseverance can be the biggest challenge of all. Given our scarcity of time, conflicting pulls (work, other children, our own interests), even fatigue or boredom (ever watch a group of five-year-olds try to "play" baseball?), it's no mean feat to just hang in there!

Making it even more difficult to stay with it, there may be other kids in the group—or maybe one in particular—whom you simply don't like. And yet you have to see these kids week after week and have them in your home. There's not much you can do about this; you don't have a choice about who ends up on your child's team or club. Therefore, try to see objectionable children through your child's eyes. For example, the kid who seems rude, or surly and arrogant, to you might be the best player on the team. And remember that fundamental law: Group members are often captivated by leaders whom parents don't like. Remember, only if another child puts your child in danger or if his behavior is morally objectionable should you vehemently criticize that child.

Granted, all this can be exhausting. I've known parents who were ready to throw in the towel after one of those days when they acted as an aide in their youngest child's classroom in the morning and, later, as chauffeur for the older kids' away game. One solution is pick and choose. As I explained in chapter 4, more is *not* better for your child— and it's certainly not better for you. Accordingly, when you survey the endless variety of choices open to your child, go with his passions. And know your own limits; when you feel overwhelmed, don't volunteer for yet another classroom or team job.

It's true that the same handful of moms and dads always seems to step up to the plate. Eager parents commit time to this activity and that and before they know it, they're drowning. So, watch out for seeping overload. Although I stress the importance of participation, sometimes in order to survive you absolutely have to say no.

Child Skills: Facing Up to Team Problems

The following child skills almost always require initial parental assistance or intervention. Once you help your child troubleshoot, she'll be better able to meet future problems on her own. The idea is to make her mindful of the hurdles and help her harness her inner strength to jump over them. In the process, she will maintain a strong, separate self while solidifying her Team Intelligence.

Breaking in without giving up

Because groups are initially rejecting rather than accepting, new children are at a disadvantage from the get-go. This is usually not an issue once the child is *on* a team but it's simply getting him to be able to participate in the first place. Failure to do so can negatively shape his core image.

For example, George, an overgrown nine-year-old whose round, pudgy face made him a dead ringer for Nickelodeon's "Doug," was distraught when roles for the monthly class play were given out to other kids. Feeling inferior and ashamed, George started misbehaving at school, sassing the teacher, falling out of his chair, being mean to other kids. Finally, he told his parents, "I don't want to go to this school anymore."

Before things really got out of hand, I encouraged his parents to try the LAPS technique with him. That is, they listened in the way I describe above, to get past vague complaints ("School stinks") and monosyllabic answers to their questions about his distress. They finally heard a specific cognitive distortion: "I'm never chosen for the play because I'm too ugly—I'm just not good-looking enough to be an actor." From there, he moved on to "I'll never be chosen for anything and I'll never have any friends."

George wasn't altogether wrong about his appearance being a factor. After all, he wasn't a "cool" leading-man type. But armed with this specific knowledge of his angst, his parents could help their son reframe his thinking and then effectively advocate for him.

"Do you want to talk to Mr. Morris, or should we?" they asked. He wanted both, so they went to the teacher as a family. Luckily, Mr. Morris was compassionate and incredibly honest. He helped George understand the ethos and rules of this particular group.

"It's true, George—in acting, appearance is a factor," said Mr. Morris. "But if you were to do something to help you get into a little better shape, that probably would make a difference." Mr. Morris said this in such a gentle way that George decided for the first time ever to try pushing himself physically. He ate less junk food and started playing soccer with the other kids. In a few weeks, he began to feel—and look—stronger.

Did George miraculously become trim—a physically fit "after" to his portly "before"? No, that's the stuff of Hollywood movies and TV specials. What was important, though, was breaking out of his self-defeating loop and beginning to develop Team Intelligence. He became more comfortable approaching teachers for help and started to understand what he was up against. By successfully following up on one small, reasonable suggestion, he was eager to undertake others. This allowed him to see that he could help himself. Not surprisingly, as George became increasingly aware of his core abilities and more confident, he was picked for several small character roles—particularly suited to his personality. Becoming a regular part of the cast—in effect, an acting "team"—was a high point of his school year. Through it all, George was still George.

Being assertive—without being pushy or getting pushed around

Some children have trouble standing up for themselves, particularly when a group's personality is comprised of aggressive players and forceful coaches. Such children tend to shy away from team participation, because the pressure makes them feel miserable. In fact, the lack of assertiveness in a child with team problems is one of the main reasons parents seek my advice. The challenge is to help a child figure out two important issues: one, what is it about the group that holds him back—perhaps he's not in sync with the ethos, or maybe the group is being actively exclusive—and, two, what about *himself* can he realistically work to change. Whatever the reason for the difficulty, *parents cannot leave children of any age alone longer than a few weeks to solve such a problem.* Feeling beaten down is potentially too damaging to a child's core spirit. Very quickly, kids can become marginalized. Even though it's impossible for parents to change a group's basic personality, they nevertheless must help children figure out a way to become part of the team—or to live peacefully outside it.

Missy, an eight-year-old who was involved in a group project at school, was supposed to help create an invention that would change life in the second millennium. But the process was changing Missy's life—for the worse. She was being pushed around by the other kids and forced into a very peripheral role. Missy not only wasn't getting any satisfaction from the project, she was becoming increasingly disheartened. By listening carefully, Mom and Dad heard her specific worry: "The other kids hate me because they think I'm dumb."

Their first step was to help Missy see that even though the group *was* being cliquish, the other kids' reaction wasn't just about her. They had been classmates since kindergarten and were excluding someone they perceived as a newcomer. Merely making her aware of group dynamics and her particular role in the equation bolstered her Team Intelligence. The next step was to help Missy figure out a reasonable way to work on herself. In other words, what could she do differently vis-à-vis the group?

Missy's mom and dad reminded her that if the whole group seemed overwhelming, she might think in terms of its individual members. Missy then realized she could call one of the friendlier kids. "Do you want to come over to play this weekend?" she asked bluntly. The girl said "Sure." Whether she was initially eager to play with Missy didn't matter. What *was* important, however, was that Missy acted instead of passively allowing her pessimistic thinking to cause her to withdraw. In addition, she learned the benefits of breaking a group into manageable size by dealing with an individual component. That concrete action made her feel better immediately. As a result of feeling more confident, other friendships came more easily.

Creating a link between self and group

Because a group can loom as a fearsome aggregate of different personalities, some children need at least one friend on the inside. If they can't partner up with someone, the team feels too impersonal and too difficult to manage. For example, so much schoolwork was done in teams that six-year-old Geoffrey was really distraught because he couldn't find a friend in his class. He told his mother, "Mommy, they don't like me. I don't have anybody to talk to, and I feel lonely inside." Geoffrey was unusually articulate, but he speaks for many kids who act up or drop out of teams. They need a buddy to feel as if they fit in.

Geoffrey, of course, had recognized a kernel of truth—many of the boys *had* been together since preschool, and this was his first year. His mom listened very carefully for both the group dynamic and Geoffrey's specific contribution to the situation. Gradually, Mom realized that Geoffrey tended to approach children in the tight-knit group in ways that almost guaranteed rejection. He often put them on the spot by asking, "Do you really want to play with me?" Or, worse, he'd ask one child to play his game when that child was already involved in another group activity. Geoffrey, sensing the group's exclusivity, was trying to push his way in, and was going about it all wrong. He needed to learn how to join activities in a manner that didn't challenge the group or violate its rules.

Geoffrey's mother helped her son practice better opening lines. "Rather than ask a question," she told him, "say what you want directly, like 'Let's play kickball together.' If you want to invite a child to our house, say very clearly, 'My mother says you can come over to my house for a play date tomorrow.' " She gave Geoffrey social guidelines as well, which helped improve his Team Intelligence: "Don't interrupt other kids in the middle of their play because it will be hard for them to say yes. Approach one kid at a time, because one-on-one is easier."

Mom also had a meeting with Geoffrey's teacher and asked him for help. "You're really my eyes and ears when he's in school," she told Mr. Gross. "I can benefit from your awareness and expertise." The teacher promised to watch what happened in class and on the playground. Mr. Gross also helped Geoffrey by "partnering" him with kids with whom there was potential for friendship.

Being a good competitor *and* doing one's "personal best"

Some children retreat from group activities—anything from math or baseball to debating—not because they're scared but because they feel conflicted about competing with friends and, possibly, outshining them. For example, eleven-year-old Rita was sent to me by her coach and her parents because, though she was a good athlete, she wanted to quit her soccer team. The more everyone told her what a great player she was and how much she was needed, the more she came up with excuses to miss practice, or to sit on the sidelines. No one knew why.

Doing LAPS with Rita, I tried to listen carefully for her specific worries as I asked, "What happens during a game?" Rita described the expression on some of her teammates' faces whenever she scored a goal. "I think they get mad at me," Rita admitted, "and I feel bad because I *like* to win." Equally distressing was her catastrophic conclusion: "If I keep scoring so many goals, none of them will want to be friends with me anymore." Rita needed to understand that while her outstanding performances could trigger *some* envy, she really had no idea what specific players thought or how they'd act in the future.

So that Rita wouldn't have to deal with the team as an entity, I suggested that she zero in on one friend in particular, "who means the most to you." Rita decided that she could approach Shelly, who had been her friend long before they both made the team. She also thought it would be a good idea to ask what her friend's facial expression meant rather than assuming the worst.

Rita finally worked up the nerve to ask, simply and directly, "Shelly, do you get mad at me when I score?" Without missing a beat, Shelly answered, "Yeah, I wish I could be that good. But it's okay . . . 'cause you're my friend." Rita heaved a sigh of relief. The two girls then developed secret hand signals that helped Rita feel connected to Shelly during a game. One finger meant "Come over—I need help," two, "Cover me—I'm going for the ball." Close friends to begin with, they became even closer. Most important, Rita didn't feel as if she had to play down her ability in order to maintain her friendships.

Living with one's own *and* the group's disappointment

Some children have such an inordinate fear of letting the team down, they'd rather quit than be part of the effort. They fear that they'll perform badly and be responsible for the team's not doing well. Children need to accept that sometimes they will deliver less-than-optimal performances—that they're bound to be disappointed in themselves and even worry that their teammates are disappointed, too. If they don't develop this awareness and acceptance, the specter of disappointment—particularly letting their teammates down—can paralyze them.

Alec, for instance, was in a school where, since kindergarten, each cluster had teams for different projects. When it came to forming the math team, Alec didn't want to participate. Each time, the teacher announced a "solve-off"—the equivalent of a math bee—Alec would create a huge ruckus. Finally, his mother asked, "What's going on with you?" She listened carefully and although she realized Alec was generally anxious about his own difficulty with math, she eventually uncovered his specific fear: "If my team loses, it will be *my* fault and all the kids will hate me forever."

In the big picture, Alec's view was accurate: Math *was* one of Alec's weaker subjects—his mistakes *would* affect the team's overall score. Some of the fiercer competitors *did* get mad when anyone came up with a wrong answer. Further, one of his team members was a competitive hothead who was really nasty about others' mistakes. But there was a bit of a cognitive distortion at work as well—allowing one boy's reaction to define the whole group's. Alec's mother tried to help him change his thinking by pointing out that the rest of the guys still chose him for the team. That allowed Alec to see that no one "hated" him and that not even the team tyrant would be angry for keeps. Feeling better, Alec actually did better—though math never became his strong suit.

Alec's parents also advocated for him. They went to his teacher, explained what was going on, and asked for Mrs. Walker's involvement: "It's clear that Alec's team won't get a medal because of his performance, but can you say something to everybody about other contributions he makes?" Mrs. Walker had never really focused on an individual child's feeling at fault for a team's overall performance. But after several better solve-offs, she told Alec, "I know your team came in third, but I loved the way you stuck with it."

Then after this small acknowledgment, an astonishing thing happened: The very next day, Alec joined the tutoring club. He volunteered to tutor a younger child, not in math, but in penmanship. During the weeks that followed, his math flubs became increasingly less important to him. And, more often than not, he came home from school in an upbeat mood, feeling better about himself than he had since fourth grade had begun.

In fact, because they emphasize the important balance between "I" and "we," all the skills that help a child acquire Team Intelligence make kids feel better about themselves. Such mastery can make a real difference in how a child negotiates a place for herself in the classroom, on the playing fields, and in after-school clubs—not to mention later in life.

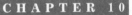
GRATITUDE

Basic Skill #10: *Expect your child to be grateful and, thereby, nurture his faith and spirituality.*

Caught in the Shift

Victor and his wife Eve, a couple I met in a workshop, told me a story about a recent outing to an amusement park with another couple and their kids. Their story strikes a chord for many families I know. The four adults and their five kids, ranging from ages four to twelve, devoted an entire day to rides, games, snacks, and souvenirs. The children reveled, while the adults suffered "Whirling Dervish" whiplash and aching feet. Each set of parents spent over a hundred dollars, but no one complained because, after all, this was old-fashioned family fun.

However, on the way to the parking lot, the families encountered a strategically located gift shop, and Vic's ten-year-old, Tara, pulled him up short. She wanted a T-shirt like her friend Jamie had gotten on the way in. Eve said no, and Tara went into a total meltdown. "It's not fair," she yelled. "How come Jamie gets one, and I don't?" And then came the line that put Victor and Eve completely over the edge: "You never do anything for me!"

I'm recounting this incident because it reflects an everyday reality. Parents like Eve and Vic, who happily give to their children, don't always realize how a child's lack of appreciation affects them. Over time, parental resentment builds until ultimately it explodes. At these intense moments, we parents can't grasp the idea that *outside* the realm of family life a completely different and more heartening trend is building. It's hard for us to believe that anything remotely resembling gratitude exists among our young.

The sharing and caring revolution

In truth, the self-centeredness we see in our children is slowly being countered by a cultural shift that Princeton sociologist Robert Wuthnow calls a "quiet revolution." He observes it in the growing number of groups ranging from those sponsored by religious organizations to twelve-step programs to less formal gatherings of folks with everyday concerns—gardeners, investors, and neighborhood parents, to name just a few.

In all of these groups, the common threads are support and information, which are weaving a new fabric of American life that holds empathy and generosity as high values. Pollster George Gallup, Jr., characterizes it as the "caring and sharing" movement, noting that 40 percent of Americans are already members of such groups; an additional 7 percent more are interested in joining; and 15 percent have been members in the past. Charitable gifts and volunteerism are also at an all-time high. In our homes, 63 percent of the population gives thanks before meals—compared with 43 percent in 1947. Indeed, despite headlines to the contrary, everywhere we look, sharing and caring is bubbling up under the surface.

Are our kids getting the message? Some are, although their numbers are hard to track. I certainly see more and more parents trying to imbue family moments with meaning instead of materialism. For example, at Thanksgiving and Christmas, some moms and dads bring their children with them to help out at shelters and soup kitchens—with an eye toward acting on the virtue of giving. Surprisingly, today's teenagers are more involved in do-gooding than ever before; they dedicate both their time and their money to charitable groups. And membership is gradually increasing in two venerable service-oriented organizations for children—the Boy Scouts and Girl Scouts of America, both of which had seen a tremendous decline in participation through the sixties and seventies.

However, make no mistake: This is a slow and often invisible metamorphosis. It's one matter to reconfigure holiday traditions or enroll our kids in the Scouts; it's quite another to change the *everyday* give-and-take between parent and child. In fact, as we peek into other people's homes or look at what's going on in our own families, there's often little evidence that a caring and sharing movement is under way. As a recent study conducted by the New York–based Public Agenda organization indicates, 44 percent of parents with children between five to twelve believe that their kids are "spoiled."

The problem is, we're caught in a paradigm shift—with child-centeredness on one side, caring and sharing on the other. In a way, it's similar to the I-versus-we dilemma I described in the previous chapter, except here we're talking about individual children versus the common good. While we parents would like to believe that we're joining society's movement in a more hopeful direction, our children seem as me-oriented as ever. We are impatient, wanting them to understand how much we do for them and how little they seem to care. At the same time, we're afraid to make our children feel guilty.

The truth is, today's child world is *not* geared toward getting kids to recognize reasons to be grateful, and we parents unwittingly feed into this ethos. Children won't become part of the caring and sharing movement unless we nudge them along and help them develop the core trait I call "Gratitude."

Why Gratitude Is Important

Children aren't selfish by nature. Indeed, as I pointed out in chapter 9, the most current research indicates that even babies are capable of some empathy. Moreover, study after study underscores the importance of developing greater empathy among human beings—particularly between parent and child. This set of findings is so new that it hasn't made its way into mainstream psychological literature. However, small pockets of clinicians have begun to grasp the revolutionary notion that parenting doesn't have to be either child-centered *or* authoritarian—until now, the two poles of parenting theory. In fact, good parenting requires what psychologists refer to as "mutuality"—a relationship in which not only is the parent attuned to her child's needs but also the child is expected to have some empathic regard for his parent. That, in fact, is the source of Gratitude.

An empathic child feels more complete. In contrast, a child without empathy and Gratitude is self-centered, unmindful, and unconnected to others—especially their parents. Indeed, if love makes a child's world go round, Gratitude holds it together in a number of important ways:

Gratitude sets the family universe in proper order. The second-century Greek scientist Ptolemy positioned earth at the center of the universe. Fifteen hundred years later, Copernicus redrew the astronomical map, correctly depicting earth as a satellite rather than the center of the universe. So it should be for each of us who make up our family constellations.

Children who possess the core trait of Gratitude grasp that they're not at the center of their world—life doesn't revolve around who they are or what they want. This was recognized years ago by the eminent pediatrician D. W. Winnicott, whose work indirectly (and, I must add, without sufficient attribution) informs that of virtually every parenting expert. Winnicott theorized that a child reaches some degree of mental health when he can understand his parents as three-dimensional human beings.

Gratitude creates a greater ongoing connection between child and parent—as well as with other adults. A child who appreciates his parents' gifts—material possessions or ephemeral "gifts," like time and attention—understands the significance and importance of giving. He gives in return, and he expresses thanks when he is given to.

Gratitude is a first step toward helping a child nurture her spiritual self. Gratitude helps a child see that she's part of a greater whole and that in the natural order of things, one gives as well as receives. Every major religion, every school of spirituality, teaches that we must be thankful to a compassionate intangible being—whether it's defined as the traditional God or another "Higher Power." A child needs this connection. With it, disappointments and losses are more tolerable because there's a sense that a greater scheme is at work, one that not only the child, but everyone else must answer to.

Gratitude reduces a child's need to consume. If children are thankful for what they have, they're less likely to feel the need for more "stuff." They feel complete and, therefore, are not as driven to press us to buy, buy, buy. Though your child still might covet the trappings of childhood—the toys, the clothes, the pop culture artifacts—having Gratitude will enable her *also* to find satisfaction in accomplishment and good deeds.

In summary, Gratitude engenders satisfaction with life, a sense of spirituality, a connection to a Higher Power, and the feeling that it's important to acknowledge the sacrifices that parents and others have made. Gratitude is compulsory—a key to raising kids with a solid core. But it is one of the most overlooked requisites of good parenting—we don't seem to get how vital it is. Gratitude works like glue, holding families together. It is a soothing balm for children as they travel the rough roads of life. Gratitude is our hope in a culture of excess. Hence our final Basic Skill:

> Basic Skill #10: Expect your child to be grateful and, thereby, nurture his faith and spirituality.

Gratitude instills a basic respect in children—a feeling of awe for the way the universe works. No child can afford to be without it. Who wouldn't want to raise a youngster who realizes that the world does not owe her and who appreciates that she's part of a larger community of life? This is the mark of a child who has a secure core.

Sadly, I don't see evidence of such feelings in many of the kids I meet, and their parents are concerned. That's why Vic and Eve were worried about Tara: Her dissatisfaction in the face of so much giving indicated shallowness and disregard. What Vic and Eve and other parents don't realize is that there's a lot they can do to change their children's ingratitude—but first they have to understand its causes.

Core Threats: The Counterforces of Gratitude

Clearly, a child's me-me-me attitude is, in part, a second-family issue. It's certainly not cool to be grateful. As I've pointed out numerous times throughout this book, the pop culture promotes a message that feeds kids' greed: "I'm number one. *My* feelings are what count." Even everyday courtesies, such as "Please" and "Thank you," are often missing from kids' vocabularies; many children nowadays feel utterly *entitled.* Tara wasn't the least bit embarrassed in front of the other kids to demand and whine; it's familiar second-family behavior. In contrast, few children would allow their friends to hear them express appreciation to an adult ("Gee, Mrs. Miller, I'm really glad about the time you're putting in with me") or a peer ("Thanks, Max. You're a good friend").

While gratitude creates a connection to the adult world that is antithetical to the second family, we can't lay the blame for me-ism solely at the second family's door. Our children's attitudes and our own reluctance to expect appreciation are influenced by other forces in the culture-at-large.

Kids don't see the cause-and-effect connection between work and the acquisition of goods. When I was a young boy, I used to go to work with my father, helping him in the small shoe store our family owned. I watched how many times he went up and down the ladder to get shoes, and how many pairs had to be tried on before a customer was satisfied. And, sometimes, after what seemed like an eternity of effort, the customer left without buying anything. In short, I saw how hard it was for my dad to make money. As a result, I had some appreciation for the food on the table and the roof over our head, no less my roller skates.

Today, kids don't get to see or, in many cases, even understand their parents' efforts. In part, it's because almost 70 percent of workers deliver services, rather than making a concrete product. Although workers based at home now comprise between 25 percent and 33 percent of the labor force—more, if you just look at working parents—they typically do consulting or other abstract services that are hard for a child to conceptualize, much less share. Hence, parents who work at home may be there physically, but their children often don't understand what they *do* any better than children whose parents are putting in twelve-hour shifts away from the house.

Gratitude has gotten a bad name. We parents fear that gratitude is a shade too close to guilt. For decades, the mental health field has embraced the notion that it's bad for people to feel guilty. In today's pop psych culture, "Gratitude" is often thought of in the same sense as words like "indebtedness," "humility," even "dependency."

Furthermore, the last twenty years, fueled by the cult of self-improvement, have seen a tremendous increase in victimhood. Some participants of twelve-step programs, pop therapy, and liberation groups seem to value grievance over gratitude. This is ironic and remarkable in that many of these programs actually promote appreciation for one's blessings and gratitude to a Higher Power. Particularly in groups devoted to "adult children," the rhetoric is often seeped in blame. Some members, who are parents themselves, spend a lot of time talking about what their parents *didn't* do, rather than what they did, how they were hurt as children, rather than what they were given.

Granted, in the last few years, we've begun to see caring and sharing tone down the gripe brigade. More of us are decrying the victim stance, as we realize that blame helps no one. All the same, the climate today is such that we're a little wary about inducing that dreaded feeling—guilt—in our kids. We don't even expect thanks from our own children. This leads me to our third, and most important, threat.

Parents give to kids whenever they can but rarely expect them to be grateful. Not wanting to quash their child's self-esteem, most parents today not only go overboard with praise, they allow their own kindnesses to go unnoticed. That's because so many of us believe that the parenting equation is totally weighted on the side of the child. They're our kids; they simply deserve what we give them. Even if a child isn't demanding, we never feel as if we give enough. At Christmas, for example, according to psychologist Marilyn Bradford, the average preschooler *asks* for 3.4 toys but *receives* (thanks to us) 11.6 toys. Some of us give to show love, others to ease our bad feelings about being absent so much of the time.

Whatever the underlying reasons, we're currently bestowing on our children more material possessions than ever before—spending on toys, for example, has soared 260 percent, up from $6.7 billion in 1980 to $17.5 billion in 1995. Yet we often don't even expect children to express gratitude or acknowledge our giving. Sure, you may ask your four-year-old to "Say thank you" when you hand her an ice-cream cone. But isn't this often a rote request? Do you really think about the significance of politeness, or how important it is for a child to develop sincere Gratitude?

And this is not only true of things we buy kids; it's also true of our time. As I pointed out in chapter 2, we are, in fact, spending more time than ever in child-oriented settings and activities. We think that it's our job to sacrifice, to turn ourselves inside out. Sometimes, these feelings are heightened if our own parents made us feel guilty about everything they did.

For example, Doris, a woman I know—a soccer mom who religiously attends every game her child plays—admitted that her own parents were masters of "guilt-tripping." As a result, Doris wanted to be different with her own children. She wanted them to experience her love as unconditional and endlessly free-flowing. Her goal was to give without expecting anything in return.

Now, I'm not advocating that we stop being generous toward our kids, but rather that we ask them to be thankful for what we give them, whether our gifts are material or the less tangible efforts of attention and time. I'm suggesting that we put Gratitude on our list of skills to foster—we need to *expect* appreciation from our children. In the process, we also need to revise our vocabulary, redefine words like "appreciation" and "humility" and "indebtedness." The truth is, if *we* don't teach Gratitude, our children aren't going to learn it anywhere else.

Parent Skills: Fostering Gratitude

It's shocking to me that in the thousands of workshops I've given, most parents admit they don't expect Gratitude. Some, like Doris, had parents who made them feel guilty for anything they did; others, influenced in part by a misreading of child-development literature, believe kids are supposed to be self-centered. Mothers and fathers throw up their hands in defeat, assuming Gratitude shouldn't be taught or expected. They hope that maybe someday, when their kids are parents themselves, they'll appreciate how much we've done for them.

There is another way. As I explained earlier, psychology is gravitating toward a focus on mutuality in relationships. Likewise, parenting has to move from child-centeredness to a truly mutual and reciprocal child/parent focus, in which Gratitude is a natural by-product. To that end, I have put together a set of parenting skills that will enable you to change your own perspective and, in turn, help foster Gratitude in your child. They are divided into two sections—the first reminds you to expect Gratitude; the second encourages you to create an atmosphere that will promote a culture of appreciation in your family.

Expecting Gratitude—without guilt

Below are pointers that will help you distinguish between Gratitude and guilt. Following that, I offer a tool called "THANK," which will remind you that you have a *right* to expect your child to appreciate all that you do and give.

Know what healthy Gratitude looks like. Granted, this important skill looks different in different children—and at different ages. And as with the nine other core-builders in this book, it's important for you to take into account your child's temperament (see chapter 1) and expressive style (chapter 3). However, because so many parents have trouble identifying what Gratitude looks like, I thought it would be a good idea to show you the difference between what healthy core-building Gratitude does for a child versus having "the gimmes" or, the opposite, feeling guilty:

A CHILD WHO FEELS HEALTHY GRATITUDE . . .

- Is not afraid to ask for help or favors.
- Will share, with siblings, with other kids.
- Is not embarrassed to express appreciation of others.
- Realizes that everyday courtesies are nice and right.
- Reciprocates with gifts and other acts of kindness.
- Feels blessed when good things happen to her and is willing to hang in and try again when bad things happen.
- Has a sense of faith in a bigger picture and sees God or a Higher Power as a loving force that looks over her.

A CHILD WHO HAS THE GIMMES . . .

- Doesn't say please and thank you—no matter how many times adults tell him it's polite.
- Doesn't seem to notice or feel good when you've gone out of your way.
- Nothing is enough; in fact, when you give a lot, it seems to stimulate more anger, more displeasure.
- Finds it hard to share even though his parents give him almost everything he wants.
- Has a tantrum or storms away angrily when he doesn't get what he asks for.
- Has no connection to God or a Higher Power, nor to anything bigger than himself.

A CHILD WHO FEELS GUILTY . . .

- Can't say no to a parent, to any other adult authority figure, or to a strong-willed child.
- Says words of appreciation but doesn't feel them.
- Doesn't like to ask for anything because of the price she pays.
- Has trouble creating boundaries; if someone give him something, he feels owned.
- Gives up easily.
- Views God or a Higher Power as a punitive being who keeps him in line.

Remember to "THANK." Gratitude is *never* optional, and you must always promote it in your child, regardless of his inborn temperament or expressive style. In other words . . .

- Even if she is an Intense/Aggressive type who has a tendency to grab things, she has to learn to stop long enough to say thanks.
- Even if he is a Reserved/Clingy child who is "too shy" to say "Thank you" to the bus driver, he has to work toward being considerate to others.
- Even if your child is an Intense/Sensitive child who hates the sweater Aunt Matilda gave him because it's too itchy, that's no excuse for his not thanking her.
- Even if your child is an Easy/Balanced child who's running off to an important game and has no time to help out, she has to learn how to balance her needs with the family's.

THANK stands for:

Teach early.

Hint at a specific thing to say or do if kids forget.

Ask for acknowledgment.

Note acts of kindness—your child's and other people's.

Know when it's normal for your child not to feel grateful.

Below is a more detailed explanation of each element:

Teach early. Even before age three, children can express basic courtesies, but you must help get the ball rolling by actually prompting consideration. For example, when your preverbal toddler extends her arms asking for a toy or cookie, give her the vocabulary of politeness, not just the cookie. It may sound old-fashioned, but tell her, "Say, 'Please,' and I'll get it for you." And, later, add, "Now say, 'Thank you.' " As kids get older, encourage them to be considerate and to reciprocate kind deeds—for example, remembering others' birthdays. Suggest making presents for other people, too, stressing the idea that it feels good to make someone else feel good. Even as your child approaches his preteen years, when politeness and common courtesy just aren't cool, hold the line. Make Gratitude a family value. Let your child clearly know, "In our home, we believe in being polite and respectful of others."

Remember, too, it's the little things that count. We might expect our children's appreciation for big-ticket items, like presents and parties and vacations, but we tend to ignore everyday exchanges that involve kindness—and deserves thanks. I often see seen small acts of kindness taken for granted. For example, little Sienna was lying on the floor watching television. When her mother, Heidi, handed her a bottle, the toddler's eyes never left the screen—her gaze never wavered. She didn't even look up, much less say "Thank you." And Mom just walked away, not even giving the exchange a second thought.

Hint at a specific thing to say or do when kids forget. The above parent/child scene underscores the importance of the "H" in THANK. What could Heidi have done instead? As she's handing her daughter the bottle, she could call Sienna's attention to what she's doing: "Here, honey. Here's your bottle. What do you say?" Naturally, it's best to start giving such hints early and to be consistent about it. When your nonverbal toddler spills his milk, you can even say the words *for* him: "Oops! Sorry, Mommy!" By the time he starts talking, you're likely to hear similar sentiments from him. When your three-year-old gets a present, make sure she thanks the giver, either in person or on the phone. And when your five-year-old complains in front of Aunt Matilda's about his new sweater, take him aside and explain, "Aunt Matilda didn't know it would feel scratchy to you. We don't want to hurt her feelings, and the nice thing would be to say 'Thank you.' " Prod gently at first, but be insistent if necessary with stronger-willed children.

Even hinting after the fact can have an impact. If your child has been rude or downright inconsiderate, review and correct your child's behavior. When three-year-old Lucia hit a playmate, Bonnie, for example, her mother didn't just stop her, she said, "Lucia, that hurts Bonnie." Then she immediately turned her attention to Bonnie ("Oh, honey, are you all right?") and apologized ("I'm so sorry that Lucia hit you"). Lucia just watched Bonnie get all her mother's attention. Competition can be an effective motivation to learn: The next time a similar incident occurred, Lucia, who had "gotten" these indirect hints, immediately said, "I'm sorry." With older children, you can be more direct. When eight-year-old Seth repeatedly interrupted his mother at the dinner table, she turned to him, saying, "You know, Seth, it hurts my feelings when you ignore the fact that I'm talking to your dad. What I have to say is important, too. I'd appreciate it if you wait your turn."

Ask for acknowledgment. If your child's effort is worth praising, so are at least some of yours. Get your child into the habit of thanking you for little things—for giving him a ride, for helping with homework, for making dinner. Of course, you should also expect to be acknowledged when you go above and beyond the call of duty. For example, when seven-year-old Amy broke her promise to clean Squiggy's hamster cage, her mother, Kim, ended up doing it. Yet it didn't occur to Amy that she ought to thank her mother.

But this isn't Amy's fault. Gratitude is dependent on our making a child aware that these little occurrences deserve thanks. I suggested to Kim that she gently ask for acknowledgment by reminding Amy of their original agreement: "Amy, I'm doing the dirty work with Squiggy. Remember, you gave me your word." Then, she should ask, "What can we do to make it easier for me and more likely you'll keep your promise next time?" And, next week, before Amy forgets about her hamster's cage, Mom shouldn't be afraid to remind her of her promise again.

Learning to ask for acknowledgment is difficult enough for most parents. But, believe it or not, sometimes we parents unwittingly discourage Gratitude by sloughing off a youngster's attempts to genuinely give thanks. Our child says, "Thanks," and we say, "Don't mention it." One mother, Regina, whom I overheard talking to her ten-year-old daughter, Dawn, on the sidelines of a soccer game, seemed to understand this instinctively. They obviously had been arguing, and suddenly Dawn said, "Mommy, I know how much you do for me. I'm really sorry." Dawn was actually acknowledging that her mother had feelings! Some mothers might have said, "Oh, don't be silly" or "Don't mention it" or "It's my pleasure." But this savvy mom didn't thwart her child's gratitude; she encouraged it by saying, "Thank you. It means a lot to me that you know it and that you can say it."

Note acts of kindness—your child's and other people's. Praise your child when he is courteous to you ("Oh, what a polite little boy you are!") or when he does something for another person ("That was very generous of you to share your jelly beans with Adam"). And be sure to point out when someone else is being kind ("Wasn't that nice of Mr. Harper to help us carry these gardening supplies to the car?").

Remember the old ad campaign that asked, "Have you hugged your child today?" That's a good rule of thumb to measure instances of generosity and thoughtfulness as well. Get into the habit of asking yourself at least once a day, "Have I pointed out any act of kindness today?" Beautiful moments happen daily in your house and outside as well. If you don't see them, it's because you've stopped paying attention. And if you've gone without noticing an act of kindness for longer than a day, you've gone too long.

Know when it's normal for your child not to feel grateful. Remember that no matter what you do, at certain times, you are *not* likely to get Gratitude from a child:

- *Times of stress,* such as moving or other situations involving family upheaval (divorce, loss of job), can cause children to do ungrateful things. The reasons for this are many—anger, fear, sadness—but what's important for you to remember is that expectations of Gratitude need to be delayed. For example, when the Youngs moved to Detroit with their four- and two-year-old children, Edwin and Mariah, they called me. The father, Jack, had been transferred suddenly. As soon as they arrived, Felicia—Mom—had gotten busy trying to get part-time work herself and, of course, finding suitable day care. Everything fell into place, but what prompted the call to me was Edwin, the older child's behavior toward the new baby-sitter. He was sullen and sometimes nasty. I explained that in the midst of all the change Edwin had experienced in such a short time, she couldn't expect her four-year-old to accept or even be polite to the day care person. Instead, she needed to focus on helping him regain a basic sense of security in his new environment. Among other things, Felicia showed the baby-sitter ways to comfort Edwin—play his favorite games, make grilled cheese sandwiches just as she did. Within a few weeks, Edwin started to warm up to the baby-sitter. One day, he even thanked her for those great sandwiches which were "almost as good as Mommy's."
- *When your child feels unappreciated,* she may have difficulty expressing appreciation to others. Libby, for example, was really trying to fit in among her third-grade peers. They continued to exclude her and treat her badly, and she began mimicking their attitude at home. She became rude, demanding, whiny, and utterly ungrateful until Dad discovered the source of her angst by doing LAPS with her.
- *During transitions and bodily changes,* Gratitude can be at a low ebb—for example, during a sudden growth spurt or in the midst of toilet teaching. When children are beginning to master any type of developmental milestone, they seem to burn out all of their reserves. Research confirms that "internal disorganization"—physiological, chemical, or biological—causes children to regress. In the face of inner vulnerability, it's hard for a child to recognize the efforts of others, harder still to express Gratitude. In this respect, they're no different from adults!

When your child is in one of these phases, don't throw in the towel altogether. It's still a good idea to *expect* Gratitude, but just remember that you might have to lower the bar a bit. Carole, the mother of six children who are now adults, had one of the wisest philosophies I've ever heard. "Rather than fight about maintaining the same level of civility and gratitude," she explained, "I always cut them some slack when they were going through a difficult time."

Then Carole added the most important point: "But I always reminded them that I was making an exception—lower expectations never became the rule." For example, when one of her daughters, Andrea, was inconsolable about an unrequited love, Carole didn't expect her to be enormously empathic toward her parents or her siblings. Carole addressed the situation directly—a good idea, because it let Andrea know exactly what was going on. "I know that you're going through a painful time," Carole told her. "I can see how preoccupied you are, but it's still not nice to expect your brothers and sisters to do all of the chores. It's okay for now—we all go through hard times, and family members pitch in to help each other out. But in a few days, I

INNER RESENTMENT: PARENT SIGNS

When your child's is ungrateful, something happens inside *you*—but most of us parents are so conditioned not to expect thanks or appreciation, we often gloss over the feelings of hurt and disappointment inside ourselves. If any of these ring true, it might be time to change your expectations.

• After a child's celebration day, you feel let down because you're not sure if he enjoyed the experience or even cared about it.

• *Your* birthday or other important adult occasions pass with little fanfare or no mention altogether.

• You're feeling increasingly resentful because of how generous you feel you are—and how little he seems to appreciate it.

• You think of her as "selfish," "lazy," an "ingrate," or you often remind her, "Life is a two-way street."

• You feel as if he has no idea what "grateful" means.

• You begin to notice how often she asks favors and how rarely she offers to help you.

expect things to get back to normal." The point is, even at times when Carole's children couldn't exhibit Gratitude, they weren't led to believe that inconsiderate or self-centered behavior was acceptable.

Creating a climate of Gratitude

The following parent skills will help you create an environment at home that will make Gratitude an integral part of your family life:

Set a good example. The single most significant step you can take toward fostering Gratitude in your child is to be a good role model. This, more than almost anything, instills in children a desire to be polite, respectful, and appreciative. It begins when your child is just a baby, and you verbally express his needs. Even though you realize he can't understand a single word, you still say, "Oh, my big boy must be hungry." When he falls as a toddler, you comfort him with hugs and even folk wisdom that's a bit over his head. And when *you* have a "boo-boo," you ask him to "kiss it and make it all better." Even though true understanding has yet to develop, these natural reactions set the stage for becoming aware of others' feelings—in short, you're strengthening his capacity for empathy.

Also, don't underestimate the importance of *your* being polite and expressing Gratitude throughout the day. Your child absorbs values when you say "Thanks a lot" to a waitress or to the man in the toll booth, when you give time or help to someone in need. Each of these acts sends an important message to your child.

As Howard, father of two, told me, "It's what our kids see *us* doing that counts." From the time his children were born, Friday-night dinners and Saturday-morning attendance at synagogue have been important. "Twenty percent of the time," he admits, "I don't feel like going on Saturday mornings. I'm exhausted from the week, and I'd just as soon stay home. But I don't." For the same reason, the couple decided never to go out on Friday nights. "There's often good music at local clubs, but we knew we couldn't ask our children to stay home for Friday-night dinners if *we* weren't willing to."

Share your beliefs with your child. Certainly, more and more Americans are embracing the religions of their childhood or joining new spiritual communities that they choose as adults. This is not surprising when you consider that 94 percent of Americans believe in God or a Universal Spirit or that 60 percent of the "sharing and caring" groups cited by George Gallup, Jr., are related to a church or other faith communities. In fact, more than 40 percent of Americans attend weekly services; church membership today almost matches figures recorded in the thirties. Robert Wuthnow's research also shows that even outside of organized religions there are spiritually oriented groups that "challenge, as well as comfort, participants; that help people in their faith journey; and encourage them to be open and honest with each other."

Spirituality and Gratitude go hand in hand. Being part of such a community not only provides support, it also alters the perspective: Individual selves are seen as small cogs in the larger wheel of humanity. But what about children who complain that it's "boring"?

Howard's answer is: "You go, and you bring them with you. I'm amazed at the number of parents who, when they hear that we go to religious services every week, say to me, 'We couldn't possibly ask our kids to do that.' "

Howard is right. If you are part of a spiritual community, and that community reflects your values and beliefs, expose your child to it. Start when she is young. Make attendance a normal, even enjoyable part of family life. Your three-year-old probably won't sit still, but you can take breaks, hand him off to an older child (who is probably looking for an excuse to take a walk!). As Howard says, "Our kids have been doing this for a long time. We just didn't give them a choice."

Another father, Albert, points out that he and his wife, Lillian, aren't rigid about Sunday church services. "We have ended up compromising some Sunday traditions. For example, we'll go to league games with them, as long as it doesn't conflict with more than a couple of Sundays in a row. Albert and Lillian know that there will be many other decisions and discussions as the kids, now eleven and eight, move into their teen years. But the values of their family and their religious community are already deeply established.

Incorporate Gratitude into your family rituals. Make Gratitude an integral part of your daily rituals and special-occasion tradition. Say grace or engage in some other ritual of thanks before eating. Have a family meeting at which everyone takes turns saying one thing to each member of the family about what he appreciates—a deed, a quality. Even children as young as two or three can participate. If you don't want to do this in a formal context, simply make appreciation part of your Sunday-night dinners. If children say prayers, encourage them

As the numbers show, more and more parents are making their way back to houses of worship. In fact, finding shelter and support in a community of fellow worshipers is central to a family's core. If you're looking for a spiritual home, here are some points to keep in mind:

• Start when your child is young.
• Find a place with a philosophy that feels good to you—it's a matter of individual taste.
• Try out the services and family activities first.
• Make attendance a family ritual.
• Connect with other families to participate in pleasurable after-service rituals, such as Sunday lunch.
• Become good friends with a small group of families within the spiritual community. This creates a secure feeling and provides like-minded playmates for your kids.

to thank God for all they have, and to ask for God's blessings on all whom they love and appreciate.

When children give gifts, help them understand the reason: A material present is a way of saying, "We appreciate you." On your birthday, toast your guests. On your child's birthday, remind her, "I bought this doll for you because I love you and am thankful that you're my child."

Keep promises. Part of appreciating another human being means coming through for that person—keeping promises. Georgia, a single mother whose children, Kim and Oliver, are six and four, told me that keeping promises is an important value in her family. "If I tell my kids they can have a certain video, and the first store I go to doesn't have it, I'll look in another store. If I don't find it, at least the kids know I tried." Even though her children are fairly young, Georgia has already seen the payoff—her kids honor their own promises. Recently, without asking her mom, Kim spoke out of turn and promised a classmate, Mindy, that she could come over after school. As it turned out, Georgia had made other plans, so it wasn't possible. "Kim felt bad because she couldn't keep her promise," recalls Georgia, "so she gave her friend Mindy one of her stuffed animals that she knew Mindy liked."

Make the invisible visible. The pre- or elementary schooler whose parents spend weeks planning his birthday party—hiring a clown, buying and wrapping favors, baking the cake, conceiving the menu, decorating the place—usually has no idea how hard they've worked to make it all happen. Tell him; make him part of the process; let him help.

It's also important to let a child participate in family business that we routinely take care of. That's why chores are so important—he sees how things get done. For example, every once in a while (assuming you own a car), you might announce to the children, "You know, I just took the car in for repairs. It took Joe nearly two hours of hard work to find out why it was making that horrible noise." This helps kids realize that things don't get fixed without someone doing it. And, what is more, you can say, "Aren't you grateful he did!" After all, the car serves everyone in the family.

This is particularly important in single-earner households where one parent, usually Dad, works out of the house. Children don't link his distant work efforts with their lifestyle. In fact, fathers often come to me lamenting the fact that their children don't understand how much they contribute to the family. When they ask the kids, "Who do you think makes the money in this family?" the younger ones often reply, "Mommy!" That's because most of what Mommy does around the house is visible.

Think ahead. Parents get into situations like Vic and Eve's at the amusement park because they don't anticipate them or explain them to their children. Hearing his story, for example, I suggested to Vic that the next time he and Eve are about to go on such an outing, they say to Tara, "How do you think we'll feel if you don't thank us?" Or "What do you think will happen if we say no to something you want?" In fact, Victor tried this approach the next time they went on a family outing, and it actually changed the picture: There were no tantrums, Tara was more appreciative, and she was aware that there had to be limits on spending.

Of course, if your child is a preteen or older, and you've already spent years giving in to his demands, old habits—both yours and his—will be harder to break. Be patient. If *you* change the dance—that is, you expect him to be grateful—even a demanding child can be transformed into a more appreciative child.

Celebrate birthdays and holidays with an eye toward fostering Gratitude. Though she can't remember the actual birthday party, Lois, now in her forties, recalls the birthday photo in which she is surrounded by so many presents, her five-year-old self barely shows. Her children, Lois laments, get even more presents on their birthdays, and it worries her. "Whatever happened to honoring the *significance* of these events?" she wonders. In fact, as I mentioned at the beginning of this chapter, many families are beginning to see the danger in this kind of excess—and they're fighting back. Some limit holiday gifts to one per child, or they have grab-bag rituals.

"We had to wean our kids down to a single present, but that gift means so much more," one mother told a TV reporter a few days after Christmas. "It really makes you think about what an individual is like and what he *really* wants—instead of running around with a long list and buying meaningless gifts for everyone," said Marla, who tried a grab-bag ritual with her family for the first time this year. Other families put less tangible types of gifts under the tree—a promise to spend fun time or an offer of help with a project. Still others make a donation to charity in a person's name to commemorate a holiday or special occasion.

In honor of a son's bar mitzvah or daughter's bat mitzvah—the Jewish rite of passage marking adulthood—some parents are interpreting mitzvah, which means "blessing," literally. And, in lieu of a giving a big party, they ask their child to choose a good deed and have his or her friends join in doing it. Think of new ways to celebrate in your family. And get your kids' ideas, too. You might be surprised; children can be incredibly sensible and giving . . . if we encourage them.

Child Skills: Making Caring Cool

As with all the core-builders in this book, your child needs your help to develop these skills. Start him early, and in time, he'll handle situations without your help.

Finding the channel of expression that feels best

To say "Thank you," some children prefer to draw a picture or write a card. Michael, four, is too shy to use words well, but his parents have encouraged him to make paintings and cutouts for people he wants to thank. Of course, if a child is more at ease with verbal expression, he should get in the habit of calling. The important key is to practice expressing Gratitude using those channels that are most natural. The more a child does this, the more genuine expressing such sentiments will feel to her and to the person on the receiving end.

Learning that sharing and giving back are part of life

We need to help children see that giving isn't a duty but rather an intrinsic part of being human. Life is not just take, take, take. Again, I see encouraging indications of change: At earlier and earlier ages, schools are placing a new kind of emphasis on the importance of sharing, on appreciating what you have and not just thinking ahead to what else you can get.

Helga has taken an approach with her children, Molly and Dale, who are now seven and nine, that I think makes a big difference—and takes this idea of sharing a step farther. When Dale was just a toddler, instead of stressing what "a good boy" Dale was for sharing, she stressed how good it made the other child feel. "Look, Dale, you made Molly smile when you gave that to her. She feels very grateful to you." The words may not have meant much to a three-year-old, but today both Dale and his sister are extremely giving children. I have no doubt this is due to their mother's subtle conditioning. They feel good about making other people feel good.

Believing that giving back is cool

Princess Diana's death in 1997 crystallized a heartening trend that began several years ago. Giving to charity is moving to a central position in the public consciousness—and not only for adults. I recently heard about a wonderful group called "Kids Care Clubs," which started when some children and parents noticed a kindly old woman's house in disrepair and thought it would be a good idea to help her by cleaning up. Word spread, and several kids grew into a whole group of boys and girls who got so enthusiastic about the job that they completely spruced up the woman's house. They felt so good about what they did they started looking around for other folks who needed help. One kind gesture grew into the creation of a local Kids Care Club, and that, in turn, lead Deborah Spaide to write the book *Teaching Your Kids to Care*. The original club has evolved into a national organization with hundreds of chapters.

There are other encouraging signs, even in the second family, that children are struggling with the idea of giving of themselves. On a recent episode of *Sabrina, the Teenage Witch,* the gang was asked to help out in a senior home. At first, the popular kids didn't think it was cool, but when they saw how much pleasure it brought, they decided it was just a little less geeky than they'd thought.

I've seen this in real life, too. Some schools have a "Secret Santa" ritual in which each child is expected to give a present or do something nice for another child anonymously. At first, the kids think it's "jerky," but when they begin to see other children's delight, their attitude changes. We need to give children these opportunities, particularly on important birthdays and holidays, when typically they're rewarded with tons of gifts and attention and are never asked to give anything in return.

Building spiritual "muscle"

It's important for children to picture themselves as part of a larger whole. Every organized religion or spiritual community, each in its own way, helps children understand that they're not number one, that there's something bigger. Belief in God, being part of an organized religion, or simply having a spiritual practice of any kind helps children feel a connection to the family of humanity. Inside a house of worship, children feel less alone. When something bad happens to a family, others are there, giving solace, helping out. They see, for instance, that when a parent has an operation, congregation members visit, fix meals, invite children over to their homes. And as I pointed out in chapter 2, these communities allow children to rub elbows with people of all ages.

Making sacrifices

As an antidote to instant gratification, we need to help children learn the meaning of *sacrifice* and to see it as a positive, affirming act. As the Talmud points out, "You save a life, you save the world." Many parents ask kids to give away outgrown toys and clothing to children who need them. Well, what about asking a child to give something *new* or

THE ABCS OF SPIRITUALITY

Being part of a spiritual community helps children learn their spiritual ABCs:

A = Activities. Children gain an appreciation of empathy and charity by *doing*. Whether they wrap Christmas gifts or paint Easter eggs for poor children or help out in a soup kitchen, these specific activities vitalize Gratitude in a profound way.

B = Beliefs. Through these beliefs, children learn a vocabulary for expressing certain feelings that they don't get in the secular world: blessed, holy, sacred. The collective beliefs of a congregation hold a child and make him feel safe.

C = Community. In every sense of the word, spirituality and religion provide "community." Children relish and absorb these connections; they help solidify a child's core.

something that he still likes? This can be a shocking concept to even a young child nowadays, but if you dare to change the assumption, you may see miraculous results.

Eleanor was appalled when her five-year-old grandson, David, counted the more than thirty Christmas gifts he received from his extended family. "David, why don't we go through these," she said, "and you decide which ones you're really going to play with." Admittedly, it was hard for David to part with his bounty, but the following day, when he and his grandma arrived at the Ronald McDonald House, five or six presents in hand, someone greeted them and gratefully accepted the gifts—his sacrifice. The recipient's warm and rather effusive response was one kind of gift David wasn't used to receiving, and it made a lasting impression.

Sacrifice can also mean going against the crowd—to make a statement about what you value and what's most important in your life. The Steins—Howard, Jane, and their two children, Sadie and Aaron—were among a fairly small minority of observant Jewish families in the Massachusetts town where they lived. One year, Halloween fell on a Friday night—a time when they routinely lit Sabbath candles and had a family dinner; the notion of "trick or treating" didn't exactly fit in. "We let them know that if they wanted to join friends, they could go out, but we just weren't comfortable about doing that," Howard recalls.

The children—all-around kids with many friends in town—decided on their own against going out. Instead, they invited another family at the synagogue for Friday-night dinner and, afterward, the adults and children sat around reading scary Jewish stories. It wasn't the first time they mixed cultures or made a compromise. But the important point here is that skipping Halloween was a sacrifice that made sense to the Stein children—and, no doubt, made them feel good about themselves.

Doing interviews for this book, I've talked to youngsters in other observant families who admit that they resented missing certain kid-focused events; many were even teased for being "goody-goodies." But, in the final analysis, they felt they hadn't given up that much compared with what they got back. In the Parsons family, for example, their four children ranged in age from one to seven when I first met them. Their parents, Ed and Justine, have always been dedicated churchgoers. Every Sunday, the six of them attended services and, afterward, went out to a wonderful lunch. Unless someone in the family was sick, nothing came between this family and their Sunday ritual. As the children got older, the usual conflicts arose between family obligations and friends—birthday parties, the occasional soccer games. But on this one morning a week, the kids were always urged to choose church over peer events, family over secular fun. To say the least, this has been a tremendous sacrifice for them.

I asked Louise, the oldest, now fifteen, to act as a spokesperson for the Parsons kids. I also was particularly interested in her reaction to the family's unfailing Sunday tradition, because she has already been through the tough years—between twelve and fifteen—when children start wanting to separate from family events.

"I've given up a lot. Sometimes I didn't like having to go to church . . . but I feel full inside," she told me, pointing to her heart. "I believe in God. I believe in my family. And I believe in my parents—they do what they say they're going to do. And you know what? I haven't lost any friends along the way."

I think Louise's statement, "I feel full inside," sums up the purpose and the hope of *Nurturing Good Children Now*. I've seen Louise grow up, and I've watched her go from a gangly middle school child into a poised young woman. She's a solid citizen and not just because she makes sacrifices for the sake of spirituality. Louise possesses many of the traits I've talked about in these pages. She is "good" in every sense of the word, because she has a secure center—a substantial core. She knows how to make choices and is confident about herself in the world. Louise's expression is one of a healthy child, brimming with confidence, determination, and happiness. That is precisely what I would like all kids to experience. And I know it is your wish, too.

INDEX

violence on, 41, 214–215
see also mass media; pop
culture; second family
"Television Ownership
Survey," 57
temperament, 14–15, 100, 267
acceptance of, 24–28
denial of, 20–21, 29
of family members, 25, 26
as innate, 12–13, 20–21, 24–28
play dates and, 39–40
recognizing of, 21–28
responding to, 29, 46–47
self-soothing and, 42–43
television and, 41
temperament styles, 8, 12, 16
Easy/Balanced, 24, 27, 30–31,
36, 38, 42, 93, 169, 269
Intense/Aggressive, 23, 25,
26, 29–30, 35, 36–37, 75, 92,
113–114, 135, 168, 171, 217,
269
Intense/Sensitive, 23, 24–25,
27, 30, 34, 36–38, 92, 113,
135, 166, 167, 168, 205,
269
Reserved/Clingy, 23–24, 29,
30, 42, 43, 92, 93, 167, 269
THANK, 267–274
thinking:
ahead, 8, 209, 213
concrete, 154
experience and, 224
linear vs. nonlinear, 91

nonlinear, 92, 93, 98
obsession vs., 187–190
Three Ss, 176–179
Three Ts, 147–152, 157
Time Bind (Hochschild), 131
Time for Life (Robinson and
Godbey), 57
time management, 164
tone, of parents, 172–173, 223,
249
toys, 266
pop culture and, 109, 263
thinking vs. reflexes and, 214
transitions, 101–102
trigger phrases, 100–101
truisms, 123
trust, 191
twelve-step programs, 88, 261,
265

"undifferentiated ego mass,"
215
"us versus them" mentality, 73

validation, 248, 249
values:
sources of teenagers', 51–52
teaching of, 61–62
values education, 6, 217
variable reinforcement, 172
verbalization, 177
victimhood, 265
video games, 18, 19, 40, 86, 215
volunteerism, 261

Waldorf schools, 235
Wall Street Journal, 129
Washington, University of, 32,
64
Wasted (Hornbacher), 186
weight, 185, 186
fitness vs., 192
obsession with, 182, 207
Westheimer, Ruth, 57
"What a Nice Kid" (Siegler), 58
*Why Marriages Succeed and
Fail* (Gottman), 32
Williams, Robin, 164
Winnicott, D. W., 263
Wolf, Naomi, 180
Wolin, Steven and Sybil, 70–71
Wonder Years, The, 56
word pairs, problem-solving
and, 220
word retrieval, 95
work:
Gratitude and, 265
materialism and, 277
Wuthnow, Robert, 261, 275

Yale University, 14
Yankelovich Youth Monitor, 38,
142, 144
yelling, 29–31

Zahn-Wexler, Carolyn, 230, 236
Zero to Three Foundation, 14,
113
Zimmerman, Jill, 185

About the Authors

Ron Taffel, Ph.D., is a noted family therapist and author of almost 100 professional and popular articles, as well as the critically acclaimed childrearing guides *Parenting by Heart* and *Why Parents Disagree.* Dr. Taffel consults with and lectures at school, religious, and community organizations around the country. He is an award-winning contributing editor to *Parents* magazine, and the founder and director of Family and Couples Treatment Services at the Institute for Contemporary Psychotherapy in New York City, where he lives with his wife and two children.

Melinda Blau is an award-winning journalist and the author of *Families Apart, Loving and Listening,* and *Our Turn,* as well as the coauthor with Dr. Taffel of *Parenting by Heart.* She is the mother of two grown children, and lives in Northampton, Massachusetts.